INTERNATIONAL ECONOMIC LAW
AND ARMED CONFLICT

NOVA ET VETERA IURIS GENTIUM

PUBLICATIONS OF THE INSTITUTE FOR PUBLIC INTERNATIONAL LAW
OF THE UNIVERSITY OF UTRECHT

SERIES A. MODERN INTERNATIONAL LAW
NUMBER 18

INTERNATIONAL ECONOMIC LAW AND ARMED CONFLICT

edited by

HARRY H.G. POST

MARTINUS NIJHOFF PUBLISHERS

DORDRECHT / BOSTON / LONDON

A C.I.P. Catalogue record for this book is available from the Library of Congress.

ISBN 0-7923-3189-3

1000401775

Published by Martinus Nijhoff Publishers,
P.O. Box 163, 3300 AD Dordrecht, The Netherlands.

Sold and distributed in the U.S.A. and Canada
by Kluwer Academic Publishers,
101 Philip Drive, Norwell, MA 02061, U.S.A.

In all other countries, sold and distributed
by Kluwer Academic Publishers Group,
P.O. Box 322, 3300 AH Dordrecht, The Netherlands.

Printed on acid-free paper

Printed in the Netherlands

PREFACE

Before writing their definitive texts, the contributors to this book had the opportunity to submit their views to a learned audience at the Second J.H.W. Verzijl Memorial Symposium, entitled 'International Economic Law During Armed Conflict'. This Symposium was organised by the Institute of Public International Law of Utrecht University and took place on the 19th February 1993 in the Senate Hall of the Academy Building in Utrecht.

The theme of the Symposium and the book seemed most appropriate as a further tribute to the memory of the great scholar in international law J.H.W. Verzijl was. His opus may be said to have begun and ended with a contribution to international law during (international) armed conflict in respect to economic activities. In his 1917 dissertation he analysed the law of prize *vis-à-vis* neutral vessels in the First World War, whereas the recent Volume XI of his monumental *International Law in Historical Perspective*, published posthumously and edited by Wybo Heere and Polona Offerhaus, also examines international prize law.[1]

The impact of (international) armed conflict on international economic law has become a subject of renewed interest since, in particular, the Iran-Iraq War of 1980-1988 and, to a lesser extent, the Falkland/Malvinas War of 1982. The military operations against Iraq during the 1990-1991 Kuwait crisis, and, more recently, the events in the former Yugoslavia have added a new dimension to this part of international law.

A record of the lively and most interesting discussions at the Second J.H.W. Verzijl Symposium is not included. However, Wolff Von Heinegg, Andrea Gioia and Nico Schrijver, who were rapporteurs at the Symposium, have made a sincere effort to use the observations of the participants, in order to transform their reports into the current parts of the book. In particular, the remarks by specially invited commentators Michael Bothe, Leslie Green and Vera Gowlland-Debas, have often been most valuable to this end. As far as their comments have not been, or could not be, included in the rapporteurs' contributions to this book, they have been reworked into special comments immediately following the reports. In addition, also those who intervened during the sessions at the Symposium have had the opportunity to submit

---

1   See on the life and work of Professor Verzijl: Pieter van Dijk, 'Jan Hendrik Willem Verzijl', in A.H.A.Soons (ed.), *International Arbitration: Past and Prospects*, Dordrecht/Boston/London 1990, pp. 1-7, and C.G.Roelofsen, *Jan Hendrik Willem Verzijl (1888-1987)*, T.M.C.Asser Instituut-The Hague, 1993.

a written text of their interventions. In this book these texts are added to each report and special commentary to which they refer.

The Institute of Public International Law is, of course, greatly indebted to the rapporteurs, the special commentators and the other participants at the Symposium whose interventions appear in this book: their contributions built up the Symposium and now make up the book.

The generous organizational and/or financial support from the following institutions is gratefully acknowledged:
- The Association for Canadian Studies in the Netherlands (who made it possible to invite Dr. Leslie Green);
- The Royal Netherlands Academy of Arts and Sciences;
- The M.A.O.C. Gravin van Bylandt Stichting;
- Utrecht University;
- The Faculty of Law of Utrecht University;
- The Department of International, Social and Economic Public Law.

The editor is also much indebted to Marlon Steine and Carla Groenestein of the Netherlands Institute for Social and Economic law Research (NISER) in Utrecht who, with great dedication and professionality, prepared the manuscript for publication, to Annebeth Rosenboom of Martinus Nijhoff Publishers who despite unexpected delays kept faith in the project, and to Marcella Kiel, Kees Roelofsen and, in particular, Monique de Boer for their most valuable assitance and support in organising the Symposium and realising the present book.

Utrecht, July 1994

Alfred Soons,
Chairman of the Second J.H.W.Verzijl Memorial Symposium

Harry Post,
Editor of *International Economic Law and Armed Conflict*

Institute of Public International Law
Faculty of Law
Utrecht University
The Netherlands

TABLE OF CONTENTS

INTRODUCTION

Harry Post

From its creation in 1945 until 1990, the Security Council of the United Nations has adopted mandatory collective sanctions only twice: in 1966 (and 1968) against Southern Rhodesia and in 1977 against the Republic of South Africa. Within the first four years since 1990, the Security Council has put another seven of those measures on record. The number of these collective sanctions, binding for (virtually) the whole world community, has thus multiplied over the past couple of years in comparison to the previous decades.

However, not only in terms of quantity, but also in terms of their substance, the Security Council's measures, notably those against Iraq and Yugoslavia (Serbia and Montenegro), may be said to have dramatically increased in scope. As before, the sanctions restrict the trade of the target states in the sense that they interfere with the trade in certain goods (primarily arms), however, as in the cases of Yugoslavia (Serbia and Montenegro) and, in particular, of Iraq, they have interfered with a much broader range of economic and other activities. For Iraq the economic part of the sanctions amounted in fact to nothing less than economic isolation.

The Security Council's sanctions of the last four years (like the South Africa and Rhodesia measures) have all been initiated by a decision under Article 39 of the UN Charter. The Council determined that all the situations to which they applied were either threats to the peace or, in the single case of the Iraqi occupation of Kuwait, a breach of the peace. Five of the seven new cases the sanctions decided upon concerned situations actually characterised by armed conflict, the two remaining ones (Lybia's possible involvement in terrorist activities, and the events in Haiti) in the view of the Security Council had the potential to develop into armed conflict. In all cases economic measures were among the steps taken to redress or to stop the situation of actual or potential armed conflict.

From an economic point of view, such a series of wide-ranging, binding measures can no longer be considered limited or incidental economic curiosities, as the sanctions against Southern Rhodesia and South Africa could still be labelled. In terms of international economic law, it might even be said that in recent years a new 'international sanctions law' is emerging with its own instruments (the Security Council Resolutions, the decisions of the Sanctions Committees, the municipal legal instruments, etc.), its own organs and institutions (the Security Council, the Sanctions

1

H.H.G. Post (ed.), International Economic Law and Armed Conflict, 1–3.
© 1994 *Martinus Nijhoff Publishers. Printed in the Netherlands.*

Committees, etc.), its own provisions on dispute settlement, on liability, on reparation, and so forth. Although this characterization is perhaps due to an academic overstatement of the importance of the developments, it is obvious that the role the Security Council has currently assumed, merits great interest from international lawyers.

Generally speaking, the subject matter of this book is the reciprocal effect of armed conflict and international economic relations. In a new or at least in a different way, the Security Council's employment of economic means just described, points to the same mutual impact of armed conflict and economic relations. However, this interrelationship already for a long time has been among the traditional concerns of international law. When war or armed conflict took place, the states directly involved have always seen their economies and their economic relations with other states being affected. Moreover, states who had little to do with the hostilities, nevertheless usually also experienced trade and other economic repercussions. From early days on international rules have been developed to regulate such situations. The rules on visit, search, diversion and capture, instruments such as blockade or the rules on termination or suspension of trade agreements and the law of neutrality provide classic examples. 'Traditional' and 'classic' do not necessarily mean that these longstanding rules are now invalid. One of the purposes of this book is to examine the state of important rules of international prize law and of fundamental principles of the law of neutrality.

The essays here collected do not pretend to provide an exhaustive general international legal perspective of the subject matter just described, nor do they examine the interrelationship of armed conflict and international relations from any other viewpoint than that of the international lawyer. They do aim at contributing to a few important *capita* of international economic law.

Firstly, one of the traditional issues in the relationship between international economic law and armed conflict is addressed: the international law of prize. Wolff Heintschel von Heinegg inquires into the modern state of international prize law. In doing so he focusses on the developments since the Second World War, thereby further treading the path set out in Volume XI of J.H.W.Verzijl's *International Law in Historical Perspective*. This essay does not only provide a survey of the law of prize as practised in modern times, but also analyses the impact of substantial changes in other parts of international law, like the general prohibition on the use of force. In his special commentary, Michael Bothe discusses the formative rules on customary law in respect to international prize law and the modalities of its continued validity in current international law. Ove Bring, Wybo Heere, André de Hoogh and Kees Roelofsen have added their comments to some of the issues raised by the rapporteur and his special commentator.

In the second essay, Andrea Gioia attempts to bring some order to what he characterizes as the 'chaotic state' of the law of neutrality. He does so, in particular, by assessing the differences in modern international law, also in view of Security Council measures, between the legal positions of 'non-belligerent' states and those who are 'genuinely' neutral. Leslie Green, as special commentator, takes issue on several substantive matters raised by the rapporteur whereby the enactment or not of binding measures by the Security Council appears once more as the modern divide within the law. Ove Bring and Dietrich Schindler contributed with additional comments to this debate.

Nico Schrijver reported on the use of economic sanctions by the Security Council. He gives an extensive survey of the Council's recent and older practice, and then continues by comparing nine sanctions cases on the basis of such criteria as their legal foundations, objectives, scope, addressees, and the like. Vera Gowlland-Debbas, in her special commentary, adds the perspective of the legal effects and consequences of the Council's economic measures for both the international and domestic legal orders. Hans-Peter Gasser and Karel Wellens appended their comments. The former referred, in particular, to the so-called 'humanitarian exception' included in several of the Security Council's economic sanctions. He stresses that it must always remain possible that relief reaches citizens in need of assistance, even though economic sanctions have interrupted the flow of goods.

THE CURRENT STATE OF INTERNATIONAL PRIZE LAW

Wolff Heintschel von Heinegg*

INTRODUCTION

Professor J.H.W. Verzijl at the age of 91 started to work on the final part of his famous *International Law in Historical Perspective* which was to be completed by two volumes on the international law of prize. His previous publications, suffice it to mention 'Le droit des prises de la Grande Guerre'[1] covering the law of prize during the First World War and the inter-war years, these two volumes were to analyse the history of prize law before 1914 and since 1939. Unfortunately, when Professor Verzijl died in 1987, the work on the first volume was not completed. Still, the editors in spite of the tremendous difficulties involved, decided to finish it. Thus, in 1992, five years after the death of Professor Verzijl, the eleventh volume of *International Law in Historical Perspective* was published.[2] It is the most comprehensive survey and analysis of the origins and developments of international prize law up to the beginning of the twentieth century and hence of inestimable value for anybody interested in that part of international law.

Since, regrettably, there will be no twelfth volume on the law of prize after 1914, the present paper, which will not nearly be as comprehensive as Verzijl and his successors, may be taken as a modest contribution to the history and development of international prize law since the end of the Second World War. To this end, in the first part, a short survey of the law of prize as practised and understood by States since 1945 will be given.[3] In that context emphasis will be on three recent military manuals, for the relevant practice of States in modern armed conflicts has been dealt with elsewhere to a considerable extent.[4] The second part is devoted to the question

---

* W. Heintschel von Heinegg, Dr.iur., Ruhr-Universität Bochum.
1 J.H.W. Verzijl, *Le droit des prises de la Grande Guerre*, Leyden 1924.
2 J.H.W. Verzijl/W.P. Heere/J.P.S. Offerhaus, *International Law in Historical Perspective*, Volume XI, Part IX-C: The Law of Maritime Prize, Dordrecht/Boston/London 1992.
3 Due to the limited space available it is not possible to also deal with blockade.
4 See, *e.g.*, R. Ottmüller, *Die Anwendung von Seekriegsrecht in militärischen Konflikten seit 1945*, Hamburg 1978; D.P. O'Connell, 'International Law and Contemporary Naval Operations', 44 *British Yearbook of International Law* (1970), pp. 19-85; D.P. O'Connell, *The Influence of Law on Sea Power*, Manchester 1975; A. Gioia/N. Ronzitti, 'The Law of Neutrality: Third States' Commercial Rights and

H.H.G. Post (ed.), International Economic Law and Armed Conflict, 5–34.
© 1994 *Martinus Nijhoff Publishers. Printed in the Netherlands.*

whether and to what extent developments in other spheres of international law, especially the outlawry of the use of force under the UN Charter, have an impact on international prize law.

A. PRIZE LAW SINCE 1945

The 1909 London Declaration[5] which is the only international document dealing with prize measures in detail, was never ratified. Even though, during the First World War, there were some attempts to adjust belligerent conduct to its rules, it has always remained a matter of controversy whether its provisions reflected customary international law.[6] The practice of States during the Second World War rather than contributing to a clarification 'distorted the law of prize beyond recognition'.[7] Since the end of World War II, the law of prize has not played an important role in armed conflicts at sea. International lawyers have, therefore, not paid too much attention to that part of international law until the recent conflict between Iran and Iraq. Hence, in order to establish whether the traditional law of prize[8] still is of legal relevance, one cannot but look beyond the actual behaviour of States during armed conflicts and to take into consideration evidences of *opinio juris* derived from military manuals.

I. The Relevance of the Iraq-Kuwait Conflict

During the 1990/91 Iraq-Kuwait conflict the Alliance forces intercepted merchant shipping bound for Iraqi ports as well as merchant shipping departing from such ports. The Alliance obviously interpreted the terms 'war material' and 'contraband' extensively. During these operations enemy as well as neutral merchant vessels were shadowed over hundreds of miles by ships and aircraft making use of satellites for communication and surveillance. During the seven months of conflict 'more than 165 ships from 19 Coalition navies challenged more than 7,500 merchant vessels, boarded 964 ships to inspect manifests and cargo holds, and diverted 51 ships carrying more

---

Duties', in: I.F. Dekker/H.H.G. Post (eds.), *The Gulf War of 1980-1988*, Dordrecht/Boston/London 1992, pp. 221-242.

5   *London Declaration concerning the Laws of Naval War* of February 26, 1909, text in 3 *American Journal of International Law* (1909) Suppl., pp. 179-220, and in: N. Ronzitti (ed.), *The Law of Naval Warfare*, Dordrecht/Boston/London 1988, pp. 223-256.

6   See, *e.g.*, F. Kalshoven, 'Commentary on the 1909 London Declaration', in: N. Ronzitti (ed.), *supra* note 5, pp. 257-275, at p. 269 ff.

7   *Ibid.*, at p. 272.

8   With regard to the traditional law see W. Heintschel v. Heinegg, 'Visit, Search, Diversion, and Capture in Naval Warfare: Part I, The Traditional Law', 29 *Canadian Yearbook of International Law* (1991), pp. 283-329.

than one million tons of cargo in violation of UNSC sanctions'.[9] The small proportion of ships boarded or diverted was due to the intelligence network implemented.[10] The Allies were able to make use of a continuously updated list of suspect shipping. Hence, it seems that in future conflicts modern technology will enable belligerents, who dispose of the necessary means, to effectively exercise ocean-wide control. This will certainly have an impact on the law of visit, search, diversion and capture. However, for two reasons the Iraq-Kuwait conflict will nevertheless not be addressed here. Firstly, it seems to be premature to endeavour to establish to what extent the traditional law will be – or already is – influenced by modern technology. Secondly, the Allied measures affecting Iraq's economy were authorized by the UN Security Council. Hence, *e.g.* the U.S. executive orders freezing Iraqi and Kuwaiti assets did not cite Trading with the Enemy legislation but rather referred to other emergency legislation as well as UN Security Council resolutions.[11] The U.S. interception notices also referred to Security Council resolutions and the inherent right of collective self-defence under Article 51 of the UN Charter.[12] Therefore, the legal nature of this conflict is unique and can hardly be generalized even though the Allies – with modifications in the area of capture and adjudication – to some extent adhered to the traditional rules.

II. 'War' as a Precondition for the Applicability of Prize Law

In State practice there are only two conflicts in which the belligerents as well as third States made the applicability of international prize law dependent upon the existence of a 'state of war': the Middle East conflict[13] and the 1965 conflict between India and Pakistan.[14] In the other conflicts that have occurred since 1945 neither the

---

9   U.S. Dept. of Defense, *Conduct of the Persian Gulf War*, Final Report to Congress, at p. 76 ff. (April 1992).

10   According to the U.S. Dept. of Defense there were not enough helicopters able to insert a full takedown team onto a vessel. Therefore, there occurred only 11 takedowns altogether; *ibid.*, at p. 78.

11   Exec. Orders No. 12, 724-25, 55 Fed. Reg. 33089-92 (1990), issued August 9, 1990, citing, *inter alia*, S.C. Res. 661, the National Emergencies Act, 50 U.S.C. paras. 1601-51 (1988), the International Emergency Economic Powers Act, *ibid.* paras. 1701-06 (1988), and the UN Participation Act, 22 *ibid.* paras. 287-87e (1988).

12   *E.g.* Special Warning No. 80, August 17, 1990, in Defense Mapping Agency Hydrographic/Topographic Center, Notice to Mariners III-1.15 (No. 36, 1990).

13   For an overview see *inter alia* Th.D. Brown, 'World War Prize Law Applied in a Limited War Situation: Egyptian Restrictions on Neutral Shipping with Israel', 50 *Minnesota Law Review* (1965-1966), p. 849 ff.; Y. Dinstein, 'The Laws of War at Sea', *Israeli Yearbook of Human Rights* (1980), p. 56 ff.; L. Gross, 'Passage through the Suez Canal of Israel-Bound Cargo and Israel Ships', *American Journal of International Law* (1957), p. 530 ff.; R. Ottmüller, *supra* note 4, at pp. 133 ff. and 180 ff.

14   See P. Sharma, *The Indo-Pakistan Maritime Conflict, 1965. A Legal Appraisal* (1970); R. Ottmüller, *supra* note 4, at p. 180 ff.

exercise of prize measures nor protests by the flag States affected were justified on the ground that there existed no 'state of war'. Rather, third States acquiesced in the exercise of the right of visit, search and capture.[15]

As regards the position taken by States in three recent military manuals[16] it is unclear whether they consider the existence of a 'state of war' necessary in order for the law of prize to come into operation.

The Canadian draft manual, in paragraph 301 ff., refers to the distinction between 'war' and 'armed conflict' and to the possibility of a *status mixtus*'. In the context of measures of economic warfare against enemy vessels and goods,[17] however, the existence of an armed conflict is seemingly considered sufficient. As regards visit and search of neutral merchant vessels, which are dealt with in the same paragraph, again no express reference to a 'state of war' is made. In paragraph 1503 the commencement of neutral status is made dependent on the existence of a 'state of war'. But according to paragraph 1514 neutral merchant shipping is to observe the rules relating to contraband as soon as, at the beginning or during the course of hostilities, the belligerents issue contraband lists.[18]

According to the German manual measures of economic warfare at sea directed against enemy merchant vessels and goods may be applied in an international armed conflict even if it does not amount to war.[19] Less clear are the rules concerning measures against neutral ships and goods. According to paragraph 209 the law of neutrality is to come into operation if there exists a 'state of war'. In paragraph 1106, however, the operation of the law of neutrality is made dependent upon an 'armed conflict of substantial extent'. The rules laid down in the paragraphs 1138 ff. concerning belligerent control of neutral merchant shipping obviously do not presuppose the existence of either a 'state of war' or of an 'armed conflict of substantial extent'.

The only unambiguous rules on the applicability of the law of prize are contained in NWP 9. In paragraph 5.1, the traditional distinction between 'war' and 'armed conflict' is abandoned. Hence, prize measures against enemy merchant vessels and goods may be resorted to in any international armed conflict.[20] As regards the law of neutrality, it is made clear in paragraph 7.1, that its coming into operation does

---

15 With regard to the reactions of States during the 1980-1988 Iran-Iraq war see A. Gioia/N. Ronzitti, *supra* note 4, at p. 231 ff.; Ch. Rousseau, 'Chronique', *Revue générale de droit international public* (1987), 139.

16 These are: *The Commander's Handbook on the Law of Naval Operations* (NWP 9 Rev. A), Washington DC 1989; Canadian Forces, *Law of Armed Conflict Manual* (Second Draft), Ottawa 1988; ZDv 15/2, *Humanitäres Völkerrecht in bewaffneten Konflikten* – Handbuch, Bonn 1992.

17 Canadian draft manual, paras. 720 ff.

18 Canadian draft manual, paras. 1514, note 2.

19 ZDv 15/2, paras. 1014-1016, 1022-1031, 1034-1036.

20 See paras. 8.2.2, 8.2.3, 8.3 and 8.4.

not depend upon the existence of a 'state of war' but, rather, upon whether the State concerned has proclaimed its neutrality or has otherwise assumed neutral status with respect to an ongoing conflict. Neutral shipping may be subjected to prize measures in any international armed conflict.[21]

III. Determination of Enemy Character

During armed conflicts at sea since the end of World War II belligerents determined the enemy character of ships, aircraft and goods in compliance with the traditional rules and the practice of States during the two World Wars.[22]

According to the three military manuals enemy character of vessels and aircraft is determined *prima facie* by the flag they are flying or by the markings they are bearing. Any vessel or aircraft owned or controlled by a belligerent possesses enemy character, regardless of whether it is operating under a neutral flag or is bearing neutral markings.[23] As regards goods found on board an enemy vessel, they are presumed to be of enemy character in the absence of proof of their neutral character.[24] Transfers are not recognized when fraudulently made for the purpose of evading belligerent capture. With regard to the determination of enemy character of the owners of vessels and goods there are, however, differences. According to paragraph 723 of the Canadian draft manual enemy character of persons may be determined by their commercial domicile in territory belonging to or occupied by an enemy belligerent. The German manual refers to the nationality of the owner or, if the owner is a stateless person, to his residence. In the case of corporations their seat is relevant.[25]

IV. Visit, Search and Diversion

In the majority of naval armed conflicts that have occurred since 1945 the belligerents exercised the right of visit and search regardless of the ships' nationality. The reactions by third States were not uniform, even though in general they acquiesced in the exercise of these belligerent rights. There are, however, two events that occurred during the Iran-Iraq war that are worth mentioning.

---

21 See para. 7.4.
22 See, *e.g.*, R. Ottmüller, *supra* note 4, at pp. 47 ff., 117 ff., 180 ff., 219 ff., 271 ff., 292 ff.
23 NWP 9, para. 7.5; ZDv 15/2, para. 1022; Canadian draft manual, para. 716.
24 ZDv 15/2, para. 1028; Canadian draft manual, para. 723.
25 ZDv 15/2, para. 1027.

When in October 1985 an Iranian warship approached the French merchant vessel *Ville d'Angers*, a French warship operating in the area positioned itself in between the two ships and warned the Iranian warship that it would not hesitate to resort to force if the Iranian endeavoured to intercept the merchant.[26] Notwithstanding this incident and the successful deterrence of the Iranian warship the *Sécretaire d'Etat français à la Mer* announced that French tankers would not be escorted by French warships.[27]

As a result of escalating attacks on Kuwaiti vessels since September 1986 the United States responded, in March 1987, to a Kuwaiti request by placing eleven of Kuwait's oil tankers under the American flag.[28] Starting from the spring of 1988 all eleven reflagged tankers were transiting the Persian Gulf escorted by United States warships. Additionally, the USA and other States deployed naval units in the Gulf and in the Strait of Hormuz in order to protect international shipping and to carry out mine-sweeping operations. In this regard it is of importance that the U.S. stressed that its actions were fully consistent with the applicable rules of international law, which clearly recognized the right of a neutral State to escort and protect ships flying its flag which were not carrying contraband.[29] The U.S. added that U.S. ships would not be carrying oil from Iraq; neither party would thus have 'any basis for taking hostile actions against U.S. naval ships or the vessels they protect'.

With regard to the right of belligerents to visit and search all merchant vessels and aircraft, whether enemy or neutral, the three manuals are analogous.[30] Even though, in general, all vessels (and aircraft) may be visited and searched, this right should be exercised 'with all possible tact and consideration'.[31] If visit and search at sea is deemed hazardous or impracticable the neutral vessel may be diverted by the summoning warship or aircraft.[32]

Paragraph 7.6 NWP 9 exempts from visit and search neutral warships, neutral state ships and neutral merchant vessels travelling under convoy of neutral warships of the same nationality. However, the 'convoy commander may be required to provide in writing to the commanding officer of an intercepting belligerent warship information as to the character of the vessels and of their cargoes which could otherwise be obtained by visit and search. Should it be determined by the convoy

26 Ch. Rousseau, *supra* note 15, p. 233.

27 Ch. Rousseau, *supra* note 15, p. 139.

28 Dept. of Defense, *A Report to the Congress on Security Arrangements in the Persian Gulf* (15 June 1987), ii (Report by the Secretary of Defense, C. Weinberger). See also M.H. Nordquist/M.G. Wachenfeld, 'Legal Aspects of Reflagging Kuwaiti Tankers and the Laying of Mines in the Persian Gulf', 31 *German Yearbook of International Law* (1988), Vol. 31, pp. 138-164.

29 See, *e.g.*, Dept. of State Bull. (June 1987), at p. 70; Dept. of State Bull. (June 1988), at p. 44.

30 NWP 9, para. 7.6; Canadian draft manual, para. 720; ZDv 15/2, paras. 1014 and 1140.

31 See, *e.g.*, Canadian draft manual, para. 720 (2); NWP 9, para. 7.6.1.

32 NWP 9, para. 7.6.1; Canadian draft manual, para. 720; ZDv 15/2, para. 1014.

commander that a vessel under his charge possesses enemy character or carries contraband cargo, he is obliged to withdraw his protection of the offending vessel, making it liable to visit and search, and possible capture, by the belligerent warship'. A similar rule is laid down in paragraph 1141 of the German manual. NWP 9 as well as the German manual are, however, silent on the consequences if the convoy commander does not comply with the said obligation.

The three manuals under scrutiny here do not differ with regard to the consequences in case of resistance to visit and search and if the summoned vessel takes to flight. In case of flight, the vessel may be pursued and brought to, by forcible means if necessary.[33] In case of active resistance to visit and search, enemy merchant ships may be attacked and destroyed,[34] neutral merchant vessels and aircraft are liable to capture.[35]

There seemingly is agreement that due to changes in warfare visit and search at sea have become hazardous or impracticable. Hence, NWP 9,[36] the Canadian[37] and the German[38] manuals directly or indirectly acknowledge the practice of issuing navicerts or aircerts in order to control the flow of goods on and over the high seas. Such navicerts or aircerts issued by one belligerent have no effect on the visit and search rights of a belligerent of the opposing side.[39]

V. Capture of Enemy Vessels and Goods

It clearly follows from the practice of States engaged in armed conflicts since World War II that they have maintained the right of capture of enemy vessels and goods. On the other hand, certain categories of enemy ships were exempted from capture. E.g., during 'Operation Sea Dragon' the U.S. Navy did not interfere with Vietnamese vessels used exclusively for fishing along the coast or with small boats employed in local trade even though Vietnam is not a party to Hague Convention XI.[40] Only after it had become evident that these ships were used for transport of ammunition etc. they lost their protected status.[41]

---

33 NWP 9, para. 7.6.1 (3); Canadian draft manual, paras. 716, 717; ZDv 15/2, paras. 1014, 1025, 1139.
34 NWP 9, para. 8.2.2.2; Canadian draft manual, para. 716; ZDv 15/2, para. 1025.
35 NWP 9, para. 7.9; Canadian draft manual, para. 717; ZDv 15/2, para. 1139.
36 Para. 7.4.2.
37 Para. 720.
38 Para. 1141.
39 NWP 9, para. 7.4.2.
40 D.P. O'Connell (1975), *supra* note 4, at p. 177.
41 D.P. O'Connell (1970), *supra* (note 4), at p. 33 ff.

According to the three manuals, enemy merchant vessels[42] and civil aircraft may be captured outside neutral jurisdiction, unless specially protected.[43] Prior exercise of visit and search is not required, provided positive determination of enemy status can be achieved by other means.[44] Leaving aside the special cases where enemy merchant vessels and aircraft may be considered legitimate military objectives[45] they may, in case of military necessity, be destroyed only after all possible measures have been taken to provide for the safety of passengers and crew.[46] Documents and papers relating to the prize should be safeguarded and, if practicable, the personal effects of passengers should be saved.[47]

With the exception of specially protected articles, all goods found on board enemy merchant vessels and aircraft may be seized.[48] Subject to a decision of a prize court they may be confiscated, unless – with the exception of contraband – it can be proved that they are of neutral character.[49]

The three manuals do not differ either with regard to the classes of enemy vessels and aircraft that are exempt from capture (and destruction).[50] A precondition for their specially protected status is that they are innocently employed in their exempt category.[51] These specially protected vessels and aircraft must not take part in the hostilities, must not hamper the movement of combatants, must submit to identification and inspection procedures, and may be ordered out of harm's way. These specifically exempt vessels and aircraft include:

1. Vessels and aircraft designated for and engaged in the exchange of prisoners (cartel vessels).
2. Properly designated and marked hospital ships, medical transports, coastal rescue craft and known medical aircraft.
3. Vessels charged with religious, non-military scientific, or philanthropic missions. (Vessels engaged in the collection of scientific data of potential military application are not exempt.)

---

42 In principle, the term merchant vessel also applies to other sea going private vessels, such as yachts and pleasure boats.
43 NWP 9, para. 8.2.2.1; Canadian draft manual, para. 716; ZDv 15/2, para. 1023. The same applies to enemy warships and military aircraft, since they are 'classical' military objectives.
44 See, *e.g.*, NWP 9, para. 8.2.2.1.
45 NWP 9, para. 8.2.2.2; Canadian draft manual, para. 716 (3-5); ZDv 15/2, para. 1025. If they are military objectives they may be attacked and sunk like enemy warships.
46 NWP 9, para. 8.2.2.1; Canadian draft manual, para. 716 (2); ZDv 15/2, para. 1026.
47 *Ibid.*
48 Canadian draft manual, para. 723 (3); ZDv 15/2, para. 1028.
49 *Ibid.*
50 NWP 9, para. 8.2.3; Canadian draft manual, para. 718; ZDv 15/2, paras. 1034 ff. and 1054 ff.
51 *Ibid.*

4. Vessels and aircraft guaranteed safe conduct by prior arrangement between the belligerents.
5. Small coastal (not deep-sea) fishing vessels and small boats engaged in local coastal trade. Such vessels and boats are subject to the regulations of a belligerent naval commander operating in the area.

Refusal by an exempt vessel or aircraft to provide immediate identification is considered to be an act of refusing to stop upon being summoned, particularly in the light of the abilities of modern communications.[52]

With regard to passenger vessels and civil airliners there are considerable differences. Whereas the Canadian draft manual obviously treats them in the same manner as enemy merchant ships or non-military aircraft, NWP 9 provides that 'civilian passenger vessels at sea and civil airliners in flight are subject to capture but are exempt from destruction'.[53] The German manual, in paragraph 1034 also exempts from destruction 'passenger ships exclusively engaged in the transport of civilians', provided they comply with the conditions lawfully imposed on them, they do not abuse their mission, or are not engaged in any other activity bringing them under the definition of a military objective. According to paragraph 1036 the same applies to civilian airliners. Civilian aircraft may be ordered to land on the ground or water in order to be searched.

The Canadian draft manual as well as NWP 9 exempt certain categories from capture as contraband.[54] According to the Canadian draft manual these are:

a. free articles, *i.e.* goods not susceptible for use in armed conflict;
b. articles intended exclusively for the treatment of wounded and sick members of the armed forces and for the prevention of disease. The particulars concerning the carriage of such articles must be transmitted to the adverse State and approved by it; and
c. articles provided for by a convention (treaty) or by special arrangement as between the belligerents.

NWP 9 is identical but more specific for two additional categories of protected articles are expressly enumerated:

3. Medical and hospital stores, religious objects, clothing, bedding, essential foodstuffs, and means of shelter for the civilian population in general, and women and children in particular, provided there is no serious reason to believe that such

---

52 NWP 9, para. 8.2.3, note 63; ZDv 15/2, para. 1035.
53 Para. 8.2.3 (6).
54 NWP 9, para. 7.4.1.2; Canadian draft manual, para. 721 (6).

goods will be diverted to other purposes, or that a definite military advantage would accrue to the enemy by their substitution for enemy goods that would thereby become available for military purposes;
4. Items destined for prisoners of war, including individual parcels and collective relief shipments containing food, clothing, medical supplies, religious objects, and educational, cultural, and athletic articles.

Since in these two manuals contraband is being dealt with in the context of neutrality and measures against neutral trade one might be inclined to restrict these rules to goods found on board neutral merchant vessels (and aircraft). In view of the purpose of the articles enumerated – with the exception of 'free articles' and probably athletic articles – one may, however, conclude that they are exempt from capture also when found on board enemy vessels.

The German manual, additionally, exempts the following objects from capture irrespective of the law of contraband:

– objects belonging to the passengers or the crew of a captured ship and intended for their personal use;
– instruments and other material belonging to relief societies;
– cultural property;
– postal correspondence of the national Prisoner of War Bureau and the Central Prisoners of War Information Agency;
– postal consignments and relief shipments destined for prisoners of war and civilian internees as well as postal consignments dispatched by these persons;
– relief shipments intended for the population of occupied territory, provided that the conditions attached by the capturing party to the conveyance of such shipments are observed; and
– relief shipments intended for the population of any territory under the control of a party to the conflict other than occupied territory.[55]

VI. Capture of Neutral Vessels and Goods

During the Middle East conflict until 1973, the 1965 and 1971 conflicts between India and Pakistan, and during the 1980-1988 Gulf War, neutral merchant shipping was severely interfered with. Belligerent measures were, however, not confined to capture. Especially during the Iran-Iraq war neutral merchant ships were exposed to

---

55 ZDv 15/2, para. 1031.

a sink-on-sight policy by both belligerents.[56] While there is agreement that the attacks on neutral tankers in the Gulf were contrary to international law – let alone the establishment of so-called exclusion zones[57] – it remains an open question under what conditions neutral merchant vessels, in the *opinio juris* of States, are liable to capture. There is, however, some evidence in the three military manuals.

Whereas it is acknowledged that in principle neutral merchant vessels and aircraft are exempt from capture,[58] according to the three manuals neutral merchant vessels and aircraft are liable to capture if engaged in any of the following activities:

1. Avoiding an attempt to establish identity
2. Resisting visit and search
3. Carrying contraband
4. Breaking or attempting to break a blockade
5. Presenting irregular or fraudulent papers; lacking necessary papers; or destroying, defacing or concealing papers
6. Violating regulations established by a belligerent within the immediate area of naval operations
7. Carrying personnel in the military or public service of the enemy
8. Communicating information in the interest of the enemy.[59]

According to paragraph 717 of the Canadian draft manual they are liable to capture also when 'operating directly under enemy control, orders, charter, employment or direction'. In paragraph 7.5.2 NWP 9 such an act as well as resistance to 'an attempt to establish identity, including visit and search' renders the vessel or aircraft liable to the same treatment as enemy merchant vessels or aircraft.

Of course, according to the Canadian as well as the U.S. manual the following activities render neutral merchant vessels and aircraft liable to destruction:

– taking a direct part in the hostilities on the side of the enemy;
– acting in any capacity as a naval or military auxiliary to the enemy's armed forces.[60]

---

56 See the examples given by A. Gioia/N. Ronzitti, *supra* note 4, at p. 231 ff.
57 See, *e.g.*, M. Bothe, 'Neutrality in Naval Warfare', in: A.J.M. Delissen/G.J. Tanja (eds.), *Humanitarian Law of Armed Conflict - Challenges Ahead. Essays in Honour of Frits Kalshoven*, Dordrecht/Boston/London 1991, pp. 387-405, at p. 400 ff.
58 See, *e.g.*, NWP 9, para. 7.4.
59 NWP 9, para. 7.9.
60 NWP 9, para. 7.5.1; Canadian draft manual, para. 717 (4). It may be added that according to the Canadian draft manual the same applies if they 'actively resist visit and search or capture; refuse to stop upon being duly summoned; or sail under convoy of enemy warships or military aircraft'.

In all other cases neutral vessels and aircraft may be destroyed only after every reasonable effort has been made to avoid destruction.[61]

As already shown, NWP 9 as well as the Canadian and the German manuals – while acknowledging that a neutral State is not obliged to forbid its subjects to engage in commerce with belligerent nations[62] – renders neutral merchant vessels and aircraft liable to capture if engaged in the carriage of contraband. While in these manuals the traditional distinction between absolute and conditional contraband is upheld formally they all agree that its relevance is of minor importance today.[63] Hence, the 'precise nature of a belligerent's contraband list may vary according to the particular circumstances of the armed conflict'.[64] The doctrine of continuous voyage is applied to both categories.[65] However, in NWP 9 it is made clear that 'although conditional contraband is liable to capture if ultimately destined for the use of an enemy government and its armed forces, enemy destination of conditional contraband must be factually established and cannot be presumed'.[66]

VII. Preliminary Conclusions

It follows from the foregoing that there is at least a tendency to adhere to the traditional law insofar as measures of economic warfare at sea are concerned. Even in international armed conflicts not amounting to 'war', ships encountered beyond neutral jurisdiction may be stopped, visited, diverted and searched regardless of their function or nationality. The only – but important – exceptions relate to neutral warships and government ships and to neutral merchant ships travelling under convoy of a neutral warship or military aircraft of the same nationality. Enemy property at sea is not exempt from capture. Insofar as certain articles exempt from capture are concerned, the 1977 Protocol Additional I seems to have had some influence. Neutral merchant vessels and aircraft are liable to capture (and partly to destruction) if they engage in activities that sustain the enemy's war fighting capability. Cargo on board neutral merchant vessels may be captured if such vessels engage in what may still be labelled unneutral service or if the goods are contraband. The distinction between absolute and conditional contraband is upheld only formally. Materially it will depend on the circumstances whether an article will be comprised in contraband lists. Finally, according to the three military manuals here under scrutiny, States seem to

---

61 See NWP 9, para. 7.9.1; Canadian draft manual, para. 717 (2) and (3); ZDv 15/2, para. 1148.
62 NWP 9, para. 7.4; ZDv 15/2, para. 1109.
63 NWP 9, para. 7.4.1; Canadian draft manual, para. 721 (1); ZDv 15/2, para. 1143.
64 Canadian draft manual, para. 721 (2).
65 NWP 9, para. 7.4.1.1; Canadian draft manual, para. 721 (3) and (4).
66 Para. 7.4.1.1.

be prepared to make use of the navicert and ship's warrant system as known from the two World Wars.

B. RESTRICTIONS ON PRIZE MEASURES

In the preceding section the law of prize has been dealt with in an isolated way. Especially, no attention has been paid to those principles and rules of international law which, generally speaking, may have an impact on the scope of applicability of international prize law. The present section is, therefore, devoted to the following controversial issues:[67]

- The possible impact of the principles regarding the use of force contained in the Charter of the United Nations – as well as in general international law – *i.e.* the modern *jus ad bellum*, on the laws of (naval) warfare and neutrality at sea and, consequently, on the law of prize.
- The problem whether the applicability of the law of prize is confined to situations in which there exists a 'state of war' or whether prize measures may be taken in any international armed conflict.

I. The Impact of the Modern *jus ad bellum* on International Prize Law

1. The Traditional View *v.* the Modern Approach

According to the traditional view, that is apparently still held by the majority of international lawyers,[68] the impact of the *jus ad bellum* on an ongoing armed conflict is confined to situations when the Security Council decides, in accordance with Chapter VII, to take action directed at the prevention or termination of hostilities.[69] In all other respects, the Charter of the United Nations is considered *lex generalis* and the law of armed conflict *lex specialis*. The purpose of the Charter

---

67 Another issue worth mentioning is the possible impact of the new law of the sea. However, the present paper has to confine itself to the two issues stated. With regard to the impact of the new law of the sea see, *e.g.* M. Bothe, *supra* note 57, at p. 402 ff.; E. Rauch, *The Protocol Additional to the Geneva Conventions for the Protection of Victims of Armed Conflicts and the United Nations Convention on the Law of the Sea: Repercussions on the Law of Naval Warfare*, Berlin 1984, at pp. 31 ff. and 132 ff.

68 See *inter alia* F. Berber, *Lehrbuch des Völkerrechts*, Vol. II, München 1969, p. 57 ff.; C.J. Colombos, *The International Law of the Sea*, 5th ed., London 1962, paras. 588 ff.; K. Ipsen, *Völkerrecht*, 3rd ed., München 1991, Chapter 15.

69 L.C. Green, 'Comments on the General Report on Visit, Search, Diversion and Capture', Round Table of Experts on International Humanitarian Law Applicable to Armed Conflicts at Sea, Bergen, 20 - 24 September 1991 (not yet published).

being to preserve or restore peace it may not regulate the conduct of the parties during an armed conflict. Hence, the sole significance of the doctrine of proportionality in relation to Article 51 UN Charter is said to be confined to an assessment of whether the initial action taken in response to an act of aggression under the plea of self-defence is in fact proportionate.[70]

The traditional view is challenged by an increasing number of scholars[71] who maintain that the *jus ad bellum* as contained in the UN Charter and in general international law has a direct impact on the conduct of hostilities. Accordingly, for a State's conduct of an armed conflict to be entirely lawful it must observe both the demands of the laws of armed conflict and the limitations imposed by the requirements of necessity and proportionality as provided for by the modern *jus ad bellum*.[72] The extended scope of application of the *jus ad bellum* is explained by the fact that States engaged in active hostilities frequently invoke the right of self-defence, thus expressing their intent to conduct hostilities within the limits of necessity and proportionality.[73] Moreover, according to one proponent of that position, in view of its object and purpose Article 2(4) UN Charter can neither be terminated nor suspended after this prohibition has been violated for that would be contrary to its peremptory character.[74] In any event, according to the modern approach, the laws of armed conflict are not superseded by the principles of necessity and proportionality.[75]

Despite the common approach described above there are, however, some significant differences as to the legal consequences. According to one author a State's conduct of an armed conflict can be in violation of international law even though that State complies with the requirements of the laws of armed conflict.[76] That would, *e.g.*, be the case if a State resorting to force for a legitimate objective conducts the ensuing hostilities in excess of what is reasonably necessary and proportionate.[77] Another proponent of that position maintains that, under the *jus ad bellum*, a

---

70 *Ibid.*
71 Chr. Greenwood, 'Self-Defence and the Conduct of International Armed Conflict', in: Y. Dinstein (ed.), *International Law at a Time of Perplexity. Essays in Honour of Shabtai Rosenne*, Dordrecht/Boston/London 1989, pp. 273-288; R. Lagoni, 'Gewaltverbot, Seekriegsrecht und Schiffahrtsfreiheit im Golfkrieg', in: W. Fürst/R. Herzog/D.C. Umbach (eds.), *Festschrift für Wolfgang Zeidler*, Vol. II, Berlin/New York 1987, pp. 1833-1867; M. Bothe, *supra* note 57, at p. 389 ff.; N. Ronzitti, 'The Crisis of the Traditional Law Regulating International Armed Conflicts at Sea and the Need for its Revision', in: N. Ronzitti (ed.), *supra* note 5, pp. 1-58.
72 Chr. Greenwood, *supra* note 71, at p. 275.
73 N. Ronzitti, *supra* note 71, at p. 3; R. Lagoni, *supra* note 71, at p. 1844.
74 R. Lagoni, 'Neutrality, the Right of Shipping and the Use of Force in the Persian Gulf', *Proceedings of the American Society of International Law* 1988.
75 N. Ronzitti, *supra* note 71, at p. 3; Chr. Greenwood, *supra* note 71, at p. 274 ff.; R. Lagoni, *ibid.*
76 Chr. Greenwood, *supra* note 71, at p. 274 ff.
77 *Ibid.*

belligerent may only make use of the *jus in bello* to that extent which is necessary and proportionate for self-defence.[78] Hence, the *jus ad bellum* is considered an additional legal yardstick for the evaluation of belligerent conduct. Yet another approach is chosen by Lagoni who believes the laws of war to apply *ab initio* within the restrictions of said principles, *i.e.* the rules of the laws of armed conflict have to be reconciled with the principles of necessity and proportionality and applied in a modified form.[79]

Unfortunately, the impact of the *jus ad bellum* on the legality of prize measures against enemy merchant vessels and goods is not being dealt with in great depth. Ronzitti confines himself to state that such measures are not in themselves inconsistent with the right of self-defence as long as they meet the test of necessity and proportionality.[80] Hence, in a large-scale conflict such measures would be justified, while in a small conflict they would be less justified or not justifiable at all.[81]

Much greater attention is paid to measures of economic warfare involving neutral vessels and goods.[82] Greenwood believes that 'except, perhaps, in a conflict on the massive scale of the two World Wars, it is unlikely that the international community would tolerate interference of that degree today'.[83] Still, a State engaged in armed conflict may be entitled to exercise the right of visit, search and capture/seizure in a 'clear case, where a neutral ship was suspected of carrying arms or combatant personnel which posed a serious threat'.[84] However, according to Greenwood, 'it seems unlikely that the condemnation of a neutral ship in prize could be justified in any but the most extreme cases'.[85] By characterising visit, search and diversion of neutral merchant vessels by Iran as necessary and proportionate for Iran's self-defence Lagoni, in his study of the 1980-1988 Iran-Iraq war, takes a similar view.[86] Ronzitti differentiates between rights of belligerents toward neutrals, on the one hand, and rights of neutrals toward belligerents, on the other. By referring to the late Professor O'Connell,[87] he considers it likely that the former category of rights has been rendered obsolete by the prohibition of the use of force under the UN Charter.[88] In any event, neutrals may not be molested in so far as they conform

---

78 N. Ronzitti, *supra* note 71, at p. 4.
79 R. Lagoni, *supra* note 71, at p. 1843 ff.
80 N. Ronzitti, *supra* note 71, at p. 4.
81 *Ibid.*
82 Chr. Greenwood, *supra* note 71, at p. 283 ff.; M. Bothe, *supra* note 57, at p. 391 ff.; N. Ronzitti, *supra* note 71, at p. 7 ff.; R. Lagoni, *supra* note 74.
83 Chr. Greenwood, *supra* note 71, at p. 284.
84 *Ibid.*
85 *Ibid.*
86 R. Lagoni, *supra* note 71, at p. 1859 ff.
87 D.P. O'Connell (1975), *supra* note 4, at p. 160.
88 N. Ronzitti, *supra* note 71, at p. 6.

with the duties of neutrality.[89] The exercise of the traditional rights of visit, search and seizure of contraband, that must be evaluated according to the requisites of necessity and proportionality, according to Ronzitti, is not in itself inconsistent with the right of self-defence, even if the rights of third States are involved.[90] For, he concludes, 'it would be completely unreasonable not to allow belligerents to take action against neutral vessels which, for instance, are loaded with a cargo of war material bound for an enemy port'.[91] Finally, Bothe maintains that the admissibility of acts of coercion under the law of neutrality, such as visit, search and blockade, 'must be evaluated both under the laws of neutrality and under the *jus contra bellum*'.[92] And, he goes on, 'since there exists no overall violent situation between a neutral and a belligerent State ... the double scrutiny principle applies not to the situation as a whole, but to the individual act of violence or coercion'.[93] However, visit and search of neutral merchant vessels which are not travelling under convoy is not considered illegal under the *jus contra bellum* because 'this does not constitute a use of force against the flag State which would be prohibited under the Charter'.[94]

It is of interest that the British government, after the interception of the British merchant vessel Barber Perseus by Iran during the Iran-Iraq war seemingly attributed to the right of self-defence a similar impact on the legality of prize measures:

> '... under Article 51 of the United Nations Charter a State such as Iran, actively engaged in an armed conflict, is entitled in exercise of its inherent right of self-defence, to stop and search a foreign merchant ship on the high seas if there is reasonable ground for suspecting that the ship is taking arms to the other side for use in the conflict ...'[95]

This statement implies that today, under the right of self-defence, the exercise of the traditional belligerent rights of visit and search of neutral merchant vessels may be considered legal only if there are reasonable grounds for suspecting that they are carrying contraband goods. If there are no such reasonable grounds for suspicion the exercise of these rights would not be necessary and proportionate for the belligerent's self-defence.

---

89 *Ibid.*
90 *Ibid.*, at p. 7.
91 *Ibid.*, at p. 10.
92 M. Bothe, *supra* note 57, at p. 393.
93 *Ibid.*
94 *Ibid.*
95 Statement by the Minister of State, Foreign and Commonwealth Office, January 28, 1986, House of Commons Debates, Vol. 90, col. 426; reprinted in: 42 *British Yearbook of International Law* (1986), at p. 583.

It is important to note in this context that the 'theory of graduated force' formulated by the late Professor O'Connell[96] differs considerably from the approach just described. Professor O'Connell starts from the premise that '... today there is the important difference that the law has changed since 1945 so as to deprive self-defensive operations of the benefit of the belligerent freedoms that classical international law endorsed for cases of naval warfare. There are now limitations upon what forces engaged in self-defence may do and where they may do it, for self-defence is not a release from all constraints but is measured reaction necessary to the occasion and proportional to the threat'.[97] Since self-defence imports restrictions of necessity and proportionality it excludes 'from the traditional range of options many types of naval operations, including visit and search on the high seas'.[98] The limitations arising from the 'theory of graduated force', however, merely apply to situations not amounting to war, *i.e.* to 'the twilight zone which is neither peace nor war'.[99] Hence, in contrast to the modern position of the scholars mentioned above, according to O'Connell, the *jus in bello* would apply without the limitations of necessity and proportionality to any situation that can be characterized 'war'. Irrespective of the objections that may be raised against the application of the *jus ad bellum* during an armed conflict[100] it is, however, doubtful whether the laws of war in order to become applicable in fact presuppose a 'state of war'.[101]

2. Appraisal

As regards the traditional view, the characterization of the laws of war as *leges speciales* superseding the *leges generales* of the *jus ad bellum* is not necessarily a cogent one. It would, *e.g.*, be in conformity with generally acknowledged principles of legal methodology to apply the *lex generalis* if the *lex specialis* contains a lacuna.[102] With regard to the laws of war one may take the position that such a lacuna exists with regard to the objective that may legitimately be pursued when it comes to the application of belligerent measures. In any event, the mere fact that the *jus in bello* applies to a given situation would not allow the conclusion that the *jus ad bellum* has been abolished altogether. It is one of the fundamental principles of modern international law that war and the use of force have ceased to be rights

---

96 D.P. O'Connell, *supra* note 4, at p. 53 ff.
97 *Ibid.*, at p. 54.
98 D.P. O'Connell (1970), *supra* note 4, at p. 27.
99 D.P. O'Connell (1970), *supra* note 4, at p. 24.
100 See *infra* notes 105 ff. and accompanying text.
101 See *infra* notes 149 ff. and accompanying text.
102 See *e.g.* U. Fastenrath, *Lücken im Völkerrecht*, Berlin 1991, p. 176 ff.; 213 ff.

which States are entitled to exercise at their unfettered discretion.[103] It would be a strange result indeed if that principle would entirely be deprived of its legal validity by the sole fact that it has been violated.[104]

However, the view that the *jus ad bellum*, even during an armed conflict, governs the legality of belligerent measures in addition to the *jus in bello* may not remain unobjected either.[105]

First, it undermines the traditional principle that rules regulating the conduct of hostilities should apply equally to both sides of the conflict, regardless of who is the aggressor, and, hence, the principle of the exclusive operation of the *jus in bello*.[106] The equal application of the laws of armed conflict can be assured only if it applies exclusively to the conduct of hostilities. Any application of further principles, like necessity and proportionality, would transform the contest into a struggle which is subject to no regulation at all.[107] All rules of warfare, and not only those of the Geneva type, are, in a sense, humanitarian in character 'inasmuch as their object is to safeguard, within the limits of the stern exigencies of war, human life and some other fundamental human rights and to make possible a measure of intercourse between enemies'.[108] For that very reason, during the war or international armed conflict respectively, 'all belligerents, including the aggressor, must be held to be under a duty to respect and are entitled to rely as among themselves on the observance of rules of warfare as generally recognized'.[109] The necessity of maintaining the equal operation of the laws of armed conflict, irrespective of the illegality on the one side, or on both sides, is not only a matter of principle but also follows from State practice. In the aftermath of World War II there was no judicial authority in support of the proposition that the aggressor is not entitled during the war to rely on those rules of warfare that bear on the actual conduct of hostili-

---

103 See *e.g.* H. Lauterpacht, 'Rules of Warfare in an Unlawful War', in: G.A. Lipsky (ed.), *Law and Politics in the World Community*, Berkeley/Los Angeles 1953, pp. 89-113, at p. 89.

104 H. Lauterpacht (*supra* note 103, at p. 90) believes that '... once a treaty has been adopted which is of a fundamental and comprehensive character, it is difficult – and probably unscientific – to act on the view that it settles only that part of the law to which it expressly refers and nothing else'.

105 We are not here concerned with situations where the Security Council has authoritatively determined the aggressor. In that case it is commonly understood that the aggressor's conduct of hostilities will be illegal even if in compliance with the laws of war.

106 See the references *supra* notes 67 and 68; also H. Lauterpacht, 'The Limits of the Operation of the Law of War', 30 *British Yearbook of International Law* (1953), pp. 206-243, at p. 212; Y. Dinstein, *War, Aggression and Self-Defence*, Cambridge 1988, at p. 147 ff.

107 H. Lauterpacht, *supra* note 103, at p. 92.

108 *Ibid.*, at p. 93.

109 *Ibid.*; also F. Berber (*supra* note 68, at p. 59) who states that the equal application of the laws of war is the most important guarantee for its observance.

ties.[110] Furthermore, the principles of equal and exclusive operation of the laws of war were reaffirmed by the 1974-1977 Diplomatic Conference. The preamble to the 1977 Additional Protocol I, in which express reference is made to the prohibition of the use of force under the UN Charter, reflects the antagonism between on the one hand, the *jus ad bellum*, which prohibits war and the use of force, and, on the other hand, humanitarian law, which establishes rules for situations which according to the *jus ad bellum* should not exist.[111] Since, however, the *jus ad bellum* is often violated there is a need to formulate rules that apply even in such situations in order to protect the victims of armed conflicts. That is made sufficiently clear by paragraph 3 ('nevertheless'). While paragraph 4 aims to protect the *jus ad bellum* against any infringement by humanitarian law, paragraph 5 allows but the conclusion that humanitarian law ignores the distinction between a legal and an illegal use of force according to the UN Charter.[112] Hence, as far as Additional Protocol I is concerned, one may argue that, according to the consensus of the negotiating parties, the *jus ad bellum* has no impact whatsoever on the legality of the conduct of hostilities as long as the Protocol applies to a given situation. Moreover, since Additional Protocol I is not restricted to purely Geneva type rules but to a great extent contains what has been considered Hague law it is suggested that the foregoing conclusion also applies to the laws of naval warfare, including international prize law: as long as the law of prize applies there is no room for the principles of necessity and proportionality derived from the modern *jus ad bellum*.

Greenwood meets some of these objections by the following arguments: In theory, the limitations inherent in the principle of self-defence will bind only the victim State, for the entire use of force by the aggressor will be contrary to Article 2(4) of the UN Charter. In practice, the *jus ad bellum* would not affect the equal application of the laws of armed conflict because a State's use of force may violate Article 2(4) without involving a breach of the *jus in bello*. Moreover, since both sides will claim to be acting in self-defence, the limitations upon the conduct of a conflict which the requirements of necessity and proportionality impose would tend to be applied equally to both parties in the conflict.[113] However, these arguments are not convincing if the impact of said principles is conceived of in such a way that the *jus in bello* may be made use of only to that extent that is necessary and proportionate

---

110 In the Hostages trial (*U.S. v. Wilhelm List et al.*) the Military Tribunal held that 'International Law makes no distinction between a lawful and unlawful occupant in dealing with the respective duties of occupant and population in occupied territory'. See also other the judgments cited by H. Lauterpacht, *supra* note 103, at p. 95 ff.

111 K.J. Partsch, in: M. Bothe/K.J. Partsch/W.A. Solf, *New Rules for Victims of Armed Conflicts*, The Hague/Boston/London 1982, p. 32 ff.

112 *Ibid.*, at p. 33.

113 Chr. Greenwood, *supra* note 71, at p. 287.

for self-defence.[114] For then one side could be prohibited from taking certain measures provided for by the *jus in bello* even though the other side would benefit from them. This also holds true if the laws of war are to apply *ab initio* within the restrictions of said principles.[115] Admittedly, Greenwood who applies the principles of necessity and proportionality in addition to, and distinct from, the *jus in bello* would not have to cope with such problems.[116] Still, the fact that the entire use of force by the aggressor will be contrary to Article 2(4) UN Charter does not necessarily imply that, leaving aside the case where the Security Council has authoritatively determined the aggressor, the principles of necessity and proportionality are of legal relevance also during an armed conflict. Moreover, there is no room for their application for the very reason that an authoritative assessment of whether a State has been acting in conformity with these principles will regularly not be possible during an ongoing conflict.[117] As Greenwood himself states, the limitations inherent in the concept of self-defence add a requirement of strategic proportionality.[118] The strategic level, however, can hardly be ascertained as long as the conflict is in progress. The same objection may be raised against the opinion held by Bothe. If the *jus contra bellum* is to be a legal yardstick for the 'action as a whole'[119] it is impossible to be applied during the conflict.

Secondly, the criteria offered by the proponents of the modern approach are too vague and hence much too easy subject to abuse. Taken at face value the legality of belligerent measures would depend on the extent of the conflict in question ('large-scale conflict'). Even if it were possible to clearly establish what a 'large-scale conflict' is, this would imply that the more rigorously a conflict is fought the more rights would accrue to the belligerents – even toward neutrals. If belligerent rights were indeed subject to the principles of necessity and proportionality this would open a wide margin of discretion lacking any clear-cut legal yardstick as provided for by the traditional and modern *jus in bello*.[120] With regard to the legality of prize measures against neutral ships and goods the proponents of the

114 As maintained by N. Ronzitti, *supra* note 71, at p. 4.
115 As maintained by R. Lagoni, *supra* note 71, at p. 1843 ff.
116 To a similar effect is the position of M. Bothe (*supra* note 57, at p. 392 ff.) who applies the *ius contra bellum* as a legal yardstick to the conflict as a whole.
117 H. Lauterpacht (*supra* note 103, at p. 98) states: 'The reasons which make it imperative to permit the full application, during the war and as between the belligerents, of the rules of war are especially cogent when we consider that in the present state of international organization there may be no means, so long as the war lasts, by which an authoritative judgement can be arrived at on the question as to which state is the aggressor'. It is submitted that this still holds true today. For the Kuwait crisis is only but an exceptional example of the functioning of the system of collective security. See also F. Berber, *supra* note 68, at p. 59.
118 Chr. Greenwood, *supra* note 71, at p. 279.
119 M. Bothe, *supra* note 57, at p. 393.
120 See *e.g.* W. Heintschel v. Heinegg, *supra* note 8, p. 288 ff.

modern approach, accordingly, do not give a satisfactory answer. They either doubt their legality altogether[121] or they consider it reasonable to maintain them.[122] They do, however, give no reason why, under the principles of necessity and proportionality, the argument of reasonableness is considered sufficient.

Thirdly and finally, it should not be left out of consideration that the *jus in bello*, as generally understood, does not confer upon belligerents unrestricted rights. This holds true with regard to methods and means of combat as well as with regard to measures of economic warfare, be they directed against enemy vessels and goods or against neutral merchant vessels and goods.[123]

From the foregoing it follows that, so long as hostilities are in progress, the 'fact of the illegality of the war undertaken by a party to the struggle in violation of its fundamental undertakings is irrelevant ... to the question of the applicability of rules of warfare in matters relating to the conduct of hostilities in the strict sense'[124] – at least insofar as the relations between the belligerents are concerned. This may be considered illogical and expressive of a serious defect in the efficacy of international law. 'However, this is the necessary result of the fact that international law, although it may prohibit war, is not always able to prevent it'.[125] Hence, under the laws of war, prize measures taken against enemy vessels and goods are in conformity with international law as long as they comply with the law of prize. Whether this is also true with regard to measures against neutral vessels and goods remains, however, undecided. We will return to that problem later.

3. A Different Approach

Although, according to the view taken here, the *jus ad bellum* has no direct impact on the conduct of hostilities this is not to say that it is superfluous. One cannot ignore altogether the development in international law that war and the use of force have ceased to be rights which States are entitled to exercise at their unfettered discretion. In the words of H. Lauterpacht 'we are not entitled to leave out of account the legal consequences of the most important of all changes which have taken place in the international legal system'.[126] Therefore, the conclusions arrived at in the preceding paragraph claim validity only for the period of ongoing hostilities and as between the belligerents. Hence, it needs to be scrutinized whether and to

---

121 Chr. Greenwood, *supra* note 71, at p. 284.
122 N. Ronzitti, *supra* note 71, at p. 10.
123 See *supra* notes 26 ff. and accompanying text.
124 H. Lauterpacht, *supra* note 103, at p. 99 ff.; also F. Berber, *supra* note 68, at p. 59 ff.
125 H. Lauterpacht, *supra* note 103, at p. 98 ff.
126 *Ibid.*, at p. 91.

what extent the *jus ad bellum* has an impact on inter-belligerent relations *ex post* and on the relations between belligerents and neutrals.

a. Inter-Belligerent Relations

With regard to the relations between belligerents it is submitted that the solution offered by H. Lauterpacht as early as 1953 is the correct one. Accordingly, after the cessation of hostilities there is room for the application of the principle that in certain spheres no rights and benefits can accrue to the aggressor from his illegal conduct.[127] That implies that the aggressor may not rely on the rules of warfare for enriching himself by acquiring title and by validly transferring it in respect of acts which are otherwise lawful, such as captures in prize.[128] According to H. Lauterpacht 'such denial of the validity of the title acquired or transferred by the aggressor would appear to be the very minimum of the consequences flowing from the illegality ... of his original action, because the operation of the rules of war, during an illegal war and in the mutual relations of the belligerents, does not follow from principle. It is contrary to principle. It follows from cogent reasons of humanity. When – and as soon as – these reasons cease to operate, the fact of the illegality of the war must be taken into account'.[129] Therefore any title acquired or transferred by the aggressor as a result of valid captures and condemnations in prize proceedings would be invalid as far as enemy ships and goods are concerned.[130]

H. Lauterpacht, in view of State practice after World War II, however, does not consider these conclusions to be in conformity with international law in force but substantially *de lege ferenda* only.[131] That may have been the correct view in 1953, even though the fact that certain legal claims are not made is not necessarily sufficient ground for denying their legal validity. Today, it is submitted, it is a principle of international law in force that, even though the conduct of hostilities during an ongoing conflict may only be evaluated by the rules of war, after the cessation of hostilities it may be judged in the light of the *jus ad bellum* whether the belligerents are entitled to benefit from the measures they have taken. The validity of this principle follows from the very fact that in the preamble of the 1977 Additional Protocol I an overwhelming majority of States has agreed that the *jus in bello* is without prejudice to the *jus ad bellum* thus recognizing that it maintains its

127 *Ibid.*, at p. 100; see also L. Oppenheim/H. Lauterpacht, *International Law*, Vol. II, 7th ed. London 1952, at p. 219 ff.
128 H. Lauterpacht, *supra* note 103, at p. 104 ff.
129 *Ibid.*, at p. 106.
130 See, *e.g.*, F. Berber, *supra* note 68, at p. 239 ff.
131 H. Lauterpacht, *supra* note 103, at p. 107.

legal effects despite the exclusive and equal operation of the laws of war.[132] If the *jus ad bellum* is to have any relevance at all it cannot be disposed of altogether for the mere fact that its prohibitions have been violated. Of course, during the conflict, *i.e.* in situations where the *jus ad bellum* has proved ineffective, it does not exert any legal consequences. Then, a special legal order applies in order to provide a minimum of legal constraints that are felt to be indispensable. If, however, the reasons for the operation of that 'order of necessity' cease to exist only those titles may be treated as valid also in peacetime that have not been acquired by a conduct contrary to the most fundamental principles of international law. It may be noted in this context that already the 1939 Harvard Research Draft on Rights and Duties of States in Case of Aggression laid down, in Article 3, that subject to the continued application of humanitarian rules 'an aggressor does not have any of the rights which it would have if it were a belligerent' and that 'titles to property are not affected by an aggressor's purported exercise of such rights'.[133]

Even though the solution offered by H. Lauterpacht is considered to be the correct one, it is believed that the reasons given need to be further elaborated. If the *jus in bello* is conceived of as creating rights on behalf of the belligerents it would indeed be a strange result if international law, on the one hand, in the form of prize law treated a title as valid, but, on the other hand, in the form of the *jus ad bellum* as invalid. That result would be justified, however, if the rules of prize law – as well as the laws of war in general – today are of a different character than common- ly – and traditionally – understood. Under the UN Charter the laws of war can no longer be characterized as granting certain novel rights international law would not recognize as long as States comply with their obligations derived from the prohibition of the non-use of force. There is indeed no cogent reason why the laws of war should allow the application of certain measures just because the States concerned are unwilling – or unable – to refrain from the use of force. Rather, the laws of war have to be conceived of as formulating duties which – as a minimum – have to be observed if States do resort to force. In other words, the restrictions contained in the rules of war are the utmost international law is ready to accept even if States are unwilling or unable to refrain from the use of armed force. Only insofar as these restrictions are not observed, the laws of war grant rights on the side of the aggrieved belligerent. Hence, belligerents, under the law of prize, are not entitled *e.g.* to capture enemy ships and goods. The law of prize simply acknowledges – as a constituent fact – that belligerents during an armed conflict are inclined to take such measures. In order to minimize the harmful effects of such conduct it formulates certain restrictions that have to be observed at any event. Accordingly, if a

---

132 See *supra* notes 111 ff. and accompanying text.
133 33 *American Journal of International Law* Suppl. (1939), pp. 819-909, at p. 886.

belligerent resorts to capture he may not capture certain categories of ships and goods.[134] Since usually both sides will take such measures, the law of prize acknowledges their validity as long as said restrictions are observed. However, that validity is limited in time, *i.e.* to the duration of the armed conflict, and subject to a final, or rather *ex post*, legal evaluation under the *jus ad bellum* which – it may be emphasized – is not superseded by the exclusive operation of the laws of war. According to the principle *ex iniuria jus non oritur* a title can be accepted as permanently valid only if it is not contrary to rules and principles that are not dispositive in character. While, by their very conduct, belligerents may agree to suspend the operation of certain peacetime rules of international law, they may not do so with regard to such rules that by the consensus of the community of States are generally acknowledged to be of a peremptory character. That is the reason why after the cessation of hostilities, on the one hand, one belligerent may not claim a certain conduct of his adversary to be contrary to, *e.g.*, the law of the sea, and why , on the other hand, he may claim the same conduct to be illegal under the *jus ad bellum*. Hence, the decisive difference with the reasoning by H. Lauterpacht lies in the characterization of the laws of war as an order of necessity that merely formulates restrictions for the conduct of hostilities. Since, accordingly, the laws of war are not apt to creating novel rights, it becomes evident that any belligerent conduct as well as the legal validity of titles acquired by such conduct necessarily have to be evaluated in the light of the *jus ad bellum* as soon as the reasons for the exclusive operation of that order of necessity have ceased to exist. Of course, if after the cessation of hostilities an authoritative determination of the aggressor (or of an excess of the right of self-defence in the light of the principles of necessity and proportionality) is unfeasible, the laws of war remain the only legal yardstick for evaluating the legality of belligerent conduct.

b. Relations between Belligerents and Neutrals

According to H. Lauterpacht the same principles ought to apply to title acquired or transferred by the aggressor as the result of valid captures and condemnations in prize proceedings relating to neutral vessels and goods.[135] Unfortunately, he does not deal with neutrality aspects in depth but deals with the laws of neutrality only in general terms. It is submitted here that the impact of the *jus ad bellum* on the law of neutrality, especially on the legality of prize measures taken against neutral

---

134 See *supra* notes 50 ff. and accompanying text.
135 H. Lauterpacht, *supra* note 103, at p. 108.

merchant vessels and goods, is different from that on the law of prize regulating measures against enemy vessels and goods.

A neutral, or rather non-participating, State may not assist the aggressor. In view of the importance and peremptory character of the *jus ad bellum* this will probably also apply to neutral merchantmen. However, this finding is safe only if there is an authoritative determination of the aggressor by the Security Council.[136] As soon as the Security Council under Article 39 UN Charter determines the aggressor, neutral flag States will be under an obligation to prohibit ships flying their flags any intercourse with the illegal belligerent.[137] If the neutral flag States do not comply with that duty the victim State will be allowed to take all necessary measures in order to prevent neutral merchant shipping from assisting the aggressor.[138] The flag States will not be entitled to protest against such measures. In view of the illegality of providing the aggressor with contraband goods, capture and seizure may still establish legally valid titles on behalf of the victim State. Prize measures taken against neutral merchant vessels and goods by the aggressor will be illegal even if they are in conformity with prize law.

Unfortunately, at least for the foreseeable future such a situation will be rather the exception than the rule. Hence, the question remains what rules and principles apply if there is no authoritative determination of the aggressor at all or if that determination can be arrived at only after the cessation of hostilities.

In these situations third States are neither obliged to determine which State is the aggressor nor do they have to prohibit their merchantmen any intercourse with any of the belligerents.[139] Therefore, neutral merchant vessels engaged in trade with a belligerent do not violate international law even if they are carrying contraband goods.[140] For the mere fact that two or more States have resorted to armed force in their relations cannot deprive neutral merchant vessels of their right of freedom of navigation and commerce. However, international law, in view of the fact that belligerents will interfere with neutral trade, has to provide standards that as a minimum have to be observed in order to minimize the harmful effects on neutral merchant shipping and commerce.[141] Again, it acknowledges as a constituent fact

---

136 See, *e.g.* Y. Dinstein, *supra* note 106, at p. 155.

137 See, *e.g.*, F. Berber, *supra* note 68, at p. 216 ff.

138 Chr. Greenwood, 'The Concept of War in Modern International Law', 36 *International Comparative Law Quarterly* (1987), pp. 283-306, at p. 299.

139 On the question whether a neutral State – relying on its own judgment – may take a position of 'benevolent' or 'qualified neutrality' (or of 'non-belligerency') see Y. Dinstein, *supra* note 106, at p. 155 ff.

140 That – it may be emphasized – is also the position under the traditional law, see W. Heintschel v. Heinegg, *supra* note 8, p. 317 ff.

141 This is – partly – acknowledged by Chr. Greenwood, when he maintains that 'whether or not non-participants have proclaimed themselves neutral in a conflict, the law of neutrality may be useful in setting an upper limit to the rights of the combatants', *supra* note 138, at p. 299.

that the belligerents will not tolerate any commerce they consider dangerous with their respective enemy. In order to achieve that goal international law has created a further order of necessity – the law of prize concerning measures against neutral vessels and goods.

Those rules – as well as probably the laws of neutrality in general – will be the exclusive legal yardstick during the period of hostilities regardless of whether the measures in question are taken by the aggressor or by the victim.[142] The reason for the exclusive operation of that body of law is to effectively protect neutral merchant vessels and property in an exceptional situation.[143] Principles of necessity and proportionality do not have an impact because they would be counterproductive to that objective. Prize measures that comply with these standards must be tolerated as long as hostilities are in progress. Even if one were prepared to share the view that any individual act of violence and coercion against neutral merchant vessels has to be evaluated both under the law of neutrality and under the *jus contra bellum*[144] that would not justify a different conclusion. For acts against individual neutral ships would not be prohibited under the Charter and acts against neutral merchant vessels under convoy are already prohibited under the law of prize.[145]

If, after the cessation of hostilities, there is an authoritative determination of the aggressor one cannot but conclude that his prize measures against neutral vessels and goods are illegal. Accordingly, he may be held liable and responsible for any damage that has resulted from visit, search, diversion and capture of neutral ships as well as from seizure of neutral goods. If possible, ships captured and goods seized will have to be returned to their owners. Otherwise, the owners will have to be compensated for their losses.[146] The victim of aggression is regularly not under such duties as far as visit, search and diversion are concerned. These measures are legal under the

---

142 E. Lauterpacht ('The Legal Irrelevance of the 'State of War'', *Proceedings American Society of International Law* (1968), pp. 58-68, at p. 63 ff.) maintains that an unlawful belligerent is not entitled to prize measures for there would be 'a genuine measure of absurdity in suggesting that a legal system which has excluded the right to have recourse to force should nonetheless permit the wrongdoer to assert belligerent rights arising out of his own wrongdoing'. Even the victim of aggression, he believes, is entitled to take prize measures only if – in the exercise of the rights under Article 51 UN Charter – that is justified by the exigencies of the situation. It needs to be taken into account, however, that according to E. Lauterpacht the right of prize can only be exercised during the existence of a state of war. Hence, his conclusions are founded on the assumption that, in principle, a state of war is incompatible with the Charter. With regard to the relevance of a state of war see *infra* notes 149 ff. and accompanying text.
143 With regard to doubts whether an aggressor State can take advantage from the law of neutrality see, *e.g.*, Chr. Greenwood, *supra* note 138, at p. 289.
144 M. Bothe, *supra* note 57, at p. 393.
145 See *supra* text subsequent to note 32.
146 This follows from the generally recognized principles and rules of State responsibility, unless there is a peace treaty regulating the details. See, *e.g.* F. Berber, *supra* note 68, at p. 239 ff.; Y. Dinstein, *supra* note 106, at p. 104 ff.; W. Heintschel v. Heinegg, 'Kriegsentschädigung, Reparation oder Schadenersatz? – Die möglichen Forderungen an den Irak nach Beendigung des Golf-Kriegs', 90 *Zeitschrift für Vergleichende Rechtswissenschaften* (1991), pp. 113-129.

law of prize as well as – *ex post* – under the *jus ad bellum*, provided the victim did not act in excess of what is considered necessary and proportionate for self-defence.[147] A different solution, however, applies as regards the legal consequences of capture and seizure. Since during the conflict there was – for what reasons soever – no authoritative determination of the aggressor, the neutral merchantmen's conduct was not illegal. Since neutrals may not be deprived of their property rights for the mere reason that two or more States were unwilling or unable to refrain from the use of force, captured ships and seized goods owned by neutrals, or rather of non-enemy character,[148] have to be returned to their legitimate owners.

If there is no *ex post* determination of the legality of the recourse to force, prize measures in conformity with the law of prize in principle remain valid. In this context, one may ask why neutrals should be obliged to submit to visit, search, and diversion only because two or more States are engaged in hostilities. Two aspects have to be observed. On the one hand, under the UN Charter the law of prize in principle cannot create rights against third parties on behalf of the belligerents. Indeed, today the traditional view of two competing rights cannot claim validity anymore. On the other hand, if the law of prize under the UN Charter has to be conceived of as an order of necessity which aims at minimizing the harmful effects of belligerent measures on neutral property, it may well create duties on behalf of those who are protected by it. Hence, according to the law of prize properly understood, neutral merchant vessels are under a duty to submit to visit, search and diversion if the belligerents make use of these measures. That is the only way to achieve the protective objective of prize law. As long as the belligerents exercise these measures within the restrictions of prize law the neutral flag States, during the conflict, cannot complain. And since, in the situation here under scrutiny, an *ex post* evaluation according to the *jus ad bellum* is not feasible, there is no further legal yardstick for evaluating the legality of such measures. If understood in that way, *i.e.* the law of prize not generating rights on behalf of the belligerents but only formulating legal restrictions for a given situation, the legal consequences of capture and seizure cannot anymore be conceived of as creating legally valid titles on behalf of the belligerents. Consequently, as a matter of logic and principle, captured neutral ships and seized neutral goods may not anymore be condemned. Title to neutral property cannot pass to the captor. Capture and seizure do not create permanently valid titles over neutral property because the scope of application of the law of prize – as an order of necessity – is limited in time as well as with regard to its legal consequences. Hence, both belligerents, after the cessation of hostilities, will be under

---

147 Chr. Greenwood (*supra* note 138, at p. 299) – though from a different approach – arrives at a similar conclusion.
148 It does not necessarily depend on ownership whether ships and goods are of enemy character; see *supra* note 22 ff. and accompanying text.

a duty to return neutral vessels captured and neutral goods seized. Admittedly, in State practice these principles have not yet been acknowledged. Hence, the conclusion offered here, which it is submitted is the correct one from the point of legal principle, is so *de lege ferenda* only. Still, it is important to draw the attention to the legal principle that under the UN Charter the laws of war and neutrality either in general or with regard to the maritime sphere have to be characterised as orders of necessity that do not create novel rights but only formulate minimum standards that have to be observed in situations which should not exist under the *jus ad bellum*.

II. The Relevance of a 'State of War'

So far as prize measures taken against enemy merchant vessels and goods are concerned, there is little evidence in recent State practice[149] as well as in the literature[150] to support the view that such measures are lawful only if there exists a 'war' in the legal sense or a 'state of war' respectively. Hence, the replacement of 'war' by 'international armed conflict',[151] that was initiated by the four Geneva Conventions of 1949 and continued by the 1977 Additional Protocol I, has also in this regard contributed to a change.

In view of the fact that in State practice attempts to exercise prize measures against neutral merchant vessels and goods in conflicts not amounting to 'war' have sometimes met with resistance, there is, in literature, considerable support for the view that 'the rules regulating the behaviour of neutrals and belligerents remain strictly dependent for their operation upon the existence of a state of war'.[152] It may be noted in this context that this view is sometimes combined with legal considerations derived from the UN Charter. Accordingly, the aggressor, while bound by rules and principles based on considerations of humanity, would never be entitled to take prize measures against neutrals for it would imply 'a genuine measure of absurdity in suggesting that a legal system which has excluded the right to have recourse to force should nonetheless permit the wrongdoer to assert belligerent rights arising out of his own wrongdoing'.[153] And since a state of war is incompatible

---

149 See *supra* note 14 ff. and accompanying text.
150 See, *e.g.*, Chr. Greenwood, *supra* note 138, at p. 294 ff.; R.W. Tucker, *The Law of War and Neutrality at Sea*, Washington 1957, at p. 23 ff.
151 See also K.J. Partsch, 'Armed Conflict', in: R. Bernhardt (ed.), 3 *Encyclopedia of Public International Law* (1982), p. 27.
152 R.W. Tucker, *supra* note 150, at p. 199 ff.; L. Delbez, 'La notion juridique de guerre', RGDIP 57 (1953), pp. 177-209; E. Lauterpacht, *supra* note 142, at p. 58; E. Castrén, *The Present Law of War and Neutrality*, Helsinki 1954, at p. 31 ff.; E. Kussbach, 'Neutral Trading', in: R. Bernhardt (ed.), 4 *Encyclopedia of Public International Law* (1982), pp. 7-9, at p. 9.
153 E. Lauterpacht, *supra* note 142, at p. 63.

with the Charter,[154] the victim of aggression would generally not be entitled to take prize measures against neutrals either, unless the creation of a state of war is justified by the exigencies of the situation.[155]

The position of the dependence of the operation of the law of prize on a 'state of war' necessarily implies a definition of the legal concept of war. That, however, involves tremendous difficulties and – it may be added – in most cases proves unsuccessful. It would, *e.g.*, be difficult to explain why the unilateral decision of one of the parties to the conflict to treat that conflict as war should have the effect of imposing duties on third States and their merchant shipping.[156] Similar difficulties exist with regard to an objective definition of war – which, by the way, has not been reached yet.[157] Despite these difficulties some authors, in view of the continued acceptance by States that war can exist as a legal institution, feel unable to abandon that position altogether.[158] Others attempt to avoid the said difficulties by characterising the exercise of belligerent rights over neutral shipping as an implicit assumption of the existence of a 'state of war'.[159] Again others, in view of the practice of States during the Iran-Iraq war, believe that the question of the existence of a formal 'state of war' is no longer of relevance.[160]

It is a typical feature of the positions just mentioned that the law of prize is considered to bring about rights and duties that do not exist prior to the outbreak of hostilities. While some accept such rights and duties only in situations that amount to war,[161] others are not prepared to deny belligerents a power of control over the flow of contraband as soon as there is actual fighting.[162] Be that as it may. According to the position taken here, it is irrelevant whether an international armed conflict may be characterised a war. The law of prize is an order of necessity which does not create novel rights on behalf of the belligerents but only duties on behalf of neutrals in order to effectively protect them against the harmful effects of belligerent measures. In other words it formulates the upper limit international law is willing to tolerate. Hence, as soon as a belligerent in fact interferes with neutral shipping and trade the law of prize is the legal yardstick with which these measures

---

154 R. Higgins, *Development of International Law through the Political Organs of the United Nations*, at p. 25.

155 E. Lauterpacht, *supra* note 142, at p. 64.

156 To the same effect see Chr. Greenwood, *supra* note 138, at p. 300.

157 F. Grob (*The Relativity of War and Peace*, New Haven 1949, at p. 179 ff.) already in 1949 has furnished ample proof for the non-existence of a 'state of war' in the legal sense.

158 *E.g.* Chr. Greenwood, *supra* note 138, at p. 305.

159 *E.g.* D. Schindler, 'Transformations in the Law of Neutrality since 1945', in: A.J.M. Delissen/G.J. Tanja (eds.), *supra* note 57, pp. 367-386, at p. 376.

160 *E.g.* M. Bothe, *supra* note 57, at p. 390.

161 See the references in note 151.

162 *E.g.* M. Bothe (*supra* note 57, at p. 390) who considers such a denial both unrealistic and inappropriate.

have to comply. Whether or not the armed conflict in question amounts to 'war' in the legal sense, is immaterial. Whether or not the belligerents were at all entitled to take such measures will depend upon an authoritative determination of the aggressor or of an excess of the right of self-defence. If that is not possible the legality of recourse to prize measures against neutral ships and goods may not be questioned anymore as long as they comply with prize law.[163]

CONCLUSIONS

The law of prize as such has not been modified extensively by the practice of States since 1945. Belligerent States are relatively free in laying down the principles according to which they wish to determine the enemy character of vessels, aircraft and goods. In principle, all ships, regardless of their nationality or function, are subject to visit, search and diversion beyond neutral territorial waters. Private enemy property, unless specially protected, is liable to capture and seizure if found outside neutral jurisdiction. Neutral vessels and goods are exempt from capture and seizure unless they contribute to the war fighting or war sustaining efforts of the respective enemy.

As far as the coming into operation of the international law of prize is concerned, it is not dependent upon the existence of a 'state of war'. As soon as belligerents, in an international armed conflict, adopt prize measures their behaviour is to be evaluated under the law of prize.

Finally, the modern *jus ad bellum* (or: *jus contra bellum*) has no direct impact on the operation of the law of prize. Hence, in principle, the law of prize is the exclusive legal yardstick during the period of ongoing hostilities. The only exception relates to a situation in which the aggressor has been authoritatively determined, *e.g.* by the UN Security Council. However, the *jus ad bellum* is of relevance in two respects. Firstly, under the UN Charter, the law of prize must be characterised an 'order of necessity'. Hence, prize measures, whether taken by the aggressor or by the victim, cannot anymore confer permanently valid legal titles over neutral private property. That also holds true if, after the end of the conflict, it is impossible to determine a violation of the *jus ad bellum*. Secondly, because of its peremptory character, the *jus ad bellum* is not totally superseded by the law of prize. *I.e.*, *ex post*, after the cessation of active hostilities, it serves as a legal yardstick even for those measures which during the conflict were taken in accordance with the law of prize.

---

163 Of course, with the consequence that prize measures generally will not create permanently valid titles over neutral property, see *supra* note 126 ff. and accompanying text.

COMMENTS

Michael Bothe[*]

I. A REMARK ON SOURCES

Wolff Heintschell von Heinegg's argument concerning the current state of the law heavily relies on military manuals recently published. This raises the question of the value of such manuals as a proof of customary international law. Von Heinegg notes, rightly so, that they constitute the expression of an *opinio juris* by a competent state organ. But manuals are perhaps more than that, they are also elements of state practice. They are directly relevant for what states, or more precisely, the armed forces as a state's organ whose practice is relevant for the purposes here discussed, actually do.

If manuals are not state practice, it has still to be asked whether and to what extent they are nevertheless relevant for the development of the law as there are many cases where the law develops without or even in spite of state practice. The best-known example of this kind of development of the law is the prohibition of the use of force, where there never was a constant state practice of abstention. Nevertheless, nobody seriously disputes, nowadays, that this prohibition exists, which can only be explained on the basis of the assumption that the law developed through a change of *opinio juris* only.

A major defect, however, of manuals, be they only an expression of *opinio juris* or also elements of state practice, is what can be called their unilateral character. Expressions of *opinio juris* and state practice are more relevant for the development of international law if they occur in international intercourse, in the relationship between two subjects of international law at least, because this is then a sign of a more general acceptance of the norm in question. Therefore, the reaction of other states is very important also in the case of manuals. This raises the question how a process could be triggered where other states could react to those manuals. What is needed, in other words, is an organized exchange between the states concerning the correctness of the statements contained in the manuals. It would be most useful if this could be arranged in appropriate fora. It must be mentioned, however, that some

---

[*]   Dr. M. Bothe, Professor of International Law, J.W. von Goethe Universität, Frankfurt a/Main.

H.H.G. Post (ed.), International Economic Law and Armed Conflict, 35–37.
© 1994 *Martinus Nijhoff Publishers. Printed in the Netherlands.*

of the recently published manuals reflect at least some international input, as drafts of the manuals were discussed at international expert meetings. This is in particular true for the German manual.

Though even if such international exchange has not yet taken place, the recent manuals will certainly have an impact as statements of the existing law. As they are published, they constitute convenient references. Anywhere where the issue will arise in practice or in theory, they will be quoted and thus create a kind of assumption that they correctly state the law. It will become more difficult, in other words, to argue that the law is different from what the manuals say. This is a well-known phenomenon in international law, namely law creation through publication. This is the whole secret of the impact the early American digests and Satow's 'Diplomatic Practice' had on international law.

II. THE CONTINUED VALIDITY OF PRIZE LAW

Von Heinegg rightly derives from the manuals and from other sources the conclusion that traditional prize law has been maintained as a matter of principle. It has not fallen into destitution. The major change is, and I agree with his conclusion, that an armed conflict is sufficient to trigger the applicability of this body of law and that no formal state of war is necessary.

The rules of prize law still being valid, the question has then to be asked whether the rules of international law pertaining to the *jus contra bellum* (I prefer that term to the traditional *jus ad bellum*) have an effect on the traditional body of prize law. In other words, the norm of the *jus contra bellum* constitutes a kind of overlay network of norms under which the old law still exists, but may, to a certain extent, take on a different shape or be deprived of some of its traditional effects.

It is important to note in this respect that the two bodies of the law, prize law as part of the *jus in bello* on the one hand, and the *jus contra bellum* (prohibition of the use of force and authorization of self-defence) on the other have not merged into one body of law. Von Heinegg rightly stresses the necessity to keep both bodies of the law distinct because otherwise the restraining effect of the laws of war would be at peril. In a situation of armed conflict, the first question to be asked always is whether a particular act is in conformity with the law of armed conflict. It is a second question whether a certain act or omission of a state also violates the *jus contra bellum* and what the possible effect of such violation could be in a given case.

In this respect, Dr. von Heinegg rightly distinguishes two questions, namely the effect of the prohibition of the use of force in the absence of a determination of the Security Council and the effect of Security Council decisions. I agree with Von Heinegg's general conclusion that in the former case, the *jus contra bellum* cannot be relevant during the conflict. Only after the conflict, the question may be asked whether acts performed in conformity with the law of war nevertheless give rise to claims for compensation because they are in violation of the *jus contra bellum*. In the absence of a binding decision on that question, that matter does not seem to be very relevant.

As regards the situation where a determination under Article 39 is made by the Security Council, I would somewhat hesitate to accept the conclusion that this mere determination completely changes the picture just drawn. It is not the determination of the wrongdoer which changes the applicable law, but the concrete consequences the Security Council derives from that determination. Where the Security Council obliges all states or certain states to interrupt any intercourse with the aggressor and to assist the victim, there is of course no room for the application of traditional rules of freedom of neutral shipping and the continuation of economic intercourse between third states and the aggressor. This implies the recognition of a power of the Security Council to modify the application of traditional rules of customary law in a given situation. It is important, it seems to me, to give that characterization of the legal situation. There is no general rule of non-application of the rules of neutrality in case of a Security Council decision, but only the principle of the primacy of Security Council decisions, derived from the Articles 25 and 103 of the Charter, over general norms of customary international law.

COMMENTS

Ove Bring[*]

I would like to congratulate Wolff von Heinegg on an interesting and well researched paper. I am particularly attracted by his approach to modern prize law as an order of necessity (an adaption to reality during an armed conflict), formulating restrictions with regard to the capture of ships, but not granting genuine belligerent rights to the parties to the conflict. This is in line with my own view of the impact of the United Nations Charter on the law of naval warfare and neutrality.[1]

Although I agree with the Rapporteur's general and partly innovative approach, I do not agree with his statement that the modern *jus ad bellum* and *contra bellum* (*i.e.* the UN Charter) 'has no direct impact on the operation of the law of prize'. I think it has. Compared to the situation in 1907, the post-1945 regime of the United Nations Charter has had a forceful influence on the law of naval warfare in the sense that it has contributed to a certain erosion of the concept of belligerent rights in its application towards states *not party to the conflict*. Reliance on the concept of belligerent rights against third states (or against the commercial shipping or other interests of third states), will in principle always contravene the Charter prohibition of the threat or use of force. The threat of military force which is always apparent with regard to belligerent capture of ships, will tend to constitute a violation of Article 2(4) of the Charter. The relationship between a belligerent state and a neutral/non-belligerent state is characterized by a condition of peace, and states not involved in an armed conflict should be able to rely on the protection afforded by the modern law of peace, *i.e.* basically the law of the UN Charter and in particular the peaceful settlement requirement of Article 2(3) and the non-use of force rule in Article 2(4). The only possible justification for military action against shipping of third states is the argument of self-defence specified as a proportionate response against a state acting in complicity with 'the aggressor' (see the Report of Andrea Gioia, *infra*, paragraph VII). Such a possible line of argumentation also testifies to the influence of the law of the UN Charter on the law of naval warfare.

* Dr. O.E. Bring is Special Legal Adviser, Ministry for Foreign Affairs, Stockholm.
1 See O.E. Bring, 'Comments', in I.F. Dekker and H.H.G. Post (eds.), *The Gulf War of 1980-1988*, The Hague 1992, pp. 243-245.

The Rapporteur has emphasized (in my view overemphasized) the need for authoritative assessment and decision-making if the law of the UN Charter is to have an influence on the law of naval warfare. It has to be remembered, though, that application of international law is not limited to cases where there is a mechanism of authoritative assessment. International law, including the law of the UN Charter, also functions as a system of self-imposed constraints. Article 2(4) thus mainly functions as a result of unilateral and *bona fide* respect for the normative framework of the international community. In fact, this is the way in which fundamental norms of inter-state behaviour are supposed to work, and this is how the main influence of the *jus ad bellum* on the law of warfare should and will manifest itself in practice.

Although my own approach to the *jus ad bellum* issue differs somewhat from that of the Rapporteur, the conclusions we reach are similar. I think, however, that the Rapporteur's thesis with regard to the non-existence of belligerents' rights *stricto senso*, and prize law as an order of necessity, would have gained even more credibility had he been able to appreciate the significant influence of the modern *jus contra bellum* on the law of naval warfare.

COMMENTS

Wybo Heere*

If I have understood the speakers behind the table correctly, two conclusions can be safely drawn: first, when there is an international armed conflict, the *jus in bello* applies, and the law of prize is part of that *jus in bello*. Secondly, the UN Charter has changed the *jus ad bellum* insofar that a belligerent can be declared officially to be the aggressor - whether war is formally declared or not. This declaration can be made during the conflict by the Security Council, or afterwards by the same Council or by a peace conference.

The reading of Wolff Heintschel von Heinegg's contribution has prompted the following questions: if the Security Council officially declares belligerent A to be the aggressor, what are the consequences for prize law? Can prize awards no longer confer a valid title on the new owner of ship or cargo, because the *causa justa*, the *bona fides* is lacking? And when the aggressor is indicated only after the conflict, what happens then? Will there be an international court of revision which can declare prize awards null and void because those awards were given by the prize court of the aggressor State? Or do we get the unfortunate lump-sum agreements which always have one thing in common, *i.e.* that the injured parties do not get their losses correctly compensated?

Another question could be: when does an (undeclared) war end, and when will it be clear that a decision on the quality of 'aggressor' will not be taken anymore, or that the possibility is still open? Marine insurers probably will be most interested in the fixation of a maximum period for this post-bellum evaluation with its possible consequences.

* W.P. Heere is Senior Lecturer at Utrecht University.

COMMENTS

André de Hoogh[*]

In response to the plea of the Organizing Committee to submit written versions of interventions, I have taken the time to elaborate somewhat more on the issue I felt it necessary to comment upon during the Symposium. That issue concerns the so-called 'principle' of auto-interpretation, or as some have put it, of auto-determination.

The urge to make my comment was triggered by certain observations of rapporteur Von Heinegg in his report (*supra*, p. 29) to the effect that:

'A neutral, or rather non-participating, State may not assist the aggressor. In view of the importance and peremptory character of the *jus ad bellum* this will probably also apply to neutral merchantmen. However, this finding is safe only when there is an authoritative determination of the aggressor by the Security Council. ... Unfortunately, at least for the foreseeable future such a situation will be rather the exception than the rule. Hence, the question remains what rules and principles apply if there is no authoritative determination of the aggressor at all or if that determination can be arrived at only after the cessation of hostilities. In these situations third States are neither obliged to determine which State is the aggressor nor do they have to prohibit their merchantmen any intercourse with any of the belligerents. Therefore, neutral merchant vessels engaged in trade with a belligerent do not violate international law even if they are carrying contraband goods.'

In the hope of being excused for the length of this quote, I have to say that I am in complete disagreement on his interpretation of the consequences that attach to the unfortunate circumstance of the Security Council not being able (for instance due to the exercise of a veto), or not willing (for instance due to the fact that the victim State has made itself unpopular), to determine which State is the aggressor in a situation of armed conflict.

* A.J.J. de Hoogh is Research Assistant at the University of Nijmegen.

Let me illustrate my opinion on the matter with an example taken from the, all too recent, past: the Iraq-Iran armed conflict that raged within the period of 1980 to 1988. With regard to that conflict the Security Council never determined which of the two States constituted the aggressor. However, little doubt exists that Iraq was the one to initiate a large scale military attack on Iran. That attack fell squarely under the terms of the prohibition of Article 2, paragraph 4, constituted an act of aggression under Article 39, and an armed attack in the sense of Article 51 of the Charter. Of course Iraq claimed to be acting in the exercise of a right of self-defence, but the facts indicate that none of the actions it attributed to Iran could be said to constitute an armed attack under Article 51. And as the Court decided in the Nicaragua Case, that criterion is the decisive one even under customary international law. Assuming the correctness of this evaluation, and considering that the Security Council did not determine Iraq to be the aggressor, could it really be said that other States were completely free to make their own evaluation of the (legal) situation and claim that nevertheless Iran was the aggressor and had initiated an armed attack against Iraq? Could they resort to countermeasures against Iran? Could they attack Iran on the basis of an alleged right of collective self-defence? Could they really call black white? Surely not!

Naturally, States at times have to appreciate the legality of acts of other States in the absence of an authoritative decision by a competent organ of an international organization. That is but a consequence of the decentralized structure and unorganized character of the relations between States. But any evaluation by a State of the facts of a certain situation and the legal rules that are applicable to it has to be made in good faith. Thus the use of the phrase 'principle of auto-interpretation (or auto-determination)' is misleading, because it incorrectly suggests that a legal principle or rule is concerned, and that legal consequences attach to the unilateral interpretation or determination made by a State. Yet that is not the case. The 'principle' of auto-interpretation or auto-determination merely constitutes a description of the reality supervening within the international community. No State can legally impose upon another State, with binding force for that other State, an interpretation or determination regarding a certain situation. Not even the parties to a conflict or dispute can do so.[1]

Now these arguments would appear to lead to the conclusion that the search for objectivity is doomed to fail in the absence of an authoritative decision by a competent organ of an international organization. But that is not so. The legality of acts always has to be judged in accordance with the applicable legal rules. States can

---

1   See on these issues the highly interesting study by Leo Gross, 'States as Organs of International Law and the Problem of Autointerpretation', in A. Lipsky, *Law and Politics in the World Community, Essays on Hans Kelsen's Pure Theory and Related Problems in International Law*, Berkeley 1953, pp. 59-89 (notes at pp. 336-351), especially pp. 74 to 87.

of course claim that certain conduct is legal or illegal, and then take action with regard to their claims. But any action taken in pursuit of a claim, or the claim of a third State, is resorted to under the presumption that the claim is well founded. If that presumption is rebutted, and the claim found to be non-existent, a State becomes accountable for its actions. And if those actions did not consist of mere retorsions, but allegedly had to be considered countermeasures or acts of self-defence, it will have incurred international responsibility rather than having justifiably invoked a circumstance precluding wrongfulness.

Furthermore, where the facts of a certain situation are clear and the content of the law beyond dispute, States are not entitled to call an internationally wrongful act lawful. And no State can justifiably proceed, on the basis of an incorrect evaluation of a situation, to provide assistance to the author State of an internationally wrongful act. In that case it would become liable of being held the accomplice of the author State, and such a State could even be seen as having committed its own internationally wrongful act (as may be seen from the rule laid down in Article 27, of the ILC Draft Articles on State Responsibility).[2]

Turning back now to the quoted part at the beginning of this comment, it may be said that no State may provide contraband goods to the aggressor State, nor allow its merchant vessels to ship contraband goods to the aggressor State. The most that a third State could do, in the absence of a decision of the Security Council as to which State is the aggressor, is to remain strictly neutral.   Clearly a third State is not obliged in the absence of an authoritative decision of the Security Council to resort to comprehensive countermeasures against the aggressor State. But it also has no right to continue its trade with the aggressor State as if in reality nothing had happened.

I would like to add a few words on the position of the Security Council. Some have argued that the question whether or not certain acts or a certain situation constitute a threat to the peace under Article 39 of the Charter is a political question, and that a decision to that effect by the Security Council could not be reviewed by the Court. Thus the Security Council would be able to order the measures of Article 41, or take action under Article 42, against a State that could in no way be considered to have committed any breach of obligations, or even to have threatened the peace. Thus the Security Council's subjective view on the matter (and let us not forget that it is only composed of 15 out of approximately 180 States) would be decisive. As Professor Bothe observed during the Symposium, it was not the intention of the original members of the United Nations, by setting up the Security Council, to install an absolute prince of medieval character. The Security Council's

---

2   Article 27 of Part I. The origin of international responsibility, in *Yearbook of the International Law Commission* (1980), Vol. II, Part Two, p. 30.

power of auto-interpretation, which is authoritative indeed, cannot be considered to amount to an absolute power of auto-determination. The Security Council has no right to say: '*La communauté internationale, c'est moi.*' The reference to international law and justice in Article 1, paragraph 1, of the Charter was inserted precisely because of the fears of the smaller States that the stronger States would impose upon them settlements with other States contrary to their rights under international law. Let us therefore not forget that the phrase goes 'Peace Through Law', and that the Security Council ought to abide by this fundamental maxim. The final word on this latter issue could be the Court's, and let us hope that in its future decision on the Lockerbie case[3] it will be daring enough to review the validity of Security Council Resolution 748(1992).

---

3   Questions of Interpretation and Application of the Montreal Convention arising from the Aerial Incident at Lockerbie (Libyan Arab Jamahiriya *vs.* United States of America); 14 April 1992, the I.C.J. ordered Provisional Measures (ICJ Reports 1992, p. 114).

COMMENTS

Kees Roelofsen*

The days of classic Prize Law as we know it from the textbooks seem to be numbered. The last volume in Verzijl's *magnum opus*, the massive Part IX-C,[1] devoted to the law of maritime prize from the Middle Ages to 1914, may soon become, together with his analysis of prize jurisdiction in World War I,[2] a monument to an extinct species of the genus of International Law. Drafts for a revised code of the law of naval warfare and maritime neutrality are now being prepared by both an ILA Committee and a Round Table of Experts invited by the International Institute of Humanitarian Law.[3] They represent attempts to adapt the law to changed circumstances, or rather, to take into account the changes in State practice and to provide for the altered base of the *jus ad bellum* under the UN Charter and customary law. This change has of course already been reflected to a certain extent in the *jus in bello* as applied in various maritime conflicts since 1945.[4] However, it is arguable to what extent changes in State behaviour during armed conflict have led to a new uniform practice. It is also rather questionable whether

* Dr. C.G. Roelofsen is senior lecturer of Public International Law at Utrecht University.

1 J.H.W. Verzijl, W.P. Heere and J.P.S. Offerhaus, *International Law in Historical Perspective, Vol. XI, Part IX-C*: The Law of Maritime Prize, Dordrecht/Boston/London 1992.

2 J.H.W. Verzijl, *Le droit des prises de la grande guerre; jurisprudence de 1914 et des années suivantes en matière de prises maritimes*, Leyden 1924.

3 Part of the work of the latter Round Table of Experts on International Humanitarian Law Applicable to Armed Conflicts at Sea is published in *Bochumer Schriften zur Friedenssicherung und zum Humanitären Völkerrecht* (1992), No. 8.

4 See D. Schindler, 'Transformations in the Law of Neutrality since 1945', in A.J.M. Delissen and G.J. Tanja (eds.), *Humanitarian Law of Armed Conflict. Challenges ahead; Essays in honour of Frits Kalshoven*, Dordrecht/Boston/London 1991, p. 367 ff.

A brief description and some comments on the present status of the law of neutrality in naval conflict is included in I.F. Dekker and H.H.G. Post (eds.), *The Gulf War of 1980-1988*, Dordrecht/Boston/London 1992, chaps. 6 and 7, contributions by Bothe, Greenwood, Bos, Gioia, Ronzitti and Bring. See also Ch. Greenwood, 'The Effects of the United Nations Charter on the Law of Naval Warfare', in *Round Table of Experts, Results of the Third Meeting of the Madrid Plan of Action* (Bergen 1991) (not yet published).

A more extensive description and analysis of State practice with regard to Prize Law in W. Heintschel von Heinegg, 'Visit, Search, Diversion and Capture; Conditions of Applicability', *ibid*. See also his 'Visit, Search, Diversion and Capture in Naval Warfare: Part I, The Traditional Law', 29 *Canadian Yearbook of International Law* (1991), pp. 283-329.

H.H.G. Post (ed.), International Economic Law and Armed Conflict, 47–50.
© 1994 *Martinus Nijhoff Publishers. Printed in the Netherlands.*

opinio juris can as yet be deduced from States' declarations on various occasions.[5] The proposed codification will therefore, even if it would seem to amount to a restatement of the traditional law of prize, have a constitutive rather than a merely declaratory character. Or, in other terms: at present the law is so uncertain that States enjoy considerable discretion whether or not to apply the traditional regime of neutrality and its sub-regime, the law of prize. In the words of Bothe one may wonder: 'What is left of traditional international law?'[6]

Bothe's answer to his own question apparently is: quite a lot, at least if we may consider the 1992 report to the ILA as reflecting his opinion.[7] Not only does the report favour the continued application of the law of prize, it even proposes to extend it to all 'armed conflicts', abandoning the requirement of a 'formal state of war'.[8] This would amount to a recognition of belligerents' jurisdiction over neutral shipping, regardless of the formal status of the conflict and of course without taking into account the status of the belligerents themselves. One of the consequences is that a State clearly engaging in a prohibited use of force will enjoy prize jurisdiction. This agrees with the traditional law of naval warfare as does indeed the report as a whole. The report's acknowledgement of the role of the Security Council in armed conflicts amounts to the recognition of a *lex specialis* which does not derogate from 'the law of neutrality, as it has developed over the centuries'.[9]

There are sound reasons for such an approach. As I have mentioned already, the traditional law of naval warfare has lost much of its impact after 1945. It was flouted by both parties during the 1980-88 Gulf War. Its reaffirmation would guarantee the rights of neutral powers and would bind belligerents to the observation of formal procedures like those before a duly constituted prize court. The condemnation of a neutral merchantman as good prize unmistakably gives rise to State responsibility. It is far more difficult to arrive at an agreed legal definition of the acts of 'volunteers' engaged in undiscriminately raiding neutral shipping with a presumed enemy destination. However, will States 'not parties to the conflict' be ready to submit to the exercise of the right of visit and search and of prize jurisdiction by

---

5   Such as the British, US and Dutch statements regarding Iranian and Iraqi exercise of belligerent rights, *cf.* Greenwood, *supra* note 4, p. 43 ff.

It is arguable to what extent the various national 'Commander's Handbooks' can be alleged in proof of the *opinio iuris* of the States concerned. In my opinion a caveat is due since States are of course not bound to abide by these regulations and may for instance well choose to declare them inapplicable in particular conflicts.

6   Delissen/Tanja (eds.), *supra* note 4, p. 387 ff.

7   *International Law Association; Cairo Conference (1992)*, Report of the International Committee on Maritime Neutrality (not yet published).

8   *Ibid*, sub 1.5 and 3.1. It is proposed to maintain the traditional right of visit and search vis-à-vis neutral commercial ships as well as the condemnation of contraband cargo and ships carrying contraband by the belligerent's prize court.

9   *Ibid*, sub 1.1.

both belligerents? Experiences from the Iran-Iraq conflict point to varied reactions of the powers concerned. Devices such as the reflagging of tankers and the institution of neutral convoys precluded to a considerable extent the exercise of Iran's superiority at sea. It may be that as Bring states 'violations of existing law ... tend to give rise to responses and reactions which lead to a progressive development of law'.[10] However, if the existing law lends itself to wide-spread abuse, should it not be discarded in favour of a new code?

An appeal for 'totally ignoring outdated customs' in the drafting of a new law of naval warfare has been made by Mrs. Doswald-Beck.[11] Though hardly couched in such drastic terms the conclusions presented at the second Verzijl Symposium by Wolff Heintschel von Heinegg have indeed the innovative character called for by Mrs. Doswald-Beck. In according only a limited validity to the effects of prize jurisdiction, subject to a final legal evaluation, Von Heinegg proposes indeed a radical transformation of the law of prize. Prize jurisdiction as a right accruing to the belligerent as such would disappear, to be replaced by a provisional power held at the discretion of the international community, presumably represented by the Security Council. Here of course serious practical objections can be raised. Is the UN and particularly the Security Council ready to undertake such a task? Would a 'provisional' exercise of prize jurisdiction not tend to degenerate into unilateral action by the 'just' belligerent whose strong moral position would permit him considerable latitude in the interpretation of the *jus in bello*? The guarantees offered to neutral powers by the traditional law might evanesce in a juridical tangle.

If such considerations show the road to reform still beset with difficulties it helps us to understand why time and again attempted reforms of prize law have failed. A reform somewhat akin in practical terms to that suggested by Von Heinegg, was proposed by Bluntschli more than a century ago and there is a long list to be made, at least since the eighteenth century, of suggestions for the abolition or mitigation of belligerent rights.[12] Verzijl in reviewing the attempts at reform of the *Institut de Droit international* rather sceptically qualified them as *vox clamantis in deserto*.[13] It remains to be seen whether contemporary proposals such as Von Heinegg's will

---

10 Dekker/Post (eds), *supra* note 4, p. 246.

11 L. Doswald-Beck, 'The International Law of Naval Armed Conflicts; the Need for Reform', 7 *The Italian Yearbook of International Law* (1988), p. 251 ff.

12 J.C. Bluntschli, *Das Beuterecht im Kriege und das Seebeuterecht insbesondere; Eine völkerrechtliche Untersuchung*, Nördlingen 1878/Amsterdam 1970. Bluntschli concludes (p. 168) that military necessity does *not* justify the continued right of capture but can merely offer an argument in favour of a temporary embargo on shipping ('mit Vorbehalt der späteren Rückgabe und der Entschädigung der Privaten'). *Cf.* also J.B. Scott (ed.), *Resolutions of the Institute of International Law dealing with the Law of Nations*, New York 1916, p. 14 ff. and *passim*.

A recent synopsis by T.E. Forland, 'The History of Economic Warfare: International Law, Effectiveness, Strategies', 30 *Journal of Peace Research* (1993), p. 151 ff.

13 Verzijl, Heere and Offerhaus, *supra* note 1, p. 133.

meet with a better fate. The retarding elements inherent in the international legislative process tend to be especially strong in a sensitive field like the laws of war. Besides, the present rather 'fluid' state of the law may well seem to suit some powers, which consider themselves able, as prospective 'neutrals' in future conflicts, to protect their own interests. They might ponder Grotius' warning that even the strong will find they need the protection of the law.[14]

14 *De Iure Belli ac Pacis*, prolegomenon 22.

NEUTRALITY AND NON-BELLIGERENCY

Andrea Gioia*

INTRODUCTION

The law of neutrality is, notoriously, in a chaotic state: whereas the status of the body of rules governing relations between belligerents (the *jus in bello* proper) has been progressively clarified by legal writers, the picture emerging from a study of the concept of neutrality in modern international law is still one of confusion.[1]

---

* Dr. A. Gioia is Senior Researcher and Acting Professor of International Law, Univeristy of Trent, Italy.

1 The crisis in the law of neutrality has been emphasized in the literature of international law at least since the end of the First World War. Among the more recent contributions to the doctrinal debate, see: Q. Wright, 'The Present Status of Neutrality', 34 *American Journal of International Law* (1940), p. 391 ff. and *idem*, 'The New Law of War and Neutrality', *Varia Juris Gentium. Questions of International Law*, Leyden 1959, p. 412 ff.; J.F. Lalive, 'International Organization and Neutrality', 24 *British Year Book of International Law* (1947), p. 72 ff.; T. Komarnicki, 'The Place of Neutrality in the Modern System of International Law', 80 *Hague Recueil* (1952, I), p. 395 ff.; C. Chaumont, 'Nations Unies et neutralité', 89 *Hague Recueil* (1956, I), p. 1 ff.; A. Verdross, 'Neutrality Within the Framework of the United Nations Organization', in *Symbolae Verzijl*, The Hague 1958, p. 410 ff.; L. Henkin, 'Force, Intervention and Neutrality in Contemporary International Law', in R.A. Falk, S.H. Mendlovitz (eds.), *The Strategy of World Order*, Vol. II, *International Law*, New York 1966, p. 335 ff.; D. Schindler, 'Aspects contemporains de la neutralité', 121 *Hague Recueil* (1967, II), p. 221 ff.; H. Blix, *Sovereignty, Aggression and Neutrality*, Stockholm 1970, p. 41 ff.; H. Meyrowitz, *Le principe de l'égalité des belligérants devant le droit de la guerre*, Paris 1970, p. 311 ff.; A. Miele, *L'estraneità ai conflitti armati secondo il diritto internazionale*, Vol. II, *La disciplina positiva delle attività statali*, Padua 1970; P.M. Norton, 'Between the Ideology and the Reality: The Shadow of the Law of Neutrality', 17 *Harvard International Law Journal* (1976), p. 249 ff.; 'The Evolution of the Notion of Neutrality in Modern Armed Conflicts', 17 *Revue de droit pénal militaire et de droit de la guerre* (1978), p. 8 ff.; L. Sico, 'Neutralità', 28 *Enciclopedia del Diritto*, Milan 1978, p. 164 ff.; W.L. Williams, 'Neutrality in Modern Armed Conflicts: A Survey of Developing Law', 90 Military Law Review (1980), p. 9 ff.; R.L. Bindschedler, 'Neutrality, Concept and General Rules', 4 *Encyclopedia of Public International Law*, Amsterdam/New York/Oxford 1982, p. 9 ff.; Y. Dinstein, 'The Laws of Neutrality', 14 *Israel Yearbook of Human Rights* (1984), p. 80 ff.; A.T. Leonhard (ed.), *Neutrality. Changing Concepts and Practices*, Lanham/New York/London 1988; M. Bothe, 'Neutrality in Naval Warfare. What is Left of Traditional International Law?', in A.J.M. Delissen, G.J. Tanja (eds.), *Humanitarian Law of Armed Conflict. Challenges Ahead. Essays in Honour of Frits Kalshoven*, Dordrecht/Boston/London 1991, p. 387 ff.; D. Schindler, 'Transformations in the Law of Neutrality Since 1945', *ibidem*, p. 367 ff.; M. Torrelli, 'La neutralité en question', 96 *Revue générale de droit international public* (1992), p. 5 ff. Other works will be quoted in the following notes.

H.H.G. Post (ed.), International Economic Law and Armed Conflict, 51–110.
© 1994 *Martinus Nijhoff Publishers. Printed in the Netherlands.*

It is a well-known fact that, although the four Geneva Conventions of 1949[2] and the first Geneva Protocol of 1977[3] contain provisions relating to neutrality, the law of neutrality consists, for the major part, of customary rules which emerged in the XVIIIth and XIXth centuries. Such rules were partially codified in 1856[4] and in 1907,[5] but, since then, several factors have cast serious doubts on their continuing relevance.

The factual conditions which were at the basis of the emergence of the law of neutrality have changed substantially. It is not necessary here to enumerate all those conditions: the fact that the international community is no longer the same as existed at the time when the law of neutrality emerged, is self-evident. Suffice it to recall that the two world wars of the XXth century have clearly shown that, at least in case of a total war involving a large number of States, the emergence of economic

2 See: Convention (I) for the Amelioration of the Conditions of the Wounded and Sick in Armed Forces in the Field (75 *United Nations Treaty Series*, p. 31 ff.), Articles 4, 8, 10, 11, 27, 32, 37, 43; Convention (II) for the Amelioration of the Condition of the Wounded, Sick and Shipwrecked Members of Armed Forces at Sea (*ibidem*, p. 85 ff.), Articles 5, 8, 10, 11, 15, 16, 17, 21, 25, 31, 32, 38, 40, 43; Convention (III) Relative to the Treatment of Prisoners of War (*ibidem*, p. 135 ff.), Articles 4, 8, 10, 11, 109, 110, 111, 114, 115, 116, 123; Convention (IV) Relative to the Protection of Civilian Persons in Time of War (*ibidem*, p. 287 ff.), Articles 4, 9, 11, 12, 24, 25, 36, 132, 140. The four conventions were signed on 12 August 1949.
3 See: Protocol (I) Additional to the Geneva Conventions of 12 August 1949, and Relating to the Protection of Victims of International Armed Conflicts, opened to signature on 12 December 1977 (1125 *United Nations Treaty Series*, p. 3 ff.), Articles 2, 9, 19, 22, 30, 31, 37, 39, 64. Mention should also be made of Article 9 of the Regulations annexed to the Convention for the Protection of Cultural Property in the Event of Armed Conflict, signed in The Hague on 14 May 1954 (249 *United Nations Treaty Series*, p. 240 ff.).
4 See: Paris Declaration Respecting Maritime Law, 16 April 1856 (15 *Martens, Nouveau Recueil Général, 1ère Série*, p. 791 ff.). The text of the 1856 declaration is also reprinted in N. Ronzitti (ed.), *The Law of Naval Warfare*, Dordrecht/Boston/London 1988, p. 61 ff., with a commentary by H. Fujita.
5 See: Convention (V) Respecting the Rights and Duties of Neutral Powers and Persons in Case of War on Land (3 *Martens, Nouveau Recueil Général, 3ème Série*, p. 504 ff.) and Convention (XIII) Respecting the Rights and Duties of Neutral Powers in Naval War (*ibidem*, p. 713 ff.). Both conventions were adopted, together with eleven other conventions and one declaration, at the Second Hague Peace Conference, on 18 October 1907. The 1907 Hague conventions were written in French; for an English translation, see: J.B. Scott (ed.), *The Hague Conventions and Declarations of 1899 and 1907*, New York 1915.
An unsuccessful attempt to further codify the laws of neutrality is represented by the unratified Declaration Concerning the Laws of Naval War, adopted in London on 26 February 1909 (text in Ronzitti, *supra* note 4, p. 223 ff., with a commentary by F. Kalshoven). At the regional level, neutrality rules were later codified in the Convention on Maritime Neutrality, adopted in Havana on 20 February 1928 by the Sixth International Conference of American States (135 *League of Nations Treaty Series*, p. 188 ff.).
In the scientific field, mention must at least be made of the Code of Rules for the Control of Radiotelegraphy in Time of War and of Aerial Warfare, formulated by the Commission of Jurists set up by the Washington Naval Conference of 1921/22, part of which deal with the law of neutrality (text in: Ronzitti, *supra* note 4, pp. 367 ff. and 381 ff.), as well as of the 1939 Harvard Research Draft Convention on Rights and Duties of Neutral States in Naval and Aerial War (text in: 33 *American Journal of International Law* (1939), *Suppl.*, p. 167 ff.).

warfare on the one hand, and advancements in military techniques on the other, have made it very difficult for States effectively to implement a policy of neutrality and to enjoy the advantages that ought to derive from such a policy, *i.e.* to suffer as little as possible the negative consequences of a war and to continue trading with belligerents relatively undisturbed.[6]

In addition, the legal framework within which the laws of neutrality historically emerged has also changed dramatically. Whereas one of the factors which contributed to the birth of neutrality as a legal institution was, undoubtedly, the legality of resorting to war, the cornerstones of modern international law are the outlawry of war as an instrument of national policy and the tendency to set up an effective system of collective security designed to apply economic and military sanctions against the States responsible for breaching the peace. As a result, a policy of strict neutrality might be considered, with some justice, as an attitude which favours the aggressor, rather than as a positive factor contributing to the localization of an armed conflict.

All these factors have exercised their influence upon the practice of States, to the extent that the question has arisen of whether the traditional rules of neutrality can still be regarded as binding rules of customary and/or treaty law. Legal writers are divided on the answer: according to one group of writers, the concept of neutrality has lost all meaning and the laws of neutrality ought to be regarded as obsolete;[7] the opposite view is taken by another group of writers, who believe that the law of neutrality has not lost its validity, especially since an effective system of collective security has proved to be very difficult to implement.[8] Among writers belonging to

---

6 Changes in the factual situation are often considered to be at the basis of the crisis in the law of neutrality. However, the argument of new conditions should not be given too much weight since, from very early times, it has recurrently been invoked by belligerents in order to justify measures which neutral States have not admitted as justified by international law: see, for example, P.C. Jessup, *Neutrality. Its History, Economics and Law*, Vol. IV, *Today and Tomorrow* [1936], New York 1976 (rep.), at p. 58 ff. New factual conditions may affect the ability or predisposition of States to rely on the law of neutrality; however, a change in the existing legal situation can only be brought about by the development of new rules of treaty and/or customary international law. On this question, see also *infra*, paragraph X, notes 211-212 and corresponding text.

7 See, for example: N. Politis, N., *La neutralité et la paix*, Paris 1935, at pp. 9 and 179; I. Fabela, *Neutralité*, Paris 1949, at pp. 156-157; N. Orvik, *The Decline of Neutrality 1914-1941*, Oslo 1953, at p. 268; C.G. Fenwick, *International Law*, 4th ed., New York 1965, at p. 727, and *idem*, 'Is Neutrality Still a Term of Present Law?', in 63 *American Journal of International Law* (1969), pp. 100-102; E. Lauterpacht, 'The 'Legal Irrelevance' of a State of War', 62 *Proceedings of the American Society of International Law* (1968), p. 58 ff., esp. at p. 68.

8 See, for example: Meyrowitz, *supra* note 1, at p. 352 ff.; Bindschedler, *supra* note 1; F.A. Boyle, 'International Crisis and Neutrality: U.S. Foreign Policy Toward the Iran-Iraq War', in A.T. Leonhard (ed.), *supra* note 1, p. 59 ff., at pp. 68-69.

Some treatises on public international law still devote detailed chapters to the law of neutrality, as do some treatises on the law of war. See, among others: L. Oppenheim, *International Law. A Treatise*, Vol. II, *Disputes, War and Neutrality*, 7th ed. by H. Lauterpacht, London/New York/Toronto 1952, at p. 624

this second group, some maintain that, although neutrality still exists as a legal institution, the laws of neutrality ought to be reconsidered in the light of the new legal framework and, in particular, of the Charter of the United Nations.[9] In this context, the view is sometimes put forward that modern international law allows for a distinction between strict neutrality and so-called 'non-belligerency' or 'qualified neutrality': according to this view, as long as the UN Security Council has not taken enforcement measures in the case of an armed conflict, third States not wishing to become parties to the conflict would have the choice either to remain neutral, thereby applying the law of neutrality, or to take any intermediate positions between neutrality and belligerency.[10]

The purpose of this report is to try and ascertain what is the status of the concept of neutrality in modern international law, whether States can now choose between strict neutrality and 'non-belligerency', and what would be, in that case, the legal consequences of an attitude of 'non-belligerency' as opposed to strict neutrality. The question of the present relevance of the concept of neutrality in the context of civil

---

ff.; G. Balladore Pallieri, *Diritto bellico*, 2nd ed., Padua 1954, at p. 371 ff.; Castrén, *The Present Law of War and Neutrality*, Helsinki 1954, at p. 421 ff.; P. Guggenheim, *Traité de droit international public*, Vol. II, Geneva 1954, at p. 493 ff.; J. Stone, *Legal Controls of International Conflict*, Sydney 1954, at p. 381 ff.; R.W. Tucker, *The Law of War and Neutrality at Sea* (Naval War College, *International Law Studies 1955*), Washington 1957, at p. 165 ff.; A.P. Sereni, *Diritto internazionale*, Vol. IV, *Conflitti internazionali*, Milan 1965, at p. 2077 ff.; R. Quadri, *Diritto internazionale pubblico*, 5th ed., Naples 1968, at p. 325 ff.; C. Rousseau, *Le droit des conflits armés*, Paris 1983, at p. 369 ff.; I. Seidl-Hohenveldern, *International Economic Law*, Dordrecht/Boston/London 1989, at p. 165 ff.

9   This seems to be the prevailing view in recent legal literature. In addition to some of the authors quoted *supra*, in notes 1 and 8, see, among others: D.W. Bowett, *Self-Defence in International Law*, Manchester 1958, at p. 156 ff.; D.P. O'Connell, *The International Law of the Sea*, Vol. II, edited by I.A. Shearer, Oxford 1984, at pp. 1094 ff. and 1141 ff.; N. Ronzitti, 'The Crisis in the Traditional Law Regulating International Armed Conflicts at Sea and the Need for Its Revision', in Ronzitti (ed.), *supra* note 4, p. 1 ff., at pp. 6-10; C. Greenwood, 'The Effects of the United Nations Charter on the Law of Naval Warfare', paper presented at the Bergen Round Table of Experts on International Humanitarian Law Applicable to Armed Conflicts at Sea (20-24 September 1991) organized by the San Remo International Institute of Humanitarian Law.

10   See especially: Komarnicki, *supra* note 1, at pp. 442-443; Guggenheim, *supra* note 8, at pp. 499-500; Schindler, 'Aspects contemporains', *supra* note 1, at p. 261 ff., *idem*, 'Commentary [on 1907 Hague Convention XIII]', in Ronzitti (ed.), *supra* note 4, p. 211, at pp. 211-213, and *idem*, 'Transformations', *supra* note 1, at p. 373. See also, among others: Oppenheim, *supra* note 8, at pp. 634-652 and 663-664; H. Kelsen, *Principles of International Law*, 2nd ed. by R.W. Tucker, New York/Chicago/S.Francisco/Toronto/ London 1966, at pp. 166-167; Miele, *supra* note 1, at p. 434 ff.; Sico, *supra* note 1, at p. 189 ff.; O. Bring, 'Comments', in I.F. Dekker, H.H.G. Post (eds.), *The Gulf War of 1980-1988*, Dordrecht/Boston/London 1992, p. 243 ff., at p. 245.

It may be interesting to recall that the view that the law of neutrality only comes into operation for States wishing to declare themselves neutral had already been formulated, as early as 1919, by a distinguished Italian author: see A. Cavaglieri, 'Belligeranza, neutralita' e posizioni giuridiche intermedie', 13 *Rivista di diritto internazionale* (1919), pp. 58 ff. and 328 ff., at pp. 341-346. For a brief analysis of earlier conceptions of 'imperfect neutrality' (Vattel) or 'limited neutrality' (Klüber), see especially: Miele, *supra* note 1, at pp. 439-446.

wars, or non-international armed conflicts, will not be addressed here.[11] Neither will this report directly address the special problems connected with the status of so-called 'permanent neutrality' of particular States.[12]

I. THE CONCEPT OF NEUTRALITY AND ITS RATIO

The political and legal factors which have contributed to the crisis in the law of neutrality have also changed the context in which the law of war, governing relations between belligerents, are to operate. However, as stated above, the present status of the *jus in bello* has been progressively clarified by legal writers: at present, it is possible to argue that, regardless of who is the aggressor and who is the victim of aggression, the laws of war – or, as they are now called, the laws of armed conflict – have to be complied with by all belligerents whenever war in the material sense exists, *i.e.* as soon as an armed conflict breaks out.[13] One may legitimately ask, therefore, why the present relevance of the law of neutrality – which, from a certain point of view, is also part of the *jus in bello* – is so much more controversial.

---

11 On this question, see, among others: Oppenheim, *supra* note 8, at pp. 659-667; Miele, *supra* note 1, at p. 479 ff.; J.W.H. Verzijl, *International Law in Historical Perspective*, Vol. X, *The Law of Neutrality*, Alphen aan den Rijn 1979, at pp. 15-16; Torrelli, *supra* note 1, at pp. 16-18.

On the special problems posed by so-called 'wars of national liberation', see also: N. Ronzitti, *Le guerre di liberazione nazionale e il diritto internazionale*, Pisa 1974, at p. 108 ff.; A. Cassese, 'Le droit international et la question de l'assistance aux mouvements de libération nationale', 19 *Revue belge de droit international* (1986), p. 307 ff.; Schindler, 'Transformations', *supra* note 1, at pp. 376-377.

12 On the more recent aspects of the status of permanent neutrality, see, among others: Guggenheim, *supra* note 8, at p. 547 ff.; Schindler, 'Aspects contemporains', *supra* note 1, at p. 295 ff., and *idem*, 'Transformations', *supra* note 1, at p. 383 ff.; L. Sico, 'Neutralizzazione', 28 *Enciclopedia del Diritto*, Milan 1978, p. 199 ff.; A. Verdross, *The Permanent Neutrality of Austria*, Vienna 1978; R.L. Bindschedler, 'Permanent Neutrality of States', 4 *Encyclopedia of Public International Law*, Amsterdam/New York/Oxford 1982, p. 133 ff.; H. Neuhold, 'The Neutral States of Europe: Similarities and Differences', in Leonhard (ed.), *supra* note 1, p. 97 ff.; Seidl-Hohenveldern, *supra* note 8, at p. 171 ff.; D. Thürer, 'Comment: UN Enforcement Measurers and Neutrality. The Case of Switzerland', 30 *Archiv des Völkerrechts* (1992), p. 63 ff.; Torrelli, *supra* note 1, at p. 31 ff.

13 The literature on the sphere of operation of the *jus in bello* is by now very substantial. Suffice it to mention: I. Brownlie, *International Law and the Use of Force by States*, Oxford 1963, at pp. 406-408; Kelsen, *supra* note 10, at p. 87 ff.; Y. Dinstein, *War, Aggression and Self-Defence*, Cambridge 1988, at pp. 12 and 145 ff.; G. Venturini, *Necessita' e proporzionalita' nell'uso della forza militare in diritto internazionale*, Milan 1988, at p. 73 ff., and the bibliography therein quoted.

According to some writers, the automatic application of the laws of war whenever war in the material sense exists is implicit in the Hague Conventions of 1899 and 1907, *supra* note 5: see, for example, Venturini, *supra* at pp. 87-89. As for the Geneva Conventions of 1949, *supra* note 2, see their common Article 2, which is also referred to in Article 1(3) of the first Geneva Protocol of 1977, *supra* note 3. See also Article 18 of the Hague Convention on cultural property of 1954, *supra* note 3, which probably best reflects the present state of customary law.

The answer is clearly that the rules governing relations between belligerents have a fundamentally humanitarian function: they emerged in order to mitigate the sufferings of the individuals affected by the hostilities and all belligerents have, in principle, an equal interest in their being respected. Consequently, even if it is no longer recognized that the outbreak of an armed conflict has the effect of suspending the operation of large parts of the laws of peace, the laws of armed conflict can easily coexist with the modern rules on the illegality of the use of force in international relations except in self-defence (the *jus ad bellum*) and with the tendency towards a system of collective security. Moreover, their continuing relevance is in keeping with the modern trend towards the protection of human rights.[14] In contrast, the function of the law of neutrality is not as immediately identifiable as 'progressive' by modern standards.

'Neutrality', in current language, means the fact of not taking part in a 'war'. As such, 'neutrality' is as old as 'war' itself. Neutrality, as a legal institution, means a condition in which relations between belligerents, on the one hand, and third States, on the other, are governed by special rules of treaty and/or customary law, constituting the law of neutrality and derogating from the rules applicable in times of peace.[15]

Historically, the law of neutrality emerged as a compromise between the conflicting interests of belligerents and States not participating in war.[16] Since the law of neutrality is a set of rules which derogate from the laws of peace, the ideal point of departure must logically be a situation in which relations between belligerents and third States were governed, in their entirety, by the laws of peace.

14 On the similarity between the humanitarian function of the *jus in bello* and the function of international rules on the protection of human rights, see, for example: A. Migliazza, 'L'évolution de la réglementation de la guerre a la lumière de la sauvegarde des droits de l'homme', 137 *Hague Recueil* (1972, III), p. 143 ff.

Some writers tend to distinguish the so-called 'Hague law', i.e. the complex of rules directly dealing with the conduct of armed hostilities, from the so-called 'Geneva law', i.e. the complex of rules having a more direct humanitarian function: see, for example, J.P.A. François, 'L'egalité d'application des règles du droit de la guerre aux parties à un conflit armé', 50 *Annuaire del'Institut de droit international* (1963, I), p. 5 ff. But the distinction is artificial and is not in keeping with recent practice: see Venturini, *supra* note 13, at pp. 99-106, and the bibliography therein quoted.

15 See, especially: Balladore Pallieri, *supra* note 8, at p. 380. See also, among others: Komarnicki, *supra* note 1, at p. 401; Oppenheim, *supra* note 8, at pp. 655-656; Castrén, *supra* note 8, at pp. 422-423; Miele, *supra* note 1, at pp. 3-7; Verzijl, *supra* note 11, at pp. 15-16.

The law of neutrality is sometimes defined in a narrow sense, *i.e.* as excluding the law of prize, even as applied to the overseas commerce of neutrals. On the current state of prize law, see the report by W.H. Von Heinegg, in this volume.

16 On the historical evolution of the law of neutrality, see especially: A. Miele, *L'estraneita' ai conflitti armati secondo il diritto internazionale*, Vol. I, *Origini ed evoluzione del diritto di neutralita'*, Padua 1970. See also, among others: P.C. Jessup, V. Deak, *Neutrality. Its History, Economics and Law*, Vol. I, *The Origins*, New York 1935; Oppenheim, *supra* note 8, at p. 623 ff.; and, of course, Verzijl, *supra* note 11.

Starting from that situation, the special rules of neutrality gradually emerged as a result, on the one hand, of the interest of belligerents in imposing ever stricter limits on 'neutral' trade with the enemy and, on the other, of the interest of third States in protecting their rights against excessive interference on the part of belligerents. The outcome of this process was a compromise by which neutral States succeeded in limiting, to a certain extent, belligerents' interference with their 'peaceful' activities, in exchange for the recognition on their part of special obligations stemming from a general principle of impartiality.

While it may be true, from a factual point of view, that the law of neutrality aims at ensuring an equilibrium between the competing interests of belligerents, on the one hand, and of neutrals, on the other,[17] it is no less true that, from a more technical point of view, the law of neutrality mainly consists of special obligations imposed upon States wishing to remain at peace towards belligerents: strictly speaking, most of the so-called 'rights of neutrals towards belligerents', which allegedly also form part of the laws of neutrality, are nothing but rights, or freedoms, which neutral States would, in any case, enjoy under the general laws of peace.[18] In other words, it is possible to argue, with some justice, that the true function of the law of neutrality is to limit the rights of neutrals in order to allow belligerents to wage war relatively undisturbed. It is not surprising, therefore, that the law of neutrality is currently rather 'unpopular'.

The problem of neutrality in modern international law is twofold. Whereas the traditional laws of neutrality automatically came into operation upon the knowledge of the outbreak of 'war' between third States, no declaration of neutrality being legally necessary,[19] it is now necessary to determine, on the one hand, whether the outbreak of an armed conflict can still have that effect, even if a formal 'state of

17 This view is widely held but is not unanimous in the literature of international law. For example, according to Verzijl, *supra* note 11, at pp. 39-40, the positive rules of neutrality 'are for a large part artificial'; they 'often make the impression of arbitrariness' and 'present a picture of an uneasily balanced set of reciprocal obligations and rights'.

18 See, for example: M. Huber, 'Die Fortbildung des Völkerrechts durch die II. Friedenskonferenz im Haag', *Das öffentliches Recht der Gegenwart. Jahrbuch 1908*, at p. 586; Balladore Pallieri, *supra* note 8, at pp. 378 and 381-383; Sereni, *supra* note 8, at pp. 2084 and 2112-2114; Miele, *supra* note 1, at pp. 52-58.

However, the prevailing view is that the law of neutrality is 'a complex of mutual rights and duties' of neutral and belligerent States: see, among others, Oppenheim, *supra* note 8, at pp. 655 and 673-675; Castrén, *supra* note 8, at pp. 422 and 439 ff.; Fenwick, *International Law, supra* note 7, at p. 729 ff.; Rousseau, *supra* note 8, at pp. 381-383. This view, which is also reflected in the titles of the fifth and thirteenth Hague conventions of 1907, *supra* note 5, will be critically examined later: see *infra*, paragraph VI, notes 93-101 and corresponding text.

19 See, for example: Komarnicki, *supra* note 1, at p. 404; Oppenheim, *supra* note 8, at pp. 653-654 and 666-667; Balladore Pallieri, *supra* note 8, at pp. 371-381; Castrén, *supra* note 8, at pp. 422-423; Guggenheim, *supra* note 8, at pp. 510-511; Stone, *supra* note 8, at p. 384; Quadri, *supra* note 8, at p. 325; Miele, *supra* note 1, at p. 13; Verzijl, *supra* note 11, at p. 4. For the opinion of Arrigo Cavaglieri, which, however, remained very much a minority opinion, see *supra* note 10.

war' is not recognized, and, on the other, whether neutrality obligations are compatible with the modern *jus ad bellum*, based on the distinction between aggression and self-defence, and with the system of collective security enshrined in the Charter of the United Nations.

II. NEUTRALITY AND THE DOCTRINE OF THE 'STATE OF WAR'

The necessary starting point for any discussion of the present relevance of the concept of neutrality should be that the mere fact of the outbreak of an armed conflict cannot, by itself, automatically bring about the application of the law of neutrality, *i.e.* cannot automatically foist traditional neutrality obligations upon all States not wishing to become party to the conflict. This simple truth seems to have been recognized by implication in the Geneva Conventions of 1949 and in the first Geneva Protocol of 1977, which apply to all cases of international armed conflict. As stated above, these conventions contain provisions relating to neutrality, but at least some such provisions are explicitly said to be applicable to 'neutral or non-belligerent Powers'[20] or to 'neutral or other States not Parties to the conflict':[21] this clearly implies that not all States not taking part in armed hostilities are always to be considered as 'neutral' States.

Even in traditional international law, the law of neutrality did not automatically come into operation upon the outbreak of any armed conflict: rather, the existence of a formal 'state of war' was usually thought to be necessary, since the law of neutrality was considered inapplicable in situations of armed conflict falling short of actual 'war', such as, for example, armed reprisals or intervention.[22] In those days, 'war' could technically be defined as a situation in which the laws of war and neutrality applied, whereas forcible measures 'short of war' were regulated, in principle, by the general laws of 'peace'. For a formal 'state of war' to come into existence, it was usually thought that a declaration of war, an ultimatum, or an implicit manifestation of the intention to wage 'war' (*animus belli*) on the part of at least one State was required.[23] In any case, it was for the States wishing to resort

---

20 See Article 4 B.(2) of the third Geneva Convention of 1949, *supra* note 2.
21 See all the articles of the first Geneva Protocol of 1977 quoted *supra*, in note 3.
22 See, for example: Balladore Pallieri, *supra* note 8, at p. 380; Castrén, *supra* note 8, at p. 423; Quadri, *supra* note 8, at pp. 287-288; Brownlie, *supra* note 13, at pp. 45-46; Venturini, *supra* note 13, at pp. 81-82, and the bibliography therein quoted.
23 See, for example: Balladore Pallieri, *supra* note 8, at pp. 4-28; Castrén, *supra* note 8, at p. 31 ff.; Quadri, *supra* note 8, at pp. 288-289; Brownlie, *supra* note 13, at pp. 26-40; W. Meng, 'War', 4 *Encyclopedia of Public International Law*, Amsterdam/New York/Oxford 1982, p. 282 ff.; Venturini, *supra* note 13, at pp. 73-84, and the bibliography therein quoted.
    The doctrine of the 'state of war' was highly artificial. A somewhat more realistic attitude was taken by writers who appeared to regard as 'war' any 'contention between States' through armed force for the

to war to bring about the application of the laws of war and neutrality. Third States could only choose between entering the war or abiding by the laws of neutrality.[24]

It is a well-known fact that, especially since the end of the Second World War, States involved in armed hostilities have been very reluctant to recognize the existence of a formal 'state of war': there have been no declarations of war and, in several cases, the existence of a 'state of war' was expressly denied by some or all belligerents.[25] This practice has led to the question of whether the laws of war and neutrality should nowadays be considered to apply in all situations of international armed conflict, irrespective of whether or not a formal 'state of war' is recognized by some or all belligerents. The answer given by modern legal writers is usually based on a distinction between the laws of war, on the one hand, and the laws of neutrality, on the other: as stated above, it is now possible to argue, on the basis of existing treaties and of State practice, that the laws of war, now universally called the laws of armed conflict, have to be complied with by all belligerents as soon as armed hostilities begin;[26] on the contrary, the view is widely held that the laws of neutrality 'remain strictly dependent for their operation upon the existence of a state of war'.[27] In other words, it is usually admitted that there is no duty on the part of third States to apply the law of neutrality if the parties to the conflict do not recognize the 'state of war'.

purpose of overpowering each other: see, especially, Oppenheim, *supra* note 8, at pp. 201-209. Oppenheim defined acts short of 'war' as 'unilateral acts of force performed by one State against another without a previous declaration of war ... so long as they are not answered by similar hostile acts by the other side, or at least by a declaration of the other side that it considers them to be acts of war' (pp. 202-203). But this latter qualification seemed to leave the door open for the possibility that a given conflict could also be considered as falling short of 'war' if *both* parties refused to qualify it as such. More generally, writers who favoured an objective definition of 'war' were confronted with the fact that there was no agreement on the criteria by which a state of 'war' could be identified: see C. Greenwood, 'The Concept of War in Modern International Law', 36 *International and Comparative Law Quarterly* (1987), p. 283 ff., at pp. 284-286; Dinstein, *supra* note 13, at pp. 7-21.

24 See, for example: Komarnicki, *supra* note 1, at p. 402; Oppenheim, *supra* note 8, at pp. 653-654; Castrén, *supra* note 8, at p. 424; Stone, *supra* note 8, at p. 383.

25 See, especially: Brownlie, *supra* note 13, at p. 384 ff.; Schindler, 'Aspects contemporains', *supra* note 1, at pp. 278-284, and *idem*, 'State of War, Belligerency, Armed Conflict', in A. Cassese (ed.), *The New Humanitarian Law of Armed Conflict*, Naples 1979, p. 3 ff., at p. 7 ff.; Greenwood, *supra* note 23, at pp. 290 ff. and 298.

26 See *supra*, paragraph II, note 13 and corresponding text.

27 Tucker, *supra* note 8, at pp. 199-200. See also, among others: Oppenheim, *supra* note 8, at p. 293(n.); Castrén, *supra* note 8, at p. 423; Guggenheim, *supra* note 8, at p. 510; Kelsen, *supra* note 10, at p. 155; Schindler, 'Aspects contemporains', *supra* note 1, at p. 288 ff., and *ibid.*, 'Transformations', *supra* note 1, at pp. 374-375; E. Kussbach, 'L'évolution de la notion de neutralité dans les conflits armés actuels', 17 *Revue de droit pénal militaire et de droit de la guerre* (1978), p. 19 ff., at pp. 25-27, and *idem*, 'Neutral Trading', 4 *Encyclopedia of Public International Law*, Amsterdam/New York/Oxford 1982, p. 7 ff., at p. 9; Bindschedler, *supra* note 1, at p. 10; Greenwood, *supra* note 23, at pp. 297-301 (but see also *infra*, note 88); Venturini, *supra* note 13, at p. 86, and the bibliography therein quoted.

The true function of the law of neutrality, as outlined above, may explain the attitude taken by modern legal writers. Indeed, recent State practice may be seen to go even further than the traditional theory of the 'state of war' allowed: whereas, in traditional international law, it was sufficient that one party to a conflict expressed its *animus belli* for the laws of neutrality to come into operation, modern practice shows a marked tendency on the part of third States not to regard themselves bound by neutrality obligations unless they choose to be so bound.[28] Given the present reluctance of belligerent States to recognize the existence of a formal 'state of war', a conflict between their opinion and that of third States may not pose difficulties in practice: even if belligerents deny the existence of a 'state of war', third States may consider it expedient to declare themselves neutral without causing too many problems to belligerents, since, as stated above, the status of neutrality really only entails special duties for neutral States.[29] The possibility remains, however, that, in a given conflict, al least one of the parties decides to exercise belligerent rights *vis-à-vis* third States, thereby implicitly recognizing, according to one view, the existence of a 'state of war'.[30] Some writers maintain that this happened in the recent Iran-Iraq conflict, since at least Iran claimed belligerent rights in respect of 'neutral' shipping in the Gulf.[31] Does this mean that third States should automatically become bound by the laws of neutrality?

28 For an examination of recent State practice in this field, see especially: Norton, *supra* note 1, p. 257 ff. See also: Schindler, 'Transformations', *supra* note 1, at p. 375. But the trend towards 'voluntary' neutrality had already emerged after the First World War: see, for example, Komarnicki, *supra* note 1, at pp. 452-456.

29 See *supra*, paragraph I, notes 17-18 and corresponding text.

For the view that third States may apply the law of neutrality even if the parties to the conflict do not recognize the existence of a 'state of war', see, among others: Oppenheim, *supra* note 8, at p. 293(n.); Guggenheim, *supra* note 8, at p. 510; Brownlie, *supra* note 13, at pp. 395-396; Kelsen, *supra* note 10, at p. 155; Kussbach, 'L'évolution', *supra* note 27, at p. 27, and *idem*, 'Neutral Trading', *supra* note 27, at p. 9; Schindler, 'Aspects contemporains', *supra* note 1, at p. 293, *idem*, *supra* note 10, at p. 212, and *idem*, 'Transformations', *supra* note 1, at pp. 375-376; Greenwood, *supra* note 23, at p. 298. Schindler rightly ponts out that this view is confirmed by the 1949 Geneva Conventions, *supra* note 2, which, as seen above, contain several provisions relating to neutral States and, at the same time, state, in common Article 2, that they apply even if a formal 'state of war' is not recognized.

30 See, for example: Schindler, 'Aspects contemporains', *supra* note 1, at pp. 293-294, and *idem*, *supra* note 25, at pp. 8 and 10-11; Greenwood, *supra* note 23, at pp. 293-294.

31 See, for example: Greenwood, *supra* note 23, at pp. 293-294, who also quotes an Iraqi statement to the effect that an 'actual state of war' existed despite the absence of a declaration of war. On Iran's practice in the Gulf war of 1980-1988, see, among others: A. Gioia, N. Ronzitti, 'The Law of Neutrality: Third States' Commercial Rights and Duties', in Dekker, Post (eds.), *supra* note 10, p. 221 ff.; D. Momtaz, 'Commentary', in A. de Guttry, N. Ronzitti (eds.), *The Iran-Iraq War (1980-1988) and the Dispatch of Western Fleets to the Gulf. A Collection of Documents and Related Commentaries on Naval Warfare*, Cambridge 1993, p. 19 ff.

According to some writers, the views of the parties to the conflict regarding the legal status of hostilities should no longer be regarded as conclusive.[32] It has been suggested that in modern international law, failing a generally accepted definition of 'war', it is for each State not taking part in armed hostilities to determine whether the conflict has attained the level of 'war', thereby causing the laws of neutrality to become operative in its relations with belligerents. It is sometimes recognized that, from this point of view, the notion of the 'state of war' is relevant only 'in that a non-participant in a conflict may couch its election to be bound by the laws of neutrality in terms of a statement that it regards the conflict as 'war''; in other words, this view 'is not very different from saying that a State is bound by the law of neutrality only if it chooses to declare itself neutral, except that it suggests that the decision may not be purely discretionary'.[33]

It seems clear, in conclusion, that the present relevance of the traditional concept of the 'state of war' is ultimately dependent upon the answer to a fundamental question: do States not wishing to become party to an armed conflict have, at least in some circumstances, a duty to abide by the laws of neutrality? Should the answer be in the negative, it would be entirely irrelevant whether a conflict does or does not qualify as 'war' under the traditional rules: third States could, in that case, choose to declare themselves neutral or to take any intermediate positions between neutrality and actual belligerency without automatically violating international law. A correct answer to this question can only be given in the light of the modern *jus ad bellum*.

III. NEUTRALITY AND THE MODERN *JUS AD BELLUM*: GROTIUS REVISITED

In traditional international law, States enjoyed an unrestricted freedom to wage war. War could be declared by any State against any other State accused of violating the first State's rigths under international law. But war could also be declared by any State in order to solve political disputes with any other State and, more generally, whenever it suited its interests. Whatever might be the cause of war, and whether or not the cause was a 'just' cause, it was thought that, by a mere act of will, any State

---

32 Some writers still maintain that, whenever the 'state of war' is recognized by belligerents, third States are bound by the law of neutrality: see, for example, Bindschedler, *supra* note 1, at pp. 10 and 13. Other writers, however, have taken the opposite view: see, especially: Wright, 'The Present Status', *supra* note 1, at p. 404; Oppenheim, *supra* note 8, at p. 221; Schindler, 'Aspects contemporains', *supra* note 1, at p. 261 ff., *idem*, *supra* note 25, at pp. 13-15, and *idem*, 'Transformations', *supra* note 1, at p. 375. It goes without saying that the characterization of one conflict as 'war' made by the parties thereto cannot be considered as automatically binding on third States if the existence of a 'state of war' is considered to be dependent on objective criteria: see, explicitly, Sereni, *supra* note 8, at p. 2081.

33 See especially: Greenwood, *supra* note 23, at pp. 300-301.

could bring about the suspension of the operation of large parts of the general law of peace and the application of the special rules regulating warfare in its relations with its elected enemies.[34] It is not surprising, in this context, that the same act of will was also thought to be sufficient to bring about the application of the special rules of neutrality in relations between belligerents and States not wishing to enter war. Indeed, in those days the law of neutrality might be seen as fulfilling an important task: since belligerents were allowed to declare war against third States, irrespective of whether or not they were responsible for a wrongful act, it could be argued that, by imposing upon third States special obligations of impartiality and by granting belligerents limited rights of interference with their trade with the enemy, the law of neutrality contributed to preventing third States' involvement in a war.

International law had not always been so indifferent to the causes of war, at least in the eyes of its most distinguished commentators. For our purposes, the opinion of Grotius is especially significant. Although Grotius distinguished between 'just' and 'unjust' causes of war, he recognized that, as far as relations between belligerents were concerned, the distinction was mainly relevant in the moral sphere, since, from the point of view of international law, both 'just' and 'unjust' wars, provided they were waged by sovereign States observing the necessary formalities, produced the same consequences, *i.e.* the application of the laws of war.[35] However, the laws of war, in Grotius's view, only concerned belligerents: as far as third States were concerned ('*qui extra bellum sunt positi*'), no special rules were applicable ('*satis constet nullum esse jus bellicum*'). Furthermore, moral considerations, which were behind the distinction between 'just' and 'unjust' causes of war, prompted Grotius to lay down two general rules: on the one hand, third States could do nothing which might strengthen a belligerent whose cause was 'unjust', or hinder the movements of a belligerent whose cause was 'just'; on the other hand, in a war in which it was doubtful whose cause was 'just', third States should treat all belligerents alike.[36]

---

34 See, for example: Oppenheim, *supra* note 8, at pp. 217 and 223; Balladore Pallieri, *supra* 8), at p. 39 ff.; Brownlie, *supra* note 13, at p. 18 ff.; Venturini, *supra* note 13, at pp. 75-76, and the bibliography therein quoted.

35 See: H. Grotius, *De jure belli ac pacis libri tres* [1646], rep. in J.B. Scott (ed.), *The Classics of International Law*, Vol. I, Oxford/London 1925, Book I, Chapter III, iv; Book II, Chapter XIII, xiii, 5; Book III, Chapter III, i, Chapter IV, Chapter VI, ii, 1, Chapter X.

36 See *ibidem*, Book III, Chapter XVII, iii, 1: 'Vicissim eorum qui a bello abstinent officium est nihil facere quo validior fiat is, qui improbam fovet causam, aut quo iustum bellum gerentis motus impediantur secundum ea quae dicta a nobis supra sunt. In re vero dubia aequos se praebere utrisque in permittendo transitu, in commeatu praebendo legionibus, in obsessis non sublevandis ...'

The phrases quoted in the text are taken from Book III, Chapter XVII, i, where Grotius also maintained that belligerents' rights against neutrals were based only on necessityAccording to Verzijl, *supra* note 11, at p. 5, Grotius's view 'was certainly not a reflection of the positive rules observed in his time'. On the place of *De jure belli ac pacis*, within the context of seventeenth-century practice see recently: C.G. Roelofsen, 'Grotius and State Practice of His Day', 10 *Grotiana* (1989), p. 3 ff.

Modern international law has, to a certain extent, moved back to the situation existing, if not in positive law[37] at least in the eyes of legal doctrine, at the times when Grotius wrote. In the XXth century, there has been a revival of the attempts to distinguish between 'just' and 'unjust' causes of war. In synthesis, the process started in 1919 with the adoption of the Covenant of the League of Nations,[38] which partially abolished the traditional freedom to wage war; it continued in 1928 with the adoption of the so-called 'Briand-Kellogg Pact',[39] which completely abolished resort to war as an instrument of national policy; and it culminated in 1948 with the adoption of the Charter of the United Nations, which contains a general prohibition on the use of force on the part of individual States, except in self-defence.[40] The Charter provisions on the use of force are by now widely regarded as declaratory of general customary law and, as such, binding upon all States; indeed, they are also

37 According to Verzijl, *supra* note 11, at p. 5, Grotius's view 'was certainly not a reflection of the positive rules observed in his time'. On the place of *De jure belli ac pacis*, within the context of seventeenth-century practice see recently: C.G. Roelofsen, 'Grotius and State Practice of His Day', 10 *Grotiana* (1989), p. 3 ff.
38 The Covenant of the League of Nation was drafted in February 1919; it was adopted by the Paris Peace Conference and became an integral part of the treaties of peace which ended the First World War. See, among others: Brownlie, *supra* note 13, at p. 55 ff.; G. Conetti, 'Societa' delle Nazioni', 17 *Enciclopedia del diritto*, Milan 1990, p. 1167 ff., and the bibliography therein quoted.
   On the problems posed by the Covenant for the operation of the law of neutrality, see especially: J.B. Whitton, 'La neutralité et la Societé des Nations', 17 *Hague Recueil* (1927, II), p. 453 ff.; R. De Nova, *La neutralità nel sistema della Società delle Nazioni*, Pavia 1935; Jessup, *supra* note 6, at p. 86 ff.; Komarnicki, *supra* note 1, at pp. 422-434; Oppenheim, *supra* note 8, at pp. 645-646; Bowett, *supra* note 9, at pp. 157-159 and 162 ff.; Fenwick, *supra* note 7, at pp. 719-720; Verzijl, *supra* note 11, at pp. 260-262; Rousseau, *supra* note 8, at pp. 381-382.
39 General Treaty for the Renunciation of War, signed in Paris on 27 August 1928 (94 *League of Nations Treaty Series*, p. 57 ff.). See, among others: S. Calogeropoulos-Stratis, *Le Pacte général de renonciation à la guerre*, Paris 1931; Brownlie, *supra* note 13, at p. 74 ff.
   On the problems posed by the Treaty for the operation of the law of neutrality, see especially: Jessup, *supra* note 6, at p. 115 ff.; Komarnicki, *supra* note 1, at pp. 434-444; Oppenheim, *supra* note 8, at pp. 642-645; Tucker, *supra* note 8, at pp. 166-171; Bowett, *supra* note 9, at p. 159 ff.; Brownlie, *supra* note 13, at p. 403; Fenwick, *supra* note 7, at pp. 720-721; Kelsen, *supra* note 10, at pp. 168-169.
40 See Articles 2(4) and 51 of the UN Charter. On the current prohibition on the use of force and on exceptions thereto, see, among others: H. Wehberg, 'L'interdiction de recours à la force; le principe et les problèmes qui se posent', 78 *Hague Recueil* (1951, I), p. 7 ff.; C.H.M. Waldock, 'The Regulation of the Use of Force by Individual States', 81 *Hague Recueil* (1952, II), p. 451 ff.; Brownlie, *supra* note 13, at pp. 112 ff. and 264 ff.; W. Wengler, 'L'interdiction de recourir à la force. Problèmes et tendences', 7 *Revue belge de droit international* (1971), p. 401 ff.; S.M. Schwebel, 'Aggression, Intervention and Self-Defence in Modern International Law', 136 *Hague Recueil* (1972, II), p. 411 ff.; J. Zourek, *L'interdiction de l'emploi de la force en droit international*, Leyden 1974; A. Cassese (ed.), *The Current Legal Regulation of the Use of Force*, Dordrecht/Boston/Lancaster 1986; Dinstein, *supra* note 13, at p. 81 ff.; Venturini, *supra* note 13, at p. 39 ff.; Ronzitti, N., 'Forza (Uso della)', 7 *Digesto delle discipline pubblicistiche*, Turin 1991, p. 1 ff., and the bibliography therein quoted.

considered to be rules of *jus cogens*, *i.e.* rules allowing for no conventional, or customary, derogations.[41]

As a result of this process, in present international law it is not only 'unjust', but it is also illegal for individual States to wage war and, more generally, to resort to military coercion, in their international relations, except when they are faced with an unlawful armed attack on the part of other States. As was advocated by Grotius, the necessity to distinguish between aggressor and victim has not had the effect of preventing the equal application of the laws of war in their mutual relations: indeed, as stated above, the *jus in bello* must now be complied with in all situations of armed conflict, irrespective of whether or not a formal 'state of war' is recognized.[42] However, the picture is very different as far as the law of neutrality is concerned. Since 'war' can no longer be declared against an 'innocent' State, the one-sidedness of the law of neutrality has become less acceptable: it is now difficult to maintain, as before, that third States' peacetime rights should be limited in exchange for the mere non-involvement in the armed conflict, which is already guaranteed by a peremptory norm of international law. Moreover, the necessity to distinguish between the aggressor and the victim of aggression has inevitable legal consequences as far as the attitude of third States is concerned; it has been rightly observed that, if the fundamental changes which have taken place in the *jus ad bellum* are to become a reality, they must be accompanied by a full realisation of their legal implications.[43]

Whether or not an armed conflict amounts to 'war' in the traditional sense, it is no longer possible to maintain that third States not wishing to enter the conflict have a legal duty to abide by the old laws of neutrality. As Oppenheim and Lauterpacht put it, 'the historic foundation of neutrality as an attitude of absolute impartiality has disappeared with the renunciation and the abolition of war as an instrument of national policy': it is now 'open to neutral States as a matter of legal right to give effect to their moral obligation to discriminate against the aggressor and to deny him, in their discretion, the right to exact from neutrals a full measure of impartiality'.[44]

---

41 This view is widely held and has been endorsed by the International Court of Justice in its 1986 decision in the Nicaragua case: see 'Case Concerning Military and Paramilitary Activities In and Against Nicaragua (Nicaragua v. United States of America) (Merits)', Judgment of 27 June 1986, *ICJ Reports 1986*, p. 14 ff., at p. 97 ff. Some writers maintain that a customary prohibition on the use of force otherwise than in self-defence had already come into existence before the adoption of the UN Charter: see, especially, Brownlie, *supra* note 13, at pp. 110-111. Other writers maintain that the customary prohibition and/or the jus cogens prohibition on the use of force have a narrower scope than the prohibition contained in the UN Charter: see, especially, N. Ronzitti, 'Use of force, Jus Cogens and State Consent', in Cassese (ed.), *supra* note 40, p. 147 ff., and *idem*, *supra* note 40, at pp. 12-13.

42 See *supra*, paragraph I, note 13 and corresponding text.

43 See: Oppenheim, *supra* note 8, at p. 221. On the problems posed by the UN prohibition on the use of force for the operation of the law of neutrality, see the authors quoted *infra*, in note 59. See also: R. De Nova, 'Neutralità e Nazioni Unite', 1 *La Comunità internazionale* (1946), p. 495 ff.

44 Oppenheim, *supra* note 8, at p. 221.

Since the law of neutrality mainly consists of special duties imposed upon third States which are expressions of a general principle of impartiality, this is tantamount to saying that, in modern international law, States are no longer obliged to abide by the laws of neutrality, whatever the status of the conflict may be.[45]

Even if our starting point were to be that changes in the *jus ad bellum* had not, *per se*, modified the traditional conditions for the operation of the law of neutrality, the situation would not in practice be very different from that briefly outlined above. First of all, it would be necessary to determine whether or not a given conflict amounted to 'war' in the traditional sense: in case of a conflict falling 'short of war', third States would not be obliged to abide by the laws of neutrality.[46] Secondly, even if the conflict amounted to 'war', the modern *jus ad bellum* would arguably provide States with 'circumstances precluding wrongfulness', which might be invoked in order to justify 'unneutral' conduct in a particular case.[47] Violations of neutrality obligations could be justified under the doctrine of collective self-defence, as enshrined in Article 51 of the UN Charter, at least in situations where the victim of aggression has requested third States' assistance against the aggressor.[48] Apart

45 In this sense, see, especially: Schindler, 'Aspects contemporains', *supra* note 1, at p. 261 ff., *idem*, *supra* note 10, at pp. 211-212, and *idem*, 'Transformations', *supra* note 1, at pp. 371-376. See also, among others: Verdross, *supra* note 1, at p. 413.

The reverse, however, is not necessarily true. The correct view is that there is no *duty* for third States to discriminate against the aggressor, unless a binding decision by the UN Security Council has been adopted in the framework of Chapter VII of the UN Charter. On this question, see *infra*, paragraph V.

46 For the view that the operation of the law of neutrality is still dependent on the existence of a formal 'state of war', see *supra*, paragraph III, notes 27-33 and accompanying text. But even if the view is accepted that the operation of the law of neutrality, like that of the *jus in bello*, is now dependent on the outbreak of any armed conflict, or of 'war' in the material sense (for this view, see the authors quoted *infra*, in note 88), discrimination against an aggressor could still be justified by collective self-defence or the law of countermeasures, as suggested in the text: see, for example, Brownlie, *supra* note 13, at pp. 395-396 and 403-404.

47 On the concept of 'circumstances precluding wrongfulness', see especially: R. Ago, 'Eigth Report on State Responsibility', Chapter V, 'Circumstances Precluding Wrongfulness', *Yearbook of the International Law Commission 1979*, Vol. II, Part One, p. 27 ff.

48 On collective self-defence, see generally and among others: Oppenheim, *supra* note 8, at pp. 650-652; Bowett, *supra* note 9, at p. 200 ff.; Brownlie, *supra* note 13, at p. 328 ff.; J. Delivanis, *La légitime défense en droit international public moderne*, Paris 1971, at p. 148 ff.; P. Lamberti Zanardi, *La legittima difesa nel diritto internazionale*, Milan 1972, at p. 276 ff.; J. Zourek, 'La notion de légitime défense en droit international', 56 *Annuaire de l'Institut de droit international* (1975), p. 1 ff., at pp. 47-48; J. Delbrück, 'Collective Self-Defence', 3 *Encyclopedia of Public International Law*, Amsterdam/New York/Oxford 1982, p. 114 ff.; J. Combacau, 'The Exception of Self-Defence in U.N. Practice', in Cassese (ed.), *supra* note 40, p. 9 ff.; Dinstein, *supra* note 13, at p. 230 ff.; Ronzitti, *supra* note 40, at pp. 22-24.

For the view that discrimination against an aggressor may be based on collective self-defence, see, for example: Komarnicki, *supra* note 1, at pp. 481-482; Castrén, *supra* note 8, at p. 434; Bowett, *supra* note 9, at pp. 179-181; Brownlie, *supra* note 13, at pp. 403-404; Henkin, *supra* note 10, at p. 349; Schindler, 'Aspects contemporains', *supra* note 1, at p. 270, and *idem*, 'Transformations', *supra* note 1, at p. 373. In this context, it should be pointed out that, although 'self-defence normally, and almost axiomatically, involves the use of armed force' (R. Ago., 'Addendum to the Eigth Report on State

from collective self-defence, it is arguable that modern international law would justify individual violations of neutrality obligations as legitimate countermeasures, *i.e.* as reprisals not involving the use of armed force.[49] However, although there is no doubt that, by unlawfully resorting to war, the guilty belligerent would violate the rights of all States, the obligation not to use force being an obligation *erga omnes*, the legality of reprisals by States other than the one directly affected by the prior violation is still very much controversial in State practice.[50]

In the opinion of the author of this report, however, the starting point should rather be that changes in the *jus ad bellum* have indeed modified the traditional conditions for the operation of the law of neutrality. Third States no longer have to justify individual violations of neutrality obligations by having recourse to a circumstance precluding wrongfulness, because there are no longer primary

---

Responsibility', *Yearbook of the International Law Commission 1980*, Vol. II, Part One, p. 13 ff., at p. 55), this should not preclude other forms of reaction against an unlawful armed attack: as Brownlie puts it, 'if force may be used to aid the victim of unlawful resort to force, other forms of partiality of a less serious matter must surely be permitted' *supra* note 13, at pp. 403-404). In this sense, see also, for example: Tucker, *supra* note 8, at p. 178; Kelsen. *supra* note 10, at pp. 172-173. *Contra*: Meyrowitz, *supra* note 1, at pp. 372-373.

The need for a request on the part of the victim of aggression has been emphasized by the International Court of Justice in the 1986 decision in the Nicaragua case, *supra* note 41, at p. 196 ff. According to Schindler, 'Transformations', *supra* note 1, at p. 374, this condition would only apply to the use of military force and not to other forms of assistance, such as economic help, 'which are generally admissible according to international law'. The correctness of this view depends, of course, on the assumption that the law of neutrality is not applicable, either because no 'state of war' is recognized or because the law of neutrality is considered to apply only if a declaration of neutrality has been effected: on this latter possibility, see *infra* in the text.

49 On reprisals or countermeasures, see generally, among others: J.-C. Venezia, 'La notion de représailles en droit international public', 64 *Revue générale de droit international public* (1960), p. 465 ff.; D.W. Bowett, 'Reprisals Involving Recourse to Armed Force', 66 *American Journal of International Law* (1972), p. 1 ff.; Ago, *supra* note 47, at p. 39 ff.; C. Leben, 'Les contre-mesures inter-étatiques et les réactions a l'illicite dans la société internationale', 28 *Annuaire français de droit international* (1982), p. 9 ff.; E. Zoller, *Peacetime Unilateral Remedies: An Analysis of Counter-Measures*, Dobbs Ferry 1984; A. de Guttry, *Le rappresaglie non comportanti la forza militare nel diritto internazionale*, Milan 1985; R. Barsotti, 'Armed Reprisals', in Cassese (ed.), *supra* note 40, p. 78 ff.; O.Y. Elagab, *The Legality of Non-Forcible Countermeasures in International Law*, Oxford 1988. On reprisals by third States, see also: M. Akehurst, 'Reprisals by Third States', 44 *British Year Book of International Law* (1970), p. 1 ff.

The view that discrimination against an aggressor may be based upon the law of reprisals had been put forward by some writers with reference to the 1928 Paris Pact, *supra* note 39: see, especially, Oppenheim, *supra* note 8, at pp. 642-645 and 651; Kelsen, *supra* note 10, at p. 168. See also the Budapest Articles adopted in September 1934 by the International Law Association (ILA, *Report of the 38th Conference*, at p. 66), as well as Article 12 of the 1939 Harvard Research Draft Convention on Rights and Duties of States in case of Aggression (33 *American Journal of International Law* (1939), *Suppl.*, p. 827 ff.).

50 On this question, and on the ongoing effort to codify the law of State responsibility by the UN International Law Commission, see the reports presented by G. Arangio-Ruiz to the ILC in 1991 (UN Docs. A/CN.4/440 and A/CN.4/440/Add.1) and 1992 (UN Docs. A/CN.4/444, A/CN.4/440/Add.1 and A/CN.4/440/Add.2).

obligations of neutrality automatically binding upon them as a result of the existence of a 'state of war': in fact, whether or not the conflict amounts to 'war', third States not wishing to declare themselves neutral are free, as a matter of principle, to discriminate against the aggressor either by entering the conflict on the side of the victim, provided there is a request on the part of this latter,[51] or by exercising the rights granted, or the freedom of action allowed for, under the general laws of peace.[52] It is only when their behaviour would be incompatible with the general laws of peace, or particular treaty obligations *vis-à-vis* the aggressor, that third States would have to invoke, where possible, a circumstance precluding wrongfulness in order to avoid reprisals. With reference to treaty obligations, however, two qualifications seem necessary. As far as treaties codifying traditional neutrality obligations are concerned,[53] it is arguable that their application is no longer dependent on the mere existence of a 'state of war': even leaving aside the question of which State should determine whether a given conflict amounts to 'war', it is now possible to maintain that the evolution of customary law has subjected their application to a declaration of neutrality, express or implied by their conduct, on the part of States not participating in 'war'.[54] As far as other treaties are concerned, it is arguable that States wishing to assist the victim of aggression could even invoke the *rebus sic stantibus* rule as a ground for suspending their application *vis-à-vis* the aggressor for the duration of hostilities.[55]

51 In this case, of course, the States in question would become co-belligerents and would, therefore, be bound by the *jus in bello*. In traditional international law, third States were free to enter the conflict on either side. In modern international law, they can only use force in collective self-defence.

52 If it is conceded that the law of neutrality does not apply unless a State chooses to declare itself neutral, it follows logically that its relations with belligerents are governed entirely by the law of peace. Therefore, no act of partiality towards one belligerent can give rise to a violation of international law if, under the general laws of peace, it amounts to the exercise of a legal right, such as the right of territorial sovereignty, or if, under the general laws of peace, such act does not constitute a violation of an international obligation *vis-à-vis* the aggrieved belligerent. On this question, however, see also *infra*, paragraph VI, notes 113-144 and corresponding text, as well as paragraph IX, notes 190-191 and 201 and corresponding text.

53 See *supra*, note 5.

54 In this sense, see especially: Schindler, *supra* note 10, at p. 215 ff. But see also other writings by the same author and by others quoted *supra*, in note 10. *Also*: Norton, *supra* note 1, at pp. 308-309.

55 See Article 62 of the 1969 Vienna Convention on the Law of Treaties (1155 *United Nations Treaty Series*, p. 331 ff.). In other words, it could be argued that the outbreak of an armed conflict, as a result of an act of aggression committed by one party to a treaty, would constitute 'a fundamental change of circumstances which has occurred with regard to those existing at the time of the conclusion of [that] treaty, and which was not foreseen by the parties'.

On the *rebus sic stantibus* rule, see generally, among others: E. Back Impallomeni, *Il principio rebus sic stantibus nella Convenzione di Vienna sul diritto dei trattati*, Milan 1974; G. Haraszti, 'Treaties and Fundamental Change of Circumstances', 146 *Hague Recueil* (1975, III), p. 1 ff.; L. Sico, *Gli effetti del mutamento delle circostanze sui trattati internazionali*, Padua 1983; G. Schwarzenberger, 'Clausula Rebus Sic Stantibus', 7 *Encyclopedia of Public International Law*, Amsterdam/New York/Oxford 1984, p. 22 ff.; P. Cahier, 'Le changement fondamental de circonstances et la Convention de Vienne de 1969 sur le

In conclusion, the situation can now be described as one in which, as a matter of principle, States not wishing to enter an armed conflict are no longer under a legal duty to abide by the traditional laws of neutrality. Such States may, in their discretion, declare themselves neutral, having regard to their own safety or to other considerations of a purely political nature, or discriminate against the aggressor without, by this fact alone, violating international law. Of course, such a situation is open to abuse since, given the 'decentralized' structure of the international legal order, each non-participating State is to decide by itself which belligerent is the aggressor and which is the victim of aggression:[56] in situations, such as, for example, the recent Iran-Iraq conflict, where both belligerents claim a 'right' of self-defence,[57] an attitude of partiality favouring one or the other belligerent could lead to unsatisfactory and dangerous results. A partial remedy is constituted by the United Nations system of collective security, to which we shall now turn. But, unless and until that system comes into play, Grotius's view that third States should treat all belligerents alike whenever it was doubtful whose cause was 'just' may still be seen as having some merit. Consequently, the question may be asked of whether post-Charter practice allows for the view that at least some of the traditional rules of neutrality can now be regarded as binding upon all States not wishing to enter an armed conflict in situations where the distinction between aggressor and victim is *prima facie* unclear. This question will be addressed later in this report.[58]

droit des traités', in *International Law at the Time of Its Codification. Essays in Honour of Roberto Ago,* Vol. I, Milan 1987, p. 163 ff.

Although the Vienna Convention does not directly deal with the legal effects of war on treaties (see Article 73 thereof), the *rebus sic stantibus* rule is sometimes referred to by modern legal writers in respect of treaties between belligerents: see, for example, B. Conforti, *Diritto internazionale,* 4th ed., Naples 1992, at pp. 131-132. In some cases, it is admitted that the same rule can have an effect on treaties between belligerents and third States: see, for example, M. Bothe, A. Cassese, F. Kalshoven, A. Kiss, J., Salmon, K.R., Simmonds, *Protection of the Environment in Times of Armed Conflict* (European Communities, Commission, Doc. SJ/110/85) 1985, at p. 47.

56 In this sense, see, for example: Wright, 'The Present Status', *supra* note 1, at p. 402; Bowett, *supra* note 9, at p. 179; Brownlie, *supra* note 13, at p. 404; Kelsen, *supra* note 10, at pp. 168-169. Contra: Sico, *supra* note 1, at p. 192. Of course, the condition by which each State is judge in its own case only exists unless and until an objective determination is made in the form of international adjudication, recognition by the international community as a whole or determination by the competent organ of a universal international organization: see, for example, M.S. Mc Dougal, F.P. Feliciano, *Law and Minimum World Public Order,* New Haven/London 1961, at p. 416.

57 See: K.H. Kaikobad, '*Ius ad bellum*: Legal Implications of the Iran-Iraq War', in Dekker, Post (eds.), *supra* note 10, p. 51 ff., at pp. 52-53. Such situations are notoriously common in post-Charter practice. Another recent example was the 1992 Falklands conflict: see, for example, A. Gioia, 'Il ricorso alla forza armata da parte argentina e la reazione britannica', in N. Ronzitti (ed.), *La questione delle Falkland-Malvinas nel diritto internazionale,* Milan 1984, p. 123 ff.

58 See *infra,* paragraphs VI-VIII.

IV. NEUTRALITY AND THE UN SYSTEM OF COLLECTIVE SECURITY

While the modern *jus ad bellum*, enshrined in the Charter of the United Nations, no longer allows for the view that States not wishing to participate in an armed conflict have to abide by all the traditional rules of neutrality, a legal duty to discriminate against the aggressor cannot reasonably be derived from the *jus ad bellum*. On the other hand, the existing system of collective security, also enshrined in the UN Charter, raises the question of whether traditional neutrality obligations are compatible with the adoption of coercive measures against a State guilty of aggression. In other words, having found that, in principle, there is no longer a duty to remain strictly neutral, it is now necessary to determine whether third States have an unrestricted freedom to remain neutral, or may sometimes be bound to end their neutral status or to deviate from traditional neutrality obligations.[59] In this paragraph, as in the preceding one, the relationship between neutrality obligations and the UN Charter will be addressed exclusively from the perspective of traditional duties of abstention, prevention and non-discrimination, which derive from a general principle of impartiality and constitute the core of the law of neutrality; other traditional duties of neutral States, such as the duty to tolerate certain activities on the part of belligerents interfering with neutral shipping, will be dealt with later in this report.[60]

The UN system of collective security is enshrined in Chapter VII of the Charter of the United Nations, dealing with 'action with respect to threats to the peace, breaches of the peace, and acts of aggression'.[61] Only the UN Security Council has the competence to take action under Chapter VII of the Charter and, mainly as a result of the so-called 'power of veto' of its five Permanent Members,[62] it is a well-known fact that the system has only partly been activated and is often ineffectual. This notwithstanding, it does not seem necessary here to address the vexed question of whether the UN General Assembly has, or has acquired, a

---

59 On the effect on neutrality of the UN system of collective security, see especially: R. De Nova, 'Neutralità e Nazioni Unite', 1 *La Comunità internazionale* (1946), p. 495 ff.; Lalive, *supra* note 1, at p. 77 ff.; Komarnicki, *supra* note 1, at p. 464 ff.; Oppenheim, *supra* note 8, at p. 645 ff.; Balladore Pallieri, *supra* note 8, at p. 388 ff.; Castrén, *supra* note 8, at pp. 433-435; Chaumont, *supra* note 1, *passim*; Tucker, *supra* note 8, at p. 171 ff.; Verdross, *supra* note 1, *passim*; Schindler, 'Aspects contemporains', *supra* note 1, at p. 243 ff.; Blix, *supra* note 1, at p. 45 ff.; Meyrowitz, *supra* note 1, at p. 342 ff.; Miele, *supra* note 1, at p. 496 ff.; Bindschedler, *supra* note 1, at p. 13; Greenwood, *supra* note 9, at p. 57 ff.; Torrelli, *supra* note 1, at p. 18 ff.

60 See *infra*, paragraphs VII-VIII.

61 On the UN system of collective security, see generally, among others: H. Kelsen, *The Law of the United Nations*, New York 1950, at p. 724 ff.; Oppenheim, *supra* note 8, at p. 159 ff.; J. Delbrück, 'Collective Security', 3 *Encyclopedia of Public International Law*, Amsterdam/New York/Oxford 1982, p. 104 ff.; B. Conforti, *Le Nazioni Unite*, 4th ed., Padua 1986, at p. 176 ff.

62 See Article 27(3) of the UN Charter.

subsidiary competence to take action under Chapter VII of the Charter.[63] Apart from the fact that the present composition of the General Assembly seems to make its involvement in the system of collective security both unlikely and undesirable in the eyes of the very States which had originally favoured it, the problems that such an involvement would pose for the purposes of this report are not substantially different from those arising out of action taken by the Security Council.

Under Article 39 of the Charter, the Security Council may, first of all, 'determine the existence of any threat to the peace, breach of the peace, or act of aggression', such determination being theoretically necessary before measures are taken, in accordance with successive articles, 'to maintain or restore international peace and security'. In practice, a precise determination that a State has committed an act of aggression has never been made by the Security Council; however, in the recent Gulf conflict, the Security Council, in Resolution 660 adopted on 2 August 1990, determined that there existed 'a breach of international peace and security' as a result of Iraq's invasion of Kuwait.[64] A determination under Article 39 has the effect that third States are undoubtedly allowed to discriminate against the aggressor, removing the possibility of abuse to which reference was made in the preceding paragraph; on the other hand, such a determination does not, *per se*, oblige third States wishing to remain neutral to deviate from their neutrality obligations.[65]

'In order to prevent an aggravation of the situation', the Security Council may further 'call upon the parties concerned to comply with such provisional measures as it deems necessary or desirable' (Article 40). The typical example is a resolution calling for a ceasefire. Whether or not a resolution under Article 40 would be binding upon the States concerned is at least debatable.[66] In any case, such a

---

63 See the so-called 'Uniting For Peace' Resolution: UN General Assembly Resolution 377(V) of 3 November 1950, 4 *Yearbook of the United Nations* (1950), pp. 193-195.

64 UN Security Council Resolution 660 (1990), adopted on 2 August 1990, by 14 votes to none, one Member (Yemen) not participating in the vote. Text in: UN, *Security Council Official Records: Forty-Fifth Year, Resolutions and Decisions of the Security Council 1990*, New York 1991, p. 19. In a later resolution, the Security Council 'considered' that Iraq's decision to order the closure of diplomatic and consular mussions in Kuwait and to withdraw the privileges and immunities of such missions and their personnel, as well as the commission of acts of violence against them and the violation of their premises, constituted 'aggressive acts': see UN Security Council Resolution 667 (1990), adopted unanimously on 16 September 1990 (*ibidem*, pp. 23-24).

65 See, for example: Wright, 'The New Law', *supra* note 1, at p. 422; Oppenheim, *supra* note 8, at pp. 651-652; Castrén, *supra* note 8, at p. 434; Bowett, *supra* note 9, at pp. 175-176; Verdross, *supra* note 1, at pp. 413-414; Sereni, *supra* note 8, at p. 2103; Greenwood, *supra* note 9, at pp. 57-58. According to one view, once the identity of the aggressor has been established by the Security Council 'Member States must do whatever they can to foil the designs of that State and to assist the party resisting aggression' (Dinstein, *supra* note 13, at p. 155; see also, for example, Komarnicki, *supra* note 1, at pp. 476 and 494). But while the spirit of the Charter undoubtedly forbids neutrality in such a case and morally requires all Member States to assist the victim of aggression, there seems to be no legal duty for States to deviate from neutrality.

66 On this question, see *infra*, paragraph VIII, notes 167-169 and corresponding text.

resolution would not oblige third States wishing to remain neutral to deviate from their neutrality obligations.[67]

Articles 41 and 42 of the Charter, dealing respectively with measures not involving the use of force and military measures against a State, constitute the core of the UN system of collective security. Under Article 41, 'the Security Council may decide what measures not involving the use of armed force are to be employed to give effect to its decisions, and it may call upon the Members of the United Nations to apply such measures'. Measures under Article 41 can be adopted either in the form of a 'recommendation', as such non-binding, or in the form of a binding 'decision'.[68] In the first instance, States wishing to remain neutral are not obliged to deviate from their neutrality obligations. However, if they do, their conduct could not be considered a violation of neutrality allowing for reprisals on the part of the belligerent concerned: in fact, compliance with a recommendation under Article 41 may be seen as a circumstance precluding wrongfulness in relations among UN Members.[69] If, on the other hand, the Security Council adopts a binding decision, member States are obliged to comply with it and this obligation prevails over the laws of neutrality: in such a case, even States wishing to remain neutral have to deviate from their neutrality obligations to the extent required by the Security Council's decision, and the belligerent State concerned is not entitled to qualify such behaviour as a violation of neutrality.[70] Of course, measures recommended or decided under Article 41 are not necessarily inconsistent with neutrality obligations: even leaving aside the question of whether there exists a formal 'state of war' giving rise to the application of the laws of neutrality, such measures may consist of actions which, *per se*, do not implicate a violation of neutrality, such as the severance of diplomatic relations.[71] In fact, the better view is that there is no general duty of

67 This view seems to be implicit in the discussion of the effect of a 'decision' under Article 40 made by Greenwood, *supra* note 9, at pp. 58-59.

68 Article 41 only seems to allow for 'decisions', but the power of the Security Council to recommend the adoption of measures not involving the use of armed force on the part of Member States is widely admitted in legal literature. In this connection, reference is sometimes made to ARticle 39 and/or to Article 24. Chapter VI of the Charter is also occasionally referred to. However, an extensive interpretation of Article 41 itself seems to provide a sounder legal basis for this power: see, especially, conforti, *supra* note 61, at pp. 187-190.

69 In this sense, see especially: Conforti, *supra* note 55, at pp. 175-178 and 343.

For the view that a recommendation under Article 39 of the Charter does not involve any Member in a duty to discriminate against the aggressor, see also, for example: Bowett, *supra* note 9, at pp. 176-177.

70 In this sense, see, among others: Lalive, *supra* note 1, at p. 80; Oppenheim, *supra* note 8, at pp. 648-649; Castrén, *supra* note 8, at p. 434; Bowett, *supra* note 9, at pp. 176-177; Verdross, *supra* note 1, at p. 414; Sereni, *supra* note 8, at p. 2103; Schindler, 'Aspects contemporains', *supra* note 1, at p. 267; Kussbach, 'L'évolution', *supra* note 27, at pp. 27-28; Greenwood, *supra* note 9. at p. 59; Torrelli, *supra* note 1, at pp. 24-26. As Komarnicki points out, 'the status of members will be that of non-belligerency so long as the aggressor does not commit an act of war against them' *supra* note 1, at p. 477).

71 In this sense, see, for example: De Nova, *supra* note 59, at p. 502.

impartiality under the law of neutrality, but only specific obligations stemming from a principle of impartiality. However, the law of neutrality *does* require that, should a neutral State decide to adopt more stringent measures than the law would require it to, it would have to apply such measures impartially to all belligerents.[72] Thus, an arms embargo or an economic embargo decreed against one belligerent only would almost certainly implicate a deviation from neutrality obligations.

The effect on the law of neutrality of military measures decided by the Security Council under Article 42 of the Charter is somewhat more difficult to assess. Under Article 42, 'should the Security Council consider that measures provided for in Article 41 would be inadequate or have proved to be inadequate, it may take such action by air, sea, or land forces as may be necessary to maintain or restore international peace and security'. Unlike measures under Article 41, which, although recommended or decided by the Security Council, necessarily have to be put into operation by Member States, action under Article 42 was clearly intended to be a *direct* action by the Security Council. However, Articles 43 to 50 of the Charter, which were designed to give the Security Council the concrete means for taking action under Article 42, have never been put into practice and are even considered by some writers as now being obsolete.[73] As a result, the Security Council has never taken direct action *against* a State deemed to be responsible for a breach of the peace or an act of aggression. So-called 'peace-keeping' operations have been undertaken in practice by UN military forces but it is at least debatable whether such operations can reasonably be considered as amounting to enforcement measures under Article 42.[74] Since peace-keeping activities are usually undertaken within a Member State and with its prior consent, the law of neutrality would not seem to be affected by such activities;[75] it may be necessary to recall, in this context, that the present role of the law of neutrality in respect of civil wars is outside the scope of this report.[76] In any case, Member States have so far never been obliged to take an active part in peace-keeping operations, since the setting up of UN forces has always taken place on a voluntary and case-by-case basis.

Indeed, in the absence of the 'special agreement or agreements' envisaged in Article 43 of the Charter, the question of whether a State can be obliged to join in a military operation decided by the United Nations, thereby not only deviating from neutrality obligations but ending its neutral status, need not be asked. In present

---

72 See *infra*, paragraph VI, notes 103-107 and corresponding text.

73 See, for example: Conforti, *supra* note 61, at pp. 195-196, and *idem*, *supra* note 55, at p. 386.

74 On UN peace-keeping operations, see, among others: Conforti, *supra* note 61, at pp. 196-199, and *idem*, *supra* note 55, at pp. 387-388; Ronzitti, *supra* note 40, at pp. 47-48.

75 For the view that UN peace-keeping operations do not affect the law of neutrality, see also, for example: Blix, *supra* note 1, at p. 53; Kussbach, 'L'évolution', *supra* note 27, at p. 30.

76 See *supra*, note 11.

circumstances, States not wishing to become militarily involved in UN activities have no duty to end their neutral status.[77]

The situation is no different where the Security Council calls for or authorizes the use of force against a State on the part of individual member States, leaving such States in command of military operations. The author of this report shares the view that a resolution of the Security Council having that purpose would, in principle, be illegitimate unless it could properly be placed in the context of Article 51 of the Charter, dealing with individual and collective self-defence:[78] arguably, such was the case as far as Resolutions Nos. 83 and 84 of 1950,[79] dealing with the Korean

77 In this sense, see, for example: Lalive, *supra* note 1, at pp. 80-81; Komarnicki, *supra* note 1, at p. 478; Chaumont, *supra* note 1, at pp. 37-38; Verdross, *supra* note 1, at p. 414; Mc Dougal, Feliciano, *supra* note 56, at p. 429; Schindler, 'Aspects contemporains', *supra* note 1, at pp. 246-247; Blix, *supra* note 1, at p. 46; Meyrowitz, *supra* note 1, at pp. 343-344 and 348; Thürer, *supra* note 12, at p. 69; Torrelli, *supra* note 1, at p. 26.

Under Article 106 of the Charter, which was to apply 'pending the coming into force of such special agreements referred to in Article 43', the parties to the Four-Nation declaration, signed at Moscow on 30 October 1943, plus France were empowered to 'consult with one another and as occasion requires with other Members of the United Nations with a view to such joint action on behalf of the Organization as may be necessary for the purpose of maintaining international peace and security'. Be the present status of this provision as it may, there would be no duty on the part of UN Members to join in military action undertaken by the five Powers 'on behalf of the Organization': see, for example, Lalive, *supra* note 1, at pp. 80-81; Chaumont, *supra* note 1, at pp. 42-43.

According to some writers, the duty of UN Members to take military action under Article 42 of the Charter would not depend upon the conclusion of the agreements envisaged in Article 43: the Security Council could 'order Members of the United Nations to declare war upon the aggressor or take armed action intended as war' (Oppenheim, *supra* note 8, at pp. 169 and 649-650). But if the view is accepted that the Security Council cannot recommend or 'authorize' the use of force on the part of individual States, then *a fortiori* it could not oblige States to use force against an aggressor: see *infra* in the text.

78 In this sense, see especially: Conforti, *supra* note 61, at pp. 194-195, and *idem*, *supra* note 55, at pp. 385-386. See also: Ronzitti, *supra* note 40, at pp. 30-31, and 45-46. However, it may well be that a different conclusion will be possible in the near future. On the basis of the practice of the Security Council and of the acquiescence therin on the part of Member States, a customary rule integrating the provisions of the UN Charter may in fact emerge. It is moreover necessary to recall that civil wars are outside the scope of this report.

79 UN Security Council Resolution 83(1950), adopted on 27 June 1950 by seven votes to one (Yugoslavia), having determined that 'the armed attack upon the Republic of Korea by forces of North Korea' constituted 'a breach of the peace', recommended 'that the Members of the United Nations furnish such assistance to the Republic of Korea as may be necessary to repel the armed attack and to restore international peace and security in the area'. Resolution 84(1950), adopted on 7 July 1950 by seven votes to none, with three abstentions (Egypt, India, Yugoslavia), welcomed 'the prompt and vigorous support which Governments and peoples of the United Nations have given to its resolutions [...] to assist the Republic of Korea in defending itself against armed attack and thus to restore international peace and security in the area'. This latter resolution also recommended 'that all Members providing military forces and other assistance pursuant to the aforesaid Security Council resolutions make such forces and other assistance available to a unified command under the United States of America', and even authorized 'the unified command at its discretion to use the United Nations flag in the course of operations against North Korean forces concurrently with the flags of the various nations participating'. Text of both resolutions in: UN, *Security Council Official Records: Fifth Year, Resolutions and Decisions of the Security Council 1950*, New York 1965, pp. 5-6.

conflict, and Resolution No. 678 of 1990,[80] dealing with the Iraq-Kuwait conflict, were concerned. This question will be referred to later in greater detail.[81] In any case, what matters here is that the Security Council could certainly not prevent States not wishing to join in military operations to declare themselves neutral,[82] nor oblige them to end their neutral status.[83]

The view has been put forward that, although not required to participate in the use of military force, third States could not rely upon the law of neutrality in the event of hostilities.[84] In this context, mention is sometimes made of Article 4 of a resolution adopted by the *Institut de Droit International* at Wiesbaden in 1975, providing that: 'Whenever United Nations forces are engaged in hostilities, Member States of the Organization may not take advantage of the general rules of the law of neutrality in order to evade obligations laid upon them in pursuance of a decision of

---

80 UN Security Council Resolution 678(1990), adopted on 29 November 1990, by twelve votes to two (Cuba, Yemen), with one abstention (China), authorized 'Member States co-operating with the Government of Kuwait, unless Iraq on or before 15 January 1991 fully implements [previously adopted] resolutions, to use all necessary means to uphold and implement resolution 660(1990) and all subsequent resolutions and to restore international peace and security'. Text in: UN, *Security Council Official Records: Forty-Fifth Year, Resolutions and Decisions of the Security Council*, New York 1991, pp. 27-28. Resolution 660 (1990) is referred to *supra*, note 64 and corresponding text.

81 See *infra*, paragraph VIII, notes 157-161 and corresponding text.

82 On practice in the Korean conflict, see: Norton, *supra* note 1, at p. 263 ff. On the attitude of Iran, Israel and Jordan during the conflict that followed the adoption of Security Council Resolution 678 (1990), *supra* note 80, see, for example: E. Robert, 'Le statut des Etats neutres dans le Golfe', in *Entre les lignes. La guerre du Golfe et le droit international*, Bruxelles 1991, p. 91 ff.; Torrelli, *supra* note 1, at pp. 27-28.

83 For the view that a resolution 'recommending' or 'authorizing' the use of force could not, *per se*, prevent individual States from retaining neutral or 'non-belligerent' status, see also, for example: Komarnicki, *supra* note 1, at p. 495; Bowett, *supra* note 9, at pp. 176-177; Schindler, 'Aspects contemporains', *supra* note 1, at p. 247; Meyrowitz, *supra* note 1, at p. 347; Greenwood, *supra* note 9, at p. 63.

Even if, as a result of the emergence of a new customary rule, the power of the Security Council to 'recommend' or 'authorize' the use of force on the part of Member States is recognized from a general point of view (see *supra*, note 78), it is unlikely that the Security Council will be empowered to *order* States to use force.

84 See, for example: Kelsen, *supra* note 61, at p. 761; Schindler, 'Aspects contemporains', *supra* note 1, at p. 267; Dinstein, *supra* note 13, at pp. 153-154; Rousseau, *supra* note 8, at p. 390; Greenwood, *supra* note 9, at p. 63. Similarly, according to Oppenheim, *supra* note 8, at p. 649, additional deviations from neutrality obligations than those decided by the Security Council under Article 41 may be required in cases where some UN Members, as a result of compliance with a 'call' from the Security Council, have become belligerents: 'in consequence of Article 2 of the Charter, the non-belligerent Members of the United Nations are under a duty to assist the United Nations and withhold assistance from the aggressor. Thus, for instance, it is not certain whether they are still entitled to admit the warships of the aggressor to their ports on a footing of equality with those of his opponent'. See also: Castrén, *supra* note 8, at p. 435; Mc Dougal, Feliciano, *supra* note 56, at pp 430-431. It is submitted that the neutral State could only be held responsible vis-à-vis the Organization in so far as its conduct could be considered as in fact amounting to assistance to the aggressor. But where, for example, a neutral State, having admitted a warship to one of its ports, complies with its duty to prevent such warship from using its territory as a base of operations of war, such conduct may not amount to assistance.

the Security Council acting in accordance with the Charter, nor may they depart from the laws of neutrality for the benefit of a party opposing the United Nations forces'.[85] This provision, *per se* not legally binding, may reasonably be considered as a corollary of the obligations laid down by Articles 2(5) and 25 of the UN Charter.[86] Yet, although there is no doubt that no member of the United Nations could lawfully give assistance to the aggressor, it is more doubtful that a general obligation to assist the victim of aggression can be derived from the Charter. Article 4 of the 1975 resolution only requires deviations from neutrality obligations 'in pursuance of a decision of the Security Council'; moreover, it relates to situations where 'United Nations forces' are engaged in hostilities and, as stated above, the idea that an 'authorization' of the use of force by Member States is equivalent to direct UN action really widens the scope of Article 42 of the Charter beyond acceptable limits. Failing a direct enforcement action by UN forces under Article 42, Articles 2(5) and 25 of the Charter only require Member States to deviate from neutrality obligations in situations where a binding decision under Article 41 has been adopted by the Security Council, and then only to the extent required by such a decision.

In conclusion, it can safely be assumed that the UN system of collective security has not abrogated the law of neutrality. Inasmuch as States do not have a duty to join in military operations undertaken or 'authorized' by the United Nations, they are free to declare themselves neutral and not to end their neutral status. However, even States wishing to remain neutral may be bound to deviate from neutrality obligations if and to the extent required by binding decisions taken by the UN Security Council under Article 41 of the Charter. Such States could still legally be qualified as neutral, but no violations of neutrality, giving rise to a 'right' of reprisal on the part of the belligerent concerned, could be attributed to them, since obligations under the Charter prevail over traditional neutrality obligations.

---

85 'Conditions of Application of Rules, other than Humanitarian Rules, of Armed Conflict to Hostilities in which United Nations Forces may be engaged', 56 *Annuaire de l'Institut de droit international* (1975), pp. 541-544, reprinted in D. Schindler, J. Toman, *The Law of Armed Conflict*, 3rd ed., Leyden 1988, at p. 907.

86 On the legal implications of these articles, especially of Article 2(5), see also, in addition to Oppenheim, quoted *supra*, in note 84: Lalive, *supra* note 1, at pp. 77-78; Kelsen, *supra* note 61, at p. 91 ff.; Castrén, *supra* note 8, at pp. 434-435; Chaumont, *supra* note 1, at pp. 33-35 and 36; Bowett, *supra* note 9, at pp. 176-178; Verdross, *supra* note 1, at p. 413; Meyrowitz, *supra* note 1, at pp. 342-347. As Bowett rightly points out, obligations under Article 2(5) 'exist solely *vis-à-vis* the United Nations. There is no obligation to render assistance to the state acting in self-defence or to discriminate in its favour'. Moreover, as Meyrowitz makes very clear, Article 2(5) of the Charter, in so far as it implies the abolition of neutrality, is only applicable in case of a collective action which is in conformity with Chapter VII: in other words, it is not applicable unless and until the special agreements envisaged in Article 43 are concluded and the Security Council takes direct military action in conformity with Article 42.

V. 'NON-BELLIGERENCY' AS A LEGAL INSTITUTION?

It follows logically from what has been said in the preceding paragraphs that modern international law does indeed seem to confirm the view that, as long as the UN Security Council has not taken enforcement measures in case of an armed conflict, third States not wishing to become party to the conflict have the choice either to remain strictly neutral or to take any intermediate positions between neutrality and belligerency. The terms 'non-belligerency' and/or 'qualified neutrality' can, therefore, usefully be employed in order to designate the situation of those States which, while not wishing to enter the conflict on the side of one belligerent, do not, at the same time, choose to be bound by traditional neutrality obligations.

Whereas neutrality can be described as a legal institution, since it derives from special rules of treaty and/or customary law, 'non-belligerency' is often qualified by legal writers as a purely factual or political notion. This qualification, however, leads to very different consequences, depending on one's view of the present status of the law of neutrality.

Those writers who still believe that the law of neutrality automatically becomes effective at the outbreak of 'war' between third States inevitably regard 'non-belligerency' as an attitude normally leading to 'a violation of the laws of neutrality' and, as an internationally wrongful attitude, giving the belligerent concerned 'the right to take reprisals'.[87] For the reasons given above, however, this view, reflecting the situation as it existed under traditional international law, is nowadays unacceptable. Some writers go even further than the traditional view and suggest that, at least *de lege ferenda*, the application of the law of neutrality should now depend, like that of the *jus in bello*, upon the mere fact of the outbreak of an armed conflict, irrespective of whether or not a formal 'state of war' is recognized; from this point of view also, 'unneutral' support for a belligerent should in any case be considered 'a violation of the law of neutrality', giving rise to 'a right of reprisal'.[88] This view is also difficult to accept since, for the reasons given above,

---

87 See, especially: Bindschedler, *supra* note 1, at p. 13. See also, among others: Tucker, *supra* note 8, at pp. 197-199; Castrén, *supra* note 8, at pp. 449-452; Sereni, *supra* note 8, at pp. 2088-2089; Quadri, *supra* note 8, at p. 327; Rousseau, *supra* note 8, at p. 371; W.H. von Heinegg, 'Visit, Search, Diversion and Capture. Conditions of Applicability', paper presented at the Bergen Round Table of Experts on International Humanitarian Law Applicable to Armed Conflicts at Sea (20-24 September 1991) organized by the San Remo International Institute of Humanitarian Law, at pp. 48-49.

88 See, especially: Bothe, *supra* note 1, at pp. 391 and 396, and *idem*, 'Neutrality at Sea', in Dekker, Post (eds.), *supra* note 10, p. 205 ff., at p. 207. But see also, among others: Brownlie, *supra* note 13, at pp. 395-396 and 400-401; Greenwood, *supra* note 9, at pp. 54-56, and *idem*, 'Comments', in Dekker, Post (eds.), *supra* note 10, p. 212 ff., at p. 212-213. See also the 1987 US Navy *Commander's Handbook on the Law of Naval Operations (NWP 9)*, Chapter 7.1. As Greenwood rightly points out *supra* note 9, at p. 55, this view raises the difficult question of the definition of 'armed conflict': a definition which may be acceptable for the purposes of ensuring the application of the humanitarian rules of the *jus in bello* may

it is at least debatable whether the traditional law of neutrality should now be given the same status as the *jus in bello*.

Other writers describe 'non-belligerency' as a political concept, as opposed to a legal one, simply because, in their view, it is a factual situation which, unlike neutrality, is not governed by specific rules of international law.[89] This view, while undoubtedly correct in principle, needs qualifications. The necessary starting point should be that relations between 'non-belligerent' and belligerent States continue, in principle, to be governed entirely by the laws of peace: the special rules of neutrality not being applicable, this seems to be the logical consequence. In other words, the situation is not very different from that existing for all States not involved in a 'war' before the laws of neutrality historically emerged. From a factual point of view, there is some truth in the view that 'non-belligerency is a name used as a modern excuse for violating the laws of neutrality and as a hope that warlike acts can be committed while escaping the consequences of belligerency'.[90] While it is true that, under traditional international law, States violating their neutrality obligations did not automatically become belligerent, the belligerent concerned could either declare war or take reprisals against them.[91] In modern international law, 'war' cannot be declared against a State unless that State is responsible for an armed attack; neither can the belligerent concerned take reprisals against 'non-belligerent' States for the mere fact that they are not abiding by traditional neutrality obligations, since these are not, in principle, binding upon them.[92]

Indeed, 'non-belligerent' States, though not bound by traditional neutrality obligations, can still enjoy the so-called 'rights of neutrals towards belligerents', which allegedly also form part of the law of neutrality. As stated above, most of these 'rights', far from being special rights enjoyed by neutral States in time of 'war', are in fact rights, or freedoms, enjoyed by all States under the general laws

---

not be appropriate for the application of the law of neutrality. Moreover, the automatic application of the law of neutrality in all situations of armed conflict, would not prevent violations of neutrality obligations being justified by collective self-defence against the aggressor.

89 See, for example, Schindler, 'Aspects contemporains', *supra* note 1, at pp. 276-277. See also: Miele, *supra* note 1, at p. 521 ff.; this latter author, however, maintains that a belligerent could react against 'unneutral' conduct on the part of 'non-belligerent' States and that violations of third States' rights under the laws of peace could be excused by the principle of 'military necessity'. This view, however, is difficult to accept: see *infra*, paragraph IX.

90 E. Borchard, 'War, Neutrality and Non-Belligerency', 35 *American Journal of International Law* (1941), p. 618 ff., at p. 624.

91 See, for example: Oppenheim, *supra* note 8, at pp. 752-753; Balladore Pallieri, *supra* note 8, at p. 382; Tucker, *supra* note 8, at pp. 258-259.

92 On reprisals against neutral and 'non-belligerent' States, see *infra*, paragraph IX.

of peace.[93] Thus the alleged right of neutral States to the inviolability of their territory is nothing but an aspect of the right of territorial sovereignty enjoyed by all States under the general laws of peace, and which is nowadays further protected by the prohibition on the use of force enshrined in the United Nations Charter.[94] Indeed, what characterizes the special law of neutrality is not the fact that a neutral State has a right to the inviolability of its territory, but rather that it has several duties of abstention, prevention and non-discrimination limiting its right of territorial sovereignty,[95] duties which the law of peace does not impose upon 'non-belligerent' States.[96] As for the alleged right of neutral States to continue trading with belligerents, nobody would certainly deny that all States enjoy a freedom to trade under the general laws of peace; again, what characterizes the law of neutrality is the fact that the so-called 'right' to trade is subject to certain limitations[97] and, in particular, to a duty to tolerate the exercise, on the part of belligerents, of certain measures, to which reference shall be made shortly.[98] Finally, according to some writers, neutral States would enjoy a right not to be involved in war, or 'a right to demand such behaviour from each belligerent as is in accordance with their attitude of impartiality'.[99] But this was clearly not a right at all at the time when the law allowed belligerents to declare war on neutral States whenever they saw fit,[100]

93   See *supra*, paragraph I, note 18 and corresponding text. Schindler maintains that the so-called 'rights of neutrals' are in fact 'not rights in the proper sense but consist, on the one hand, in the duty of belligerents to respect neutral territory and, on the other hand, in the negation of duties of neutrals which might be presumed if they were not expressly denied'; given examples of this latter category of 'rights' are the 'rights' referred to in Articles 7, 10, 11 and 26 of the 1907 Hague Convention (XII), *supra* note 5. See: Schindler, *supra* note 10, at pp. 213-214 and 215-217, and *idem*, 'Transformations ...', *supra* note 1, at pp. 378-379. As far as the duty to respect neutral territory is concerned, the author's contention is not easy to understand, since, if there is such a duty, then there is a corresponding right; the point should rather be that this right is not a special right conferred by the law of neutrality, but flows from the general laws of peace. As for the 'negation of duties of neutrals which might be presumed if they were not expressly denied', the fact that such special duties do not exist can only mean that third States continue to enjoy the rights and freedoms which they enjoy under the general laws of peace. In any case, the author rightly concludes that all the so-called 'rights of neutrals' can be considered 'as belonging to customary law and as applying to neutrals and non-belligerents alike'.

94   As Schindler rightly points out, the Charter prohibition on the use of force goes beyond the traditional law of neutrality 'in so far as a belligerent may no longer, as was the case under pre-Charter law, use force in neutral waters when the other belligerent or the neutral State violate neutrality to its detriment. Only if a belligerent is the victim of an armed attack in neutral waters may it lawfully use force in self-defence' *supra* note 10, at p. 216). On the use of force by one belligerent to redress violations of neutrality, see also *infra*, paragraph IX, especially notes 183-189 and corresponding text.

95   For this view, see especially: Balladore Pallieri, *supra* note 8, at pp. 381-382.

96   See *infra*, paragraph VI.

97   For this view, see especially: Balladore Pallieri, *supra* note 8, at p. 382.

98   See *infra*, paragraphs VII and VIII.

99   See, for example: Oppenheim, *supra* note 8, at pp. 673-674.

100 For this view, see especially: Balladore Pallieri, *supra* note 8, at p. 382.

whereas in modern international law, a right not to be involved in armed hostilities is enjoyed by all States not guilty of an armed attack.

In principle, therefore, 'non-belligerent' States enjoy all the traditional 'rights of neutral States',[101] without being bound by traditional neutrality obligations. The fact, however, remains that the outbreak of an armed conflict substantially changes the factual conditions in which international norms have to operate, also in respect of relations between belligerent and 'non-belligerent' States. One may legitimately ask, therefore, whether this fact, which was historically at the basis of the emergence of the laws of neutrality, has influenced post-Charter practice to the extent that at least some of the traditional duties of neutral States can now be considered to bind neutral and 'non-belligerent' States alike. This question appears to be particularly relevant in situations where the United Nations system of collective security proves to be ineffectual and where the distinction between the aggressor and the victim of aggression is difficult or virtually impossible to make: *in such situations*, one could agree that the concept of neutrality may still provide, as Grotius himself seemed to recognize, for a balance of interest between the belligerents on the one hand, and those not participating in the war on the other.[102] However, it is suggested that the question of whether some of the traditional duties of neutral States can now be regarded as binding on all States not party to a conflict, cannot be properly answered on the basis of abstract, and debatable, reasons of policy, but rather depends on the evolution of customary law, *i.e.* on the practice of States and on their *opinio juris*. The question may also be raised of whether modern practice has imposed upon all States not party to an armed conflict certain duties that the traditional law of neutrality did not contemplate. Should the answer to either of these questions be a positive one, it would follow that 'non-belligerency' could no longer be dismissed as a purely political category: 'non-belligerency' would rather have to be considered, like neutrality, as a legal institution, a condition in which relations between belligerents and third States are governed by special rules applicable in times of armed conflict and derogating from the general laws of peace.

Modern practice does seem to lend some support to the view that, in some situations, some of the traditional duties of neutral States are now considered to be binding on all States not party to an armed conflict, irrespective of whether or not they have declared themselves neutral and irrespective of whether or not the conflict is recognized as amounting to a formal 'war'. Indeed, it is also possible to see a clear tendency to impose upon States not party to a conflict certain duties which did not form part of the traditional law of neutrality. On the other hand, other traditional

---

101 In this sense, see, especially: Schindler, *supra* note 93.
102 For Grotius's view, see *supra*, paragraph III, notes 35-36 and corresponding text.

duties of neutral States are clearly regarded as binding only on States wishing to remain stricly neutral.

VI. 'NON-BELLIGERENT' STATES AND TRADITIONAL DUTIES OF ABSTENTION, PREVENTION AND NON-DISCRIMINATION

Traditional neutrality obligations can be classified in two main categories. The first category consists of obligations stemming from a general principle of impartiality. The principle of impartiality, however, is not a *normative* principle, *i.e.* a principle from which rights and duties direcly derive for neutral States: it is rather a principle which was historically at the basis of the emergence of the laws of neutrality and which can be derived by way of abstraction from existing rules of treaty and/or customary law.[103] There is, therefore, no general duty of impartiality for neutral States.[104] There are rather specific duties of abstention, such as the duty to abstain from directly supplying belligerents with arms, munitions, vessels, and military

103 On the concept of general principles of international law and on the distinction between principles which are mainly abstractions from a mass of positive rules and so-called 'normative' principles, see especially: R. Ago, *Lezioni di diritto internazionale*, Milan 1943, at p. 65; G. Sperduti, *L'individuo nel diritto internazionale*, Milan 1950, at p. 5 ff.; A. Cassese, *International Law in a Divided World*, Oxford 1986, at pp. 126-127. Examples of the first category are the principles of effectiveness and of good faith: the function of such principles, which are at the basis of the development of several rules of customary law but are not direct sources of rights and obligations, is mainly to help interpreting existing rules of international law. See also *infra*, note 184, on the principle of military necessity. Examples of the second category are the principles of the freedom of the high seas, of self-determination of peoples and the prohibition on the use of force in international relations: such principles are conceptually difficult to distinguish from ordinary norms of customary law, except where they have been recognized as principles of *jus cogens*. It goes without saying that we are not dealing here with the so-called 'general principles of law recognized by civilized nations' within the meaning of Article 38(1) of the Statute of the International Court of Justice.
104 For this view, see especially: G. Ottolenghi, *Il rapporto di neutralità*, Turin 1907, at p. 222 ff.; Cavaglieri, *supra* note 10, at p. 66 ff.; Balladore Pallieri, *supra* note 8, at pp. 387-388; Sereni, *supra* note 8, at pp. 2112-2113 and 2116 ff.; Miele, *supra* note 1, at p. 271 ff. A similar view seems to have also been taken by Stone, *supra* note 8, at p. 383. As Professor Miele points out, this view is in keeping with both the history of the law of neutrality and the recent practice of States, which allows for a distinction between the law of neutrality and a 'policy of neutrality': although there have been cases in which third States have adopted a policy of strict impartiality going beyond what was required by existing rules of international law, such States have usually made it clear that their attitude was not dictated by a sense of legal obligation. The contrary view, however, is widely held in the literature of international law: see, for example, De Nova, *supra* note 38, at p. 6 ff.; Oppenheim, *supra* note 8, at pp. 675-676; Tucker, *supra* note 8, at p. 202 ff.; Kelsen, *supra* note 10, at p. 156; Quadri, *supra* note 8, at p. 326. These conflicting views are mainly based on different interpretations of the residual duty of non-discrimination of neutral States, on which see *infra*, note 107.

provisions, and from granting them loans and subsidies;[105] there are also specific duties of prevention, such as the duty to prevent belligerents from carrying out certain activities within their territories and to prevent private persons subject to their authority from carrying out certain other activities.[106] However, as stated above, the law of neutrality does require that, should a neutral State choose to adopt more stringent measures, such measures apply to all belligerents without discrimination: for example, a neutral State is not bound to prevent the export or transit, for the use of either belligerent, of arms, munitions, or, in general, of anything which could be of use to any army or fleet; however, should it choose to establish an arms embargo, it would have to prevent trade in arms with both belligerents.[107]

Duties of abstention and prevention, as well as the residual duty of non-discrimination, undoubtedly constitute the 'essence' of neutrality. In principle, such duties only apply to States choosing to be strictly neutral.[108] To assert that

---

105 See, for example: Oppenheim, *supra* note 8, at p. 738 ff.; Balladore Pallieri, *supra* note 8, at pp. 407-408; Castrén, *supra* note 8, at p. 474 ff.; Guggenheim, *supra* note 8, at p. 536 ff.; Stone, *supra* note 8, at p. 389-390; Tucker, *supra* note 8, at p. 206 ff.; Sereni, *supra* note 8, at p. 2122 ff.; Miele, *supra* note 1, at p. 378 ff.; Rousseau, *supra* note 8, at pp. 394-399 and 434-436. See also Article 6 of the 1907 Hague Convention XIII, *supra* note 5.

106 See, for example: Oppenheim, *supra* note 8, at pp. 687 ff. and 713 ff.; Balladore Pallieri, *supra* note 8, at pp. 391 ff. and 408 ff.; Castrén, *supra* note 8, at p. 481 ff.; Guggenheim, *supra* note 8, at p. 520 ff.; Stone, *supra* note 8, at pp. 385-389, 390 ff.; Tucker, *supra* note 8, at p. 218 ff.; Sereni, *supra* note 8, at p. 2125 ff.; Miele, *supra* note 1, at pp. 299 ff. and 396 ff. See also: Articles 4 and 5 of the 1907 Hague Convention V and Articles 8 and 25 of the 1907 Hague Convention XIII, *supra* note 5.

107 The precise content of this residual duty of non-discrimination is often at the basis of the doctrinal debate on the existence of a general duty of impartiality for neutral States. The existing conventions only provide for such a residual duty in specific cases: see Article 9 of the 1907 Hague Convention V (dealing with restrictions on the use of telegraph, telephone cables and wireless telegraphy apparatus and/or on the trade in arms, munitions of war or, in general, in 'anything which can be of use to any army or fleet') and Article 9 of the 1907 Hague Convention XIII (dealing with restrictions on the admission of belligerent warships or of their prizes in neutral waters); both conventions are quoted *supra*, note 5. Some of the writers quoted *supra*, in note 104, seem to believe that there is no general duty of non-discrimination going beyond what is provided for in these conventions, since their provisions cannot be extensively applied. In particular, a duty of non-discrimination is sometimes said to exist only in so far as military activities, as opposed to economic activities, are concerned. See also, for example: Guggenheim, *supra* note 8, at p. 517 ff. This view was also taken by Switzerland at the time when it adhered to the League of Nations on the understanding that the adoption of economic sanctions would not be incompatible with neutrality obligations: see, for example, Schindler, 'Aspects contemporains', *supra* note 1, at pp. 256-257. However, the better view is probably that there *is* a residual customary duty of non-discrimination for neutral States: such States are obliged to apply equally to all belligerents any restrictions freely imposed by themselves on their relations with belligerents, including restrictions on private economic activities. But the duty of non-discrimination means the duty to treat belligerents formally, not materially, on the basis of equality. Moreover, such duty is not equivalent to a general duty of impartiality, since it does not cover activities which may be detrimental to one belligerent in the conduct of war, such as, typically, the expression of sympathy with one belligerent and disapproval of the other on the part of the neutral State or of its nationals.

108 See especially: Schindler, *supra* note 10, at pp. 214, 217-219, 220-221, and *idem*, 'Transformations', *supra* note 1, at pp. 379-380.

they still automatically apply to all States not party to hostilities at the outbreak of 'war' between third States seems to be rather unrealistic, given the present reluctance of States to recognize the existence of a formal 'state of war'. To assert, on the other hand, that such duties nowadays become effective as a result of the mere outbreak of an armed conflict seems to defy the evidence. State practice clearly shows that States do not regard themselves bound by such duties unless they choose to declare themselves neutral.[109] With reference to the trade in arms and war material, it is highly significant, for example, that a recent Italian statute, dealing with import, export and transit controls on armaments, has, in principle, prohibited the export and transit of war materials 'towards Countries in a state of armed conflict, *in violation of the principles of Article 51 of the United Nations Charter*'.[110] This clearly shows that Italy regards itself free, if not morally bound, to discriminate against the State responsible for an armed attack.

But what if the distinction between aggressor and victim is *prima facie* difficult, or impossible, to draw? It may be significant, in this respect, that in the Iran-Iraq conflict, a conflict in which it had not identified the aggressor, the Security Council repeatedly called upon 'all' States not party to the conflict to refrain from acts which might lead to the continuation and to a further escalation and widening of the conflict.[111] On the other hand, State practice in the same conflict would rather seem to confirm that 'non-belligerent' States do not consider themselves bound by neutrality obligations even in such situations: indeed, even some States which had officially adopted a policy of 'neutrality' did not always stricly conform to neutrality obligations.[112] While the attitute of these latter States might be considered, with some justice, as a violation of international law, the same could not easily be said as far as the attitude of other 'non-belligerent' States was concerned.

As stated above, the structure of the international legal order is such that, in the absence of a determination by the UN Security Council, each 'non-belligerent' State is allowed to decide by itself which belligerent is the aggressor and which is the victim of aggression, and to act accordingly.[113] The resulting situation, however, may lead to very serious consequences. Indeed, even if an attitude of 'non-

---

109 See the authors quoted *supra*, in note 28.
110 Law No. 185 of 9 July 1990 (author's translation; emphasis added). Text in: *Gazzetta Ufficiale della Repubblica Italiana*, No. 167, 14 July 1990, and reprinted in 73 *Rivista di diritto internazionale* (1990), p. 1048 ff. For a commentary on this law, see: A. Bianchi, 'Esportazione e transito di armamenti: profili di diritto internazionale', 75 *Rivista di diritto internazionale* (1992), p. 65 ff.
111 See: UN Security Council Resolutions 514(1982), 522(1982), 540(1983), 582(1986), 598(1987).
112 See, for example: Gioia, Ronzitti, *supra* note 31, at p. 226 ff. On the alleged 'neutrality' of the United States, see also the critical analysis by Boyle, *supra* note 8.

For the view that State practice does not seem to confirm the existence of a duty of impartiality in situations where the distinction between aggressor and victim is unclear, see, for example: Schindler, 'Aspects contemporains', *supra* note 1, at pp. 271-272, and *idem, supra* note 10, at p. 212.
113 See *supra*, note 56 and corresponding text.

belligerency' is not considered as constituting, *per se*, a violation of international law, the aggrieved belligerent might perceive the behaviour of a 'non-belligerent' State as amounting, in certain circumstances, to complicity with the aggressor: this may be the case, in particular, where a 'non-belligerent' State supplies the enemy with arms or war materials, or where it grants loans or subsidies to the enemy. Where a 'non-belligerent' State goes as far as allowing its territory to be used by the enemy to carry out military operations, the aggrieved belligerent might even perceive such behaviour as constituting in itself an act of aggression. The question of possible reactions to 'unneutral' behaviour on the part of 'non-belligerent' States will be addressed later in this report.[114] At this stage, it is important to stress that, at least *de lege ferenda*, traditional neutrality obligations may still be regarded as fulfilling an important task in all situations where the UN system of collective security is ineffectual and where the distinction between aggressor and victim is *prima facie* unclear, *i.e.* where both belligerents claim a 'right' of self-defence.

The fact that 'non-belligerent' States are not bound by neutrality obligations, in so far as these implicate an attitude of impartiality, does not preclude the possibility that modern international law imposes upon such States – and, indeed, upon all States not party to an armed conflict – some other duties of abstention and/or prevention flowing from principles other than that of impartiality. For example, as far as the trade in arms and war materals is concerned, State practice shows a marked tendency to impose upon all States a duty to abstain – as well as a duty to prevent private persons – from supplying belligerents with arms the employment of which is prohibited under the *jus in bello*, and from helping them to produce such arms. With particular reference to chemical weapons, the employment of which is prohibited under a 1925 Geneva Protocol as well as under existing customary law,[115] practice in the Iran-Iraq conflict showed a tendency on the part of third States to establish or apply specific export controls on certain chemicals used in producing chemical weapons to both Iran and Iraq.[116] On 9 May 1988, in its Resolution No. 612, the UN Security Council called upon all States 'to continue to apply or to establish strict control on the export to the parties to the conflict of chemical products serving for the production of chemical weapons'.[117] Another resolution adopted by the Security

---

114 See *infra*, paragraph IX.
115 See: Protocol for the Prohibition of the Use in War of Asphyxiating, Poisonous or Other Gases, and of Bacteriological Methods of Warfare, signed on 17 June 1925 (94 *League of Nations Treaty Series*, p. 65 ff.). On the customary nature of the prohibition, see, among others: M. Bothe, *Das völkerrechtliche Verbot des Einsatzes chemischer und bakteriologischer Waffen*, Köln/Bonn 1973, and *idem*, 'Chemical Warfare', in 3 *Encyclopedia of Public International Law*, Amsterdam/New York/Oxford 1982, p. 83 ff.
116 See, for example: Gioia, Ronzitti, *supra* note 31, at p. 231.
117 UN Security Council Resolution 612(1988), adopted unanimously on 9 May 1988. Text in: UN, *Security Council Official Records: Forty-Third Year, Resolutions and Decisions of the Security Council*, New York 1989, at p. 10.

Council on 26 August 1988 again called upon all States, this time from a general point of view, 'to continue to apply, to establish or to strengthen strict control of the export of chemical products serving for the production of chemical weapons, *in particular to parties to a conflict*, when it is established or when there is substantial reason to believe that they have used chemical weapons in violation of international obligations'.[118] The recently adopted convention on chemical weapons, which, once entered into force, will apply in time of armed conflict also, will implicitly impose upon States not party to a conflict a duty to ensure that chemical weapons, as well as chemicals and equipment likely to be used for the purposes of chemical warfare, are not transferred to belligerent States.[119]

If this tendency gives rise to the birth of a customary rule binding upon all States, the result will be that international law will impose upon all States not engaged in an armed conflict, irrespective of whether the conflict amounts to 'war' and irrespective of the distinction between aggressor and victim, obligations more far-reaching than traditional neutrality obligations: on the one hand, as far as chemical products are concerned, they would not necessarily fall into the category of 'war materials', given their possible use for peaceful purposes; on the other hand, as stated above, neutral States were not obliged, under the traditional rules, to prevent their nationals from trading in arms or war materials. In this latter respect, some writers maintain that, in view of the fact that the international trade in arms is now subject to State controls in most countries, the traditional distinction between State trade and private trade should be regarded as obsolete: according to this view, States wishing to preserve neutrality would now have to prevent the export of arms and war materials to belligerents on the part of their nationals.[120] Be that as it may, such an obligation could certainly not be said, in present circumstances, to be binding upon 'non-belligerent' States.

---

118 UN Security Council Resolution 620(1988), adopted unanimously on 26 August 1988. Text: *ibidem*, at p. 12 (emphasis added).

119 Convention on the Prohibition of the Development, Production, Stockpiling and Use of Chemical Weapons and on Their Destruction, opened for signature in Paris on 13 January 1993. The text of the convention is contained in the Report of the Conference on Disarmament dated 3 September 1992. On the application of the convention in time of armed conflict, see: A. Gioia, 'The CWC and Its Application in Time of Armed Conflict', in M. Bothe, N. Ronzitti, A. Rosas, *Chemical Weapons Disarmament: Strategies and Legal Problems*, to be published in Stockholm in 1994.

120 This view is often put forward in a *de lege ferenda* perspective. See, among others: Stone, *supra* note 8, at pp. 383-384 and 408 ff.; Mc Dougal, Feliciano, *supra* note 56, at p. 437 ff.; W. Friedman, *The Changing Structure of International Law*, London 1964, at pp. 346-349; Sereni, *supra* note 8, at p. 2105; Miele, *supra* note 1, at pp. 396-408; Seidl-Hohenveldern, *supra* note 8, at p. 170. Other writers, however, believe that the distinction should be retained: see, for example, Kussbach, 'Neutral Trading', *supra* note 27, at p. 9. But, as Kelsen pointed out, the practice of 'neutral' States would rather seem to point to the obsolescence of the traditional rules: see *supra* note 10, at pp. 156-158.

VII. 'NON-BELLIGERENT' STATES AND TRADITIONAL BELLIGERENT RIGHTS: THE LAW OF CONTRABAND

The second category of neutral duties consists of duties to tolerate certain acts on the part of belligerents which interfere with 'peaceful' activities, *i.e.* activities allowed under the general laws of peace, undertaken by their nationals or by private ships flying their flag (so-called 'duties of acquiescence'). Leaving aside the 'right of angary' of belligerents,[121] such duties mainly concern maritime warfare: they consist of the duty to tolerate the exercise by either belligerent 'of the right to punish neutral merchantmen for breach of blockade or attempted breach of blockade, carriage of contraband, or rendering unneutral service to the enemy, and, accordingly, to visit, search, and eventually capture them'.[122] Indeed, it can probably be asserted that, in some circumstances, even apart from cases in which neutral merchant vessels can properly be said to have acquired enemy character, belligerents may also attack such vessels: this is the case when a ship persistently refuses to stop on being duly summoned or otherwise actively resists visit and search.[123]

The view is sometimes put forward that all States not party to an armed conflict have nowadays to tolerate such acts, be they neutral or 'non-belligerent' and

---

121 The right of angary can be defined as the right of belligerents 'to destroy, or use, in case of necessity, for the purpose of offence and defence, neutral property on their territory, or on enemy territory, or on the open sea' (Oppenheim, *supra* note 8, at p. 761). There is, however, a duty to pay compensation for any damage done to neutral property. On the right of angary, see also, among others: Balladore Pallieri, *supra* note 8, at p. 384; Castrén, *supra* note 8, at p. 509 ff.; Guggenheim, *supra* note 8, at p. 531 ff.; Miele, *supra* note 1, at p. 95 ff.; Verzijl, *supra* note 11, at pp. 242-245 and 293-294; R. Lagoni, 'Angary, Right of', 3 *Encyclopedia of Public International Law*, Amsterdam/New York/Oxford 1982, p. 18 ff.; Rousseau, *supra* note 8, at p. 465 ff.

The better view is that the right of angary derives from a specific rule of customary law rather than from the concept of military necessity as a general principle of the law of war and neutrality or from the concept of the state of necessity as a circumstance precluding wrongfulness: see *infra*, note 184. It is at best doubtful, however, that the rule is still applicable and, even more so, that it applies irrespective of the recognition of a 'state of war' and, in any case, in relations between belligerents and 'non-belligerent' States.

122 Oppenheim, *supra* note 8, at p. 673. In particular, on the traditional law of contraband, see, among others: Oppenheim, *supra* note 8, at p. 798 ff.; Balladore Pallieri, *supra* note 8, at p. 414 ff.; Castrén, *supra* note 8, at p. 545 ff.; Tucker, *supra* note 8, at p. 263 ff.; Quadri, *supra* note 8, at p. 328 ff.; Miele, *supra* note 1, at p. 144 ff.; Verzijl, *supra* note 11, at p. 331 ff.; W. Meng, 'Contraband', 3 *Encyclopedia of Public International Law*, Amsterdam/New York/Oxford 1982, p. 122 ff.; Rousseau, *supra* note 8, at p. 465 ff.. On the traditional law of blockade, see the authors quoted *infra*, paragraph VIII, in note 145.

123 See the 1936 London Procès-Verbal Relating to the Rules of Submarine Warfare Set Forth in Part IV of the Treaty of London of 22 April 1930 (173 *League of Nations Treaty Series*, p. 353 ff.). See also, among others: Tucker, *supra* note 8, at pp. 336-337; E.I. Nwogugu, 'Commentary', in Ronzitti (ed.), *supra* note 4, p. 353 ff., at pp. 355-356; W.J. Fenrick, 'The Merchant Vessel as a Legitimate Target in the Law of Naval Warfare', in Delissen, Tanja (eds.), *supra* note 1, p. 425 ff., at p. 427; W.H. von Heinegg, 'Visit, Search, Diversion and Capture in Naval Warfare. Part 1: The Traditional Law', 29 *Canadian Yearbook of International Law* (1991), p. 283 ff., at pp. 318-319.

irrespective of whether or not a formal 'state of war' is recognized. This view is usually based on considerations of expediency: it is often said that 'such measures would indeed not have any justification if they were limited to States which are genuinely neutral'.[124] However, while such considerations may have considerable weight *de lege ferenda*, it is suggested that, *de lege lata*, a correct evaluation of this view entirely depends on the evolution of customary law after the entry into force of the UN Charter: if one accepts that, in principle, relations between belligerent and 'non-belligerent' States are to be governed by the general laws of peace, it is only on the basis of the practice of such States, and on their *opinio juris*, that special duties, eventually corresponding to the traditional duties of neutral States, can be said to have emerged for all States not party to an armed conflict. In this context, it would not be sufficient to point out that States which have exercised traditional belligerent rights since 1945 'have never made a distinction between genuine neutrals and other States not parties to the conflict':[125] the attitude of 'non-belligerent' States should also be taken into account.

In the opinion of the author of this report, it is not possible to assert that belligerent rights can nowadays be exercised in all situations of armed conflict, irrespective of the distinction between aggressor and victim. In a situation where the Security Council has identified one State as the aggressor, or as the State responsible for a 'breach of the peace' under Article 39 of the Charter, and, arguably, in other situations where the distinction is clear-cut, third States cannot be expected to tolerate the exercise of belligerent rights on the part of the aggressor.[126] The situation is different as far as the State acting in self-defence is concerned. It may probably still be asserted that neutral States have to tolerate the exercise of traditional belligerent rights on the part of the victim of aggression. On the other hand, whether the other 'non-belligerent' States have a similar duty is not so clear.

According to some writers, the concept of self-defence allows for the view that belligerent rights may be exercised against States not party to an armed conflict.[127] This view is presented as being both logical and desirable and seems to have been taken by some States, such as the United Kingdom, both when being a party to a

---

124 Schindler, 'Transformations', *supra* note 1, at p. 379. For the view that, at least *de lege ferenda*, the right of visit and search should be recognized in all situations of international armed conflict, see also, for example: Bothe, *supra* note 88, at pp. 206, 209, 210; Greenwood, *supra* note 88, at p. 213.
125 Schindler, *supra* note 124.
126 In this sense, see also, for example: Greenwood, *supra* note 9, at pp. 57-58.
127 See especially: O'Connell, *supra* note 9, at pp. 1109-1112 and 1141 ff.; C. Greenwood, 'Self-Defence and the Conduct of International Armed Conflict', in Y. Dinstein (ed.), *International Law at a Time of Perplexity*, Dordrecht/Boston/London 1989, p. 273 ff., at p. 283 ff., *idem*, *supra* note 9, at pp. 45-53, and *idem*, *supra* note 88, at pp. 215-216. See also: Ronzitti, *infra*, note 130. A rather more cautious attitude is taken by: Von Heinegg, *supra* note 87, at p. 43.

conflict[128] and when taking a position of 'non-belligerency'.[129] In this respect, it seems necessary to clear the way of possible misunderstandings. Moving from the premiss that the law of neutrality is, in principle, still applicable, it is possible to maintain that the modern law of self-defence has had an effect on the conditions for the exercise of traditional belligerent rights: from this point of view, one could argue that, even if a formal 'state of war' is recognized, traditional belligerent rights can nowadays only be exercised in situations where the requirements of necessity and proportionality, which are usually said to be essential conditions for the admissibility of a plea of self-defence, are met.[130] But our premiss is rather that the traditional law of neutrality is *not* applicable in relations between belligerent and 'non-belligerent' States. From this point of view, there can be no doubt that self-defence cannot, *by itself*, excuse violations of third States' rights.[131] Moreover, the argument, which is sometimes put forward, that the law of self-defence would have a restraining effect on belligerents seems to be contradicted by practice: belligerent States have invoked self-defence in order to justify measures that the traditional law of neutrality would *not* justify, such as 'total exclusion zones' and the like, to which reference shall be made shortly.[132] To this author it seems clear that construing self-defence as allowing for violations of third States' rights is tantamount to opening Pandora's box and may have very dangerous consequences, especially in situations where both belligerents claim a 'right' of self-defence.

On the other hand, the concept of self-defence may not always be necessary in order to justify the exercise of traditional belligerent rights. Whereas self-defence is, arguably, the only circumstance precluding the wrongfulness of acts involving a 'use

128 On British practice in the 1982 Faklands conflict, see, for example: G. Venturini, '*Ius in bello* nel conflitto anglo-argentino', in Ronzitti (ed.), *supra* note 57, at p. 210 ff. The law of self-defence was also invoked by Pakistan during the 1965 conflict with India: see P. Sharma, *The Indo-Pakistan Maritime Conflict 1965. A Legal Appraisal* (1970), at p. 9.

129 In the Iran-Iraq conflict, the British position appeared to be that belligerent measures against neutral shipping would only be lawful if they satisfied the requirements of self-defence: see, for example, Gioia, Ronzitti, *supra* note 31, at pp. 232 and 234; C.J. Greenwood, 'Remarks', 82 *Proceedings of the American Society of International Law* (1988), p. 158 ff.; A.V. Lowe, 'Commentary', in De Guttry, Ronzitti (eds.), *supra* note 31, p. 241 ff.

130 This seems to be the position taken by N. Ronzitti, *supra* note 9, at pp. 6-7.

131 On this question, see, for example: D. Schindler in 14 *Syracuse Journal of International Law and Commerce* (1988), at p. 594; Bothe, *supra* note 1, at pp. 394-395.

As Ago rightly points out, the fundamental difference between self-defence and state of necessity lies precisely in the fact that the State acting in self-defence responds by force to forcible wrongful action carried out by another, whereas the State acting in a state of necessity adopts 'a form of conduct inconsistent with an international obligation' *vis-à-vis* another State 'which has committed no international wrong against the State taking the action' *supra* note 48, at pp. 53-54). Whether violations of third States' rights can be excused by a state of necessity, however, is controversial: see *infra*, paragraph IX notes 182-189 and corresponding text.

132 See *infra*, paragraph IX.

of force' under Article 2(4) of the UN Charter,[133] interference with third States' commercial shipping may not constitute a 'use of force' under that Article. If a right of visit and search is claimed in relation to 'non-belligerent' commercial shipping, this would certainly entail a derogation from the right of free navigation on the high seas, *i.e.* from third States' right to exercise exclusive authority over vessels flying their flag; but if a merchant ship 'is ordered or even forced to stop in order to facilitate a visit, this does not constitute a use of force against the flag State which would be prohibited under the Charter'.[134] This leaves the door open for the possibility that post-1945 practice has made it lawful for belligerents to exercise, in some situations, at least some of the traditional rights, without at the same time allowing for derogations from the current regulation of the use of force under the UN Charter.

Practice in the Iran-Iraq conflict showed a tendency to allow belligerents to exercise a right to visit and search third States' merchant vessels in order to ascertain whether they were carrying contraband of war, irrespective of whether the State concerned had adopted an attitude of strict neutrality or one of 'non-belligerency': Iran's decision to exercise that right was widely acquiesced in by third States.[135] However, while in a situation where the distinction between aggressor and victim is somewhat blurred it can easily be admitted that both belligerents enjoy, in principle, a right of visit and search,[136] the same cannot be said where the UN Security Council has identified one State as the aggressor or as the State responsible for a 'breach of the peace': as stated above, in this latter case, and, possibly, in other cases where the distinction is clear-cut, only the victim of aggression is allowed to exercise that right.

It is more doubtful whether both belligerents or, as the case may be, the victim of aggression can also still enforce their right of visit and search by attacking and,

---

133 See, for example: Ago, *supra* note 47, at p. 53.

134 Bothe, *supra* note 1, at p. 393. Article 2(4) of the UN Charter prohibits the use of force by States 'in their international relations', and then only 'against the territorial integrity or political independence of any State, or in any other manner inconsistent with the purposes of the United Nations'. According to one view, Article 2(4) would cover any use of force by a State on or above the high seas and, in general in areas not subject to any State's exclusive jurisdiction: see, in particular, Ronzitti, *supra* note 40, at p. 10; Conforti, *supra* note 55, at p. 358 (but see also Conforti, *supra* note 61, at p. 193). But where coercion is used against private ships the situation is far from clear. For example, there are established customary rules allowing, in exceptional cases, for interference with the right of free navigation on the high seas: see Articles 19, 22 and 23 of the 1958 Geneva Convention on the High Seas (450 *United Nations Treaty Series*, p. 82 ff.). Are these rules to be considered as also derogating from the prohibition on the use of force 'in international relations'?

135 See, for example: Gioia, Ronzitti, *supra* note 31, at p. 232.

136 However, it may be that an authoritative determination of the aggressor takes place after the end of armed hostilities. In this case, it is arguable that the aggressor may be held 'liable and responsible for any damage that has resulted from visit, search, diversion and capture as well as from seizure of neutral goods' (W. Heintschel von Heinegg's report, p. 30, in this volume).

if necessary, destroying, merchant vessels persistently refusing to stop or otherwise actively resisting visit and search. Attacks on neutral merchant vessels may be considered, *per se*, as violating not only the rule on freedom of navigation on the high seas, but also rules on the protection of aliens and their property[137] and, arguably, even rules on the protection of fundamental human rights;[138] whether or not they would also constitute a prohibited 'use of force' under Article 2(4) of the UN Charter is unclear. Account should be taken, in this connection, of the 1974 UN General Assembly Resolution on the Definition of Aggression,[139] whose Article 3(d) mentions the attack on the 'marine merchant fleet' of another State among acts qualifying as acts of aggression. However, it is at least debatable whether this provision, *per se* not legally binding, corresponds to customary law; moreover, it is also debatable whether attacks on individual merchant vessels are covered by Article 3(b).[140] Inasmuch as an act of aggression implies a use of force of a certain gravity, a policy of indiscriminate economic warfare, involving attacks on sight on neutral merchant vessels in order to prevent them from contributing to the enemy's war

137 The better opinion is that the customary rules on the protection of aliens and their property are also applicable on the high seas and, more generally, in areas not subject to a State's exclusive jurisdiction: thus, even vessels not flying the flag of any State, though not enjoying the protection granted by the rule on freedom of navigation, are not outside the law altogether. For this view, see especially: M. Giuliano, *I diritti e gli obblighi degli Stati*, Padua 1956, at pp. 375-376, and 469.

138 International rules on the protection of human rights mainly consist of conventional rules. However, it is increasingly recognized that some fundamental principles of humanity have acquired a general customary character and that such principles are applicable to the protection of all individuals in all situations. Some decisions and advisory opinions of the International Court of Justice are especially relevant in this connection: see *ICJ Reports 1949*, at pp. 4 and 22; *ICJ Reports 1951*, at p. 23; *ICJ Reports 1980*, at p. 42. In the literature of international law, see especially: T. Meron, *Human Rights and Humanitarian Norms as Customary Law*, Oxford 1989, at p. 79 ff. Among such fundamental principles, the one protecting the right to life is especially relevant in respect of attacks on merchant vessels, at least where no attempt is made to place their crews in safety.

139 UN General Assembly Resolution 3314(XXIX), adopted without vote on 14 December 1974. Text in: 28 *Yearbook of the United Nations* (1974), pp. 846-848. On this resolution, see, among others: J. Zourek, 'Enfin une définition de l'agression', 20 *Annuaire français de droit international* (1974), p. 9 ff., M. Bothe, 'Die Erklärung der General-versammlung der Vereinte Nationen über die Definition der Aggression', 18 *German Yearbook of International Law* (1975), p. 127 ff., C.T. Eustathiadès, 'La définition de l'agression adoptée aux Nations Unies et la légitime défense', 28 *Revue héllenique de droit international* (1975), p. 5 ff.; P. Rambaud, 'La définition de l'agression par l'O.N.U.', 80 *Revue générale de droit international Public* (1976), p. 835 ff.; B. Broms, 'The Definition of Aggression', 154 *Hague Recueil* (1977, I), p. 305 ff.; B.B. Ferencz, 'Aggression', 3 *Encyclopedia of Public International Law*, Amsterdam/New York/Oxford 1982, p. 1 ff.; B.V.A. Röling, 'The 1974 Definition of Aggression', in Cassese (ed.), *supra* note 40, p. 413 ff.; Dinstein, *supra* note 409 at p. 119 ff.

140 The negative view is taken, for example, by: Bothe, *supra* note 1, at p. 394, and *idem*, *supra* note 88, at p. 209. *Contra*, see, for example: Greenwood, *supra* note 88, at pp. 213-215. See also the 1987 US Navy Handbook, *supra* note 88, Chapter 3.11.1, which refers both to the 'doctrine' of self-defence and to the 'doctrine' of protection of nationals, in order to allow for 'the use of proportionate force by US warships and military aircraft when necessary for the protection of US flag vessels and aircraft, US citizens (whether embarked in US or foreign flag vessels), and their property against unlawful violence in and over international waters'.

effort, may indeed be considered as giving rise to acts of aggression, under the 1974 Definition, against the flag States concerned;[141] but the use of the necessary degree of coercion in order to force individual merchant vessels to submit to visit and search should not necessarily be considered as amounting to an act of aggression.

On the other hand, practice in the Iran-Iraq conflict has also confirmed that 'non-belligerent' States can lawfully prevent belligerents from exercising their right of visit and search by assembling merchant vessels in a convoy protected by warships.[142] Whereas the status of a neutral convoy under the traditional law of neutrality was the object of some controversy,[143] there is no doubt that, under modern international law, belligerents cannot attack vessels travelling under 'non-belligerent' convoy, since such an attack would constitute an act of aggression against the flag State of the convoying warship.[144]

VIII. 'NON-BELLIGERENT STATES' AND THE TRADITIONAL LAW OF BLOCKADE

Whether modern international law still allows belligerents to enforce a blockade *vis-à-vis* 'non-belligerent' vessels approaching the enemy coast, or a part of it, is considerably more controversial.[145] It is possible to maintain, in this case also, that, to the extent that merchant ships 'are prevented from going to or from the blockaded port, such action is not a violation of the prohibition of the use of force'.[146] On the other hand, the law of blockade implicates a considerably greater interference with third States' commerce than the law of contraband.

141　On this question, see also *infra*, paragraph IX.

142　See, for example: Gioia, Ronzitti, *supra* note 31, at pp. 238-239. As Bothe rightly points out, 'where a warship simply escorts ships flying its flag to and from a neutral port, this does not constitute a use of force' *supra* note 88, at p. 208). The question of whether escorting constitutes 'innocent passage' to which a warship is entitled under the general rules of the law of the sea need not be asked whenever the convoy navigates on the high seas or traverses a State's territorial sea with its prior consent.

143　See, for example: Oppenheim, *supra* note 8, at pp. 849-851 and 858-859; Verzijl, *supra* note 11, at pp. 90 ff., 179-180, 245-248; R. Stodter, R., 'Convoy', 3 *Encyclopedia of Public International Law*, Amsterdam/New York/Oxford 1982, p. 128 ff.

144　For this view, see also, for example: Bothe, *supra* note 1, at p. 394, and *idem*, *supra* note 88, at p. 210.

145　On the traditional law of blockade, see, among others: Oppenheim, *supra* note 8, at p. 167 ff.; Balladore Pallieri, *supra* note 8, at p. 428 ff.; Castrén, *supra* note 8, at p. 290 ff.; Tucker, *supra* note 8, at p. 283 ff.; Quadri, *supra* note 8, at p. 330 ff.; Miele, *supra* note 1, at p. 135 ff.; L. Weber, 'Blockade', 3 *Encyclopedia of Public International Law*, Amsterdam/New York/Oxford 1982, p. 46 ff.

146　Bothe, *supra* note 1, at p. 394. Whether attacks on merchant vessels attempting to breach blockade would constitute a 'use of force' and an act of 'aggression' under the 1974 Definition (note 139), is open to question: see *supra*, paragraph VII, notes 137-141, and corresponding text.

Practice in the Iran-Iraq conflict showed a reluctance on the part of some States to allow for measures of economic warfare other than the visit and search of merchant ships for the purpose of preventing them from carrying contraband of war bound for enemy territory.[147] Practice in the same conflict also confirmed doubts on the present relevance of the concept of blockade: in modern naval conflicts, belligerents tend to ignore the traditional rules on naval blockade and to adopt more stringent measures of economic warfare which the law of neutrality would not allow. Recent trends in economic warfare will be briefly examined in the next paragraph. Inasmuch as blockade can still be regarded as a viable method of warfare, the question remains of whether third States still have to tolerate the resulting interference with their commercial shipping.[148]

With respect to situations where the Security Council has recommended or decided enforcement measures against one State under Article 41 of the UN Charter, the question has been raised of whether the State acting in self-defence is entitled 'to intercept shipping and aircraft bound for its adversary in order to enforce the sanctions resolution';[149] depending on the list of goods covered in the resolution, this might imply greater powers than the traditional law of contraband would confer on belligerent States and could in fact amount to the institution of a blockade, especially where ships coming from enemy ports are also involved.

In the recent Gulf conflict, the United States, claiming a right of collective self-defence in response to requests from 'the legitimate government of Kuwait', announced that it would 'intercept the import and export of commodities and products to and from Iraq and Kuwait' that had been prohibited by Security Council Resolution 661(1990), which had imposed an almost total economic embargo against Iraq,[150] and that 'failure of a ship to proceed as directed' would result in 'the use of the minimum level of force necessary to ensure compliance'.[151] A similar announcement was made by the United Kingdom.[152] After these announcements, the Security Council eventually adopted, on 25 August, Resolution 665(1990)

---

147 See, for example: Gioia, Ronzitti, *supra* note 31, at p. 233-234.
148 Several writers have pointed out that formal blockade seems to have become an obsolete method of warfare: see the authors quoted *infra*, in note 171. But at least some writers maintain that blockade is still a valid legal concept: see, for example, Ronzitti, *supra* note 9, at pp. 9-10; Bothe, *supra* note 10, at pp. 397-399 and *idem*, *supra* note 88, at p. 210. According to Miele, *supra* note 1, at p. 218 ff., one should distinguish between situations of limited and localized armed conflict, to which the traditional rules still apply, and situations of total war, which are governed by different legal principles.
149 Greenwood, *supra* note 9, at pp. 59-61.
150 UN Security Council Resolution 661(1990), adopted on 6 August 1990 by thirteen votes to none, with two abstentions (Cuba and Yemen). Text in: UN, *Security Council Official Records: Forty-Fifth Year, Resolutions and Decisions of the Security Council*, New York 1991, at p. 20.
151 US Special Warning Note No. 80 of 17 August 1990. Text in: E. Lauterpacht, C.J. Greenwood, M. Weller, D., Bethlehem (eds.), *The Kuwait Crisis: Basic Documents*, Vol. I, Cambridge 1991, at p. 248. See also the Press Release of 16 August 1990, *ibidem*, at p. 247.
152 See: *ibidem*, at pp. 245-246.

expressly demanding States co-operating with Kuwait to adopt 'measures commensurate to the specific circumstances' to stop merchant ships and inspect their cargo, in order to enforce Resolution 661.[153] As a result, some kind of blockade was instituted against Iraq.[154]

The adoption of Resolution 665(1990) posed a number of difficult problems, one of which was its legality under Article 41 or Article 42 of the UN Charter.[155] This problem can only be touched upon in the context of this report. With respect to the State directly affected, the institution of a blockade undoubtedly constitutes, *per se*, a violation of Article 2(4) of the Charter and an act of aggression under Article 3(c) of the 1974 Definition of Aggression;[156] therefore, a resolution deciding or recommending measures amounting to a blockade against a State could certainly not be based on Article 41 of the Charter. Blockade is explicitly mentioned by Article 42 among possible measures that the Security Council may take in order to 'maintain or restore international peace and security'. However, as stated above, it is doubtful that the Security Council can delegate its powers under Article 42 to individual States: this writer shares the view that a resolution 'recommending', 'authorizing', or even 'demanding', expressly or by implication, the imposition of a blockade on the part of individual States would be illegitimate, unless it could properly be placed in the context of Article 51 of the Charter.[157] In the Gulf conflict, the States co-operating with Kuwait could be seen as acting in collective self-defence.[158] While Article 51 does not subject action in self-defence to a previous authorization on the part of the Security Council, it *does* require that such action ends when the Security Council 'has taken measures necessary to maintain international peace and security'. Of course, precisely what measures constitute such 'necessary measures'

---

153 UN Security Council Resolution 665(1990), adopted on 25 August 1990 by thirteen votes to none, with two abstentions (Cuba and Yemen), called upon 'Member States co-operating with the Government of Kuwait which are deploying maritime forces to the area to use such measures commensurate to the specific circumstances as may be necessary under the authority of the Security Council to halt all inward and outward maritime shipping, in order to inspect and verify their cargoes and destinations and to ensure strict implementation of the provisions related to such shipping laid down in resolution 661(1990)'. Text in UN, *supra* note 150, at pp. 21-22.

154 In this sense, see, for example: Bothe, *supra* note 1, at p. 398.

155 See, for example: F. Presutti, 'L'uso della forza per garantire l'applicazione di misure non implicanti l'uso della forza: il caso della risoluzione n. 665 del Consiglio di Sicurezza', 73 *Rivista di diritto internazionale* (1990), p. 380 ff. See also the report by N.J. Schrijver in this volume.

156 *supra* note 139.

157 See *supra*, paragraph IV, notes 78-81 and corresponding text.

158 The 'inherent right of individual and collective self-defence, in response to the armed attack by Iraq against Kuwait, in accordance with Article 51 of the Charter' had been affirmed by UN Security Council Resolution 661 (1990), *supra* note 150.

is a highly controversial question;[159] but, in any case, a Security Council resolution, such as Resolution 665(1990) and indeed the much more important Resolution 678(1990),[160] has the effect of removing all doubts on the possibility for the victim of aggression and its allies to resort to military measures of self-defence or to continue acting in self-defence, and/or on the necessity and proportionality of individual measures of self-defence.[161]

What are the implications of all this for the 'non-belligerent' States? As stated above, it is neither possible nor strictly necessary to justify traditional belligerent measures against third States' shipping on the sole basis of self-defence.[162] In order to justify such measures, it would rather be necessary to prove that specific rules of customary law have emerged as a result of post-1945 practice, allowing both belligerents or, as the case may be, the victim of aggression, to derogate from the rules protecting freedom of navigation. But whereas State practice seems to allow for the exercise of a right of visit and search in order to ensure that merchant ships do not carry contraband of war, it is much more doubtful whether customary law still allows belligerents to enforce a maritime blockade *vis-à-vis* the 'non-belligerent' States. Where the Security Council asks or authorizes States acting in self-defence to enforce a blockade, third States can reasonably be expected to tolerate the necessary interference with their commercial shipping: in such a situation, it is *not* the fact that the States concerned are acting in self-defence, but the fact that such States are complying with a Security Council resolution which constitutes a circumstance precluding wrongfulness in relations among UN Members.[163] In fact, where a resolution 'authorizing' a blockade is legitimate in the context of Article 51, *its effects on States not party to the conflict* can be justified under Article 41 of the Charter, inasmuch as they do not necessarily implicate, as seen above, a derogation from the regulation of the use of force.[164]

---

159 On this question, see, among others: Kelsen, *supra* note 61, at p. 801 ff.; Bowett, *supra* note 48, at p. 195; Delivanis, *supra* note 48, at pp. 55-56; Lamberti Zanardi, *supra* note 48, at pp. 263-264; Zourek, *supra* note 48, at pp. 50-51; Dinstein, *supra* note 40, at pp. 196-197; D.W. Greig, 'Self-Defence and the Security Council: What Does Article 51 Require?', 40 *International and Comparative Law Quarterly* (1991), p. 306 ff., at p. 389 ff.

160 *supra* note 80.

161 In this sense, see especially: G. Gaja, 'Il Consiglio di Sicurezza di fronte all'occupazione del Kuwait: il significato di una autorizzazione', 73 *Rivista di diritto internazionale* (1990), pp. 696-697; O. Schachter, 'United Nations Law in the Gulf Conflict', 85 *American Journal of International Law* (1991), p. 452 ff., at pp. 459-461; Conforti, *supra* note 55, at p. 385.

162 See *supra*, paragraph VII, notes 133-134 and 137-140, and corresponding text.

163 On the legal effects of recommendations by UN organs, see *supra*, paragraph V, note 69 and corresponding text.

164 It is precisely for this ambivalent character of Resolution 665(1990) that some commentators have considered it as falling 'somewhere in between' Articles 41 and 42: see Schrijver, in this volume. The question is complicated by possible terminological disputes on the meaning of the expression 'use of force' as employed in Article 2(4) of the UN Charter. There is no doubt that the institution of a blockade

On the other hand, where the Security Council is unable or unwilling to 'authorize' States acting in self-defence to enforce a blockade, 'non-belligerent' States do not seem to be prepared to allow for derogations from the rights they enjoy under the general laws of peace: it is significant, in this respect, that in the short interval between the adoption of Security Council Resolutions 661 and 665 (1990), there was considerable opposition on the part of third States to the US and UK decision to set up some kind of maritime blockade against Iraq in order to enforce economic sanctions.[165] *A fortiori*, it would be very difficult to admit that belligerents could enforce a blockade in situations where the Security Council has not even recommended or decided the adoption of economic sanctions.

One last question needs to be touched upon in this context. It has been suggested that 'when the Security Council adopts a decision under Chapter VII of the Charter calling upon the parties to a conflict to cease firing, that decision is binding and, in principle, a State which refuses to abide by the resolution (even if it had originally been acting in self-defence) will be acting unlawfully if it continues to use force'; therefore, 'that ought to have the same effects with regard to the exercise of rights against neutrals' as in the case where the Security Council has identified one State as the aggressor, *i.e.* third States could lawfully resist attempts to exercise belligerent rights on the part of the State refusing to abide by the cease-fire resolution.[166]

An evaluation of this view clearly depends on whether or not one accepts its fundamental premiss, *i.e.* the binding character of cease-fire resolutions adopted by the Security Council under Article 40 of the UN Charter. This question cannot adequately be dealt with in the context of this report. Suffice it to make it clear that this author shares the view that Security Council resolutions under Article 40 can never create binding obligations: the fact that Article 40 says that 'the Security Council shall duly take account of failure to comply' with the provisional measures it has recommended can only be a reference to the further measures the Council can take under Articles 41 and 42 of the Charter, *i.e.* measures which can be taken

---

amounts to a 'use of force' against the blockaded State under that Article; but the enforcement of a blockade vis-à-vis third States' shipping may not amount to a 'use of force' under the same article: see *supra* in note 162.

An interesting precedent (also referred to by Schrijver) is represented by UN Security Council Resolution 221(1966) (20 *Yearbook of the United Nations* (1966), p.112). By that resolution, the Security Council, at a time when mandatory sanctions against Southern Rhodesia had not yet been imposed, called upon the United Kingdom 'to prevent, by the use of force if necessary, the arrival at Beira of vessels reasonably believed to be carrying oil destined for Southern Rhodesia'. At least to the extent that such 'use of force' merely consisted in the diversion of private ships, it was certainly not a 'use of force' which would have been prohibited by Article 2(4) of the Charter: see also Conforti, *supra* note 61, at p. 193.

165 In this sense, see, for example: Greenwood, *supra* note 9, at p. 61.

166 Greenwood, *supra* note 9, at p. 58.

irrespective of a failure to comply with provisional measures.[167] It may be significant, in this respect, that, in the Iran-Iraq conflict, Resolution 598(1987), which had 'demanded' a cease-fire, was mainly treated by States as though it had to be accepted by both parties before it became binding:[168] in other words, it was not treated differently from previous resolutions, which had merely 'called' for a cease-fire.[169]

IX. STATES NOT PARTY TO AN ARMED CONFLICT AND CURRENT TRENDS IN ECONOMIC WARFARE

Practice in modern armed conflicts aboundantly demonstrates the existence of a tendency on the part of belligerent States to adopt measures of economic warfare which would not be justified under the traditional law of neutrality. Only a few examples will be given here. In the first place, although the traditional law of contraband was always somewhat ambiguous in stating precisely what kinds of goods belonged to the class of contraband of war, the tendency in modern conflicts has been to unduly enlarge the list of contraband articles.[170] Secondly, whereas the traditional law required a blockade to be declared and effectively maintained by a naval force sufficient really to prevent access to, and egress from, the enemy's coast,

---

167 In this sense, see especially: Conforti, *supra* note 61, at pp. 183-186. The contrary view, however, is widely held in legal literature. Suffice it to mention, for example, Oppenheim, *supra* note 8, at pp. 166-167.

168 UN Security Council Resolution 598(1987), adopted unanimously on 20 July 1987. Text in: 41 *Yearbook of the United Nations* (1987), p. 223. On the legal implications of this resolution, see especially: P. Tavernier, 'Le caractère obligatoire de la résolution 598 (1987) du Conseil de Sécurité relative à la guerre du Golfe', 1 *European Journal of International Law* (1990), p. 278 ff.

169 This is recognized by Greenwood himself, *supra* note 166.

170 The precise definition of contraband of war has been the subject of disputes between belligerent and neutral States from very early times. The 1909 unratified London Declaration, *supra* note 5, drew a distinction between 'absolute' and 'conditional' contraband; it listed articles exclusively used in war, which may, without notice, be treated as 'absolute' contraband (Article 22) as well as articles, 'susceptible of use in war as well as for purposes of peace', which may, equally without notice, be treated as 'conditional' contraband (Article 24). Belligerents were allowed to add further articles to both lists, by means of a duly notified declaration (Articles 23 and 25); but articles, listed in Article 28, 'which are not susceptible of use in war', may not be declared contraband of war (Article 27). Subsequent State practice has caused widespread scepticism on the present relevance of the rules embodied in the 1909 Declaration: see, for example, Mc Dougal, Feliciano, *supra* note 56, at p. 481 ff.; Sereni, *supra* note 8, at p. 2147 ff.; Miele, *supra* note 1 at p. 159 ff.; O'Connell, *supra* note 9, at pp. 1142-1144; Kalshoven, *supra* note 5, at pp. 272 and 273-274.

modern practice has introduced the so-called 'long-distance blockade', the blockade of entire coasts, often undeclared and maintained exclusively by aircraft.[171]

Indeed, modern techniques of warfare, especially submarine and air warfare, have made it often inexpedient for belligerents to respect the traditional requirements of the law of neutrality, which did not allow for attacks on neutral merchant vessels except in very limited circumstances. Modern practice has seen the setting up of 'war zones' or 'exclusion zones', *i.e.* zones in which all ships, neutral or enemy, are subject to sinking on sight.[172] Moreover, even apart from the creation of such zones, belligerents often tend to attack without warning all merchant vessels, neutral or enemy, whose activities they regard as economically advantageous for the enemy, irrespective of whether or not these vessels carry contraband or perform 'unneutral service', and with no attempt being made to place their crews in safety.[173] The so-called 'tanker war', which was so striking an aspect of the Iran-Iraq conflict, is only the latest example of this unfortunate tendency.[174]

What are the legal consequences of these modern trends for the States not party to an armed conflict? The question arises, first of all, of whether at least some acts constituting violations of neutral States' rights can be justified as reprisals. As stated above, in traditional international law belligerents faced with violations of neutrality on the part of third States could either declare war – which, however, they could do in any case – or take reprisals against them; in modern international law, war cannot be declared against a State not guilty of an armed attack, and reprisals involving the use of armed force, within the meaning of Article 2(4) of the UN Charter, are not

171 According to the 1909 London Declaration, *supra* note 5, a blockade, in order to be binding, had to be declared (Article 8) and maintained by a force sufficient really to prevent access to the enemy's coast (Article 2, which referred to the 1856 Paris Declaration, *supra* note 4). Blockade was, historically, a purely naval institution and a blockade maintained exclusively by aircraft was often considered unlawful: see, for example, Oppenheim, *supra* note 8, at p. 781. In this respect also, subsequent practice has caused considered scepticism on the present relevance of the traditional rules: see, for example, Mc Dougal, Feliciano, *supra* note 56, at p. 490 ff.; Sereni, *supra* note 8, at p. 2152; Miele, *supra* note 1, at p. 159 ff.; O'Connell, *supra* note 9, at pp. 1153-1154; Kalshoven, *supra* note 5, at pp. 272 and 274; Ronzitti, *supra* note 9, at pp. 9-10.

172 The traditional law of war at sea only allowed for the setting up of 'operational zones' in the 'theatre of war', *i.e.* in the area where naval hostilities were actually taking place, thereby prohibiting or restricting movements of neutral vessels or aircraft: see, for example, Tucker, *supra* note 8, at p. 300. On the modern practice of 'war zones' or 'exclusion zones', see especially: O'Connell, *supra* note 9, at pp. 1109-1112; W.J. Fenrick, 'The Exclusion Zone Device in the Law of Naval Warfare', 24 *Canadian Yearbook of International Law* (1986), p. 91 ff.; Kalshoven, *supra* note 5, at p. 274; Ronzitti, *supra* note 9, at pp. 40-41; Bothe, *supra* note 1, at pp. 400-401.

173 On modern techniques of economic warfare, see, among others: Tucker, *supra* note 8, at p. 181 ff.; Miele, *supra* note 1, at p. 197 ff.; Verzijl, *supra* note 11, at p. 252 ff. See also the authors quoted *infra*, in note 209.

174 On Iraq's practice, see: A. Gioia, 'Commentary', in De Guttry, Ronzitti (eds.), *supra* note 31, p. 57 ff., at p. 61 ff. On Iran's practice, see: Momtaz, *supra* note 31, at p. 29 ff.

allowed.[175] In addition, an act of reprisal must be reasonably proportionate to the prior violation of international law to which it is a response, and, except perhaps in cases of emergency, it must be preceded by an attempt to redress the situation by other peaceful means. Finally, there is at least a tendency in modern international law to prohibit reprisals involving violations of fundamental human rights.[176] As seen above, interference with third States' shipping may not always be seen as amounting to a violation of the prohibition on the use of force in international relations;[177] however, a policy of indiscriminate economic warfare, involving attacks without warning on neutral merchant vessels may indeed be seen as amounting to an act of aggression against the flag States concerned.[178] Moreover, even leaving aside the requirements of proportionality and subsidiarity, it is at best debatable whether reprisals involving the sinking on sight of neutral merchant vessels would be in keeping with the modern trend towards the protection of fundamental human rights.[179]

However, modern practice clearly shows that belligerent States tend sometimes to justify unlawful measures of economic warfare not as reactions to 'unneutral' behaviour on the part of third States, but rather as a response to the enemy's prior resort to similar measures aimed at suppressing their own legitimate trade relations with third States.[180] This seems to raise the question of whether such measures can be justified as belligerent reprisals, a question which should be answered in the negative: while belligerent reprisals may cause incidental injury to neutrals, reprisals involving direct violations of third States' rights are always to be considered unlawful.[181] The *tu quoque* argument, when used to justify violations of the rights

---

175 See *supra*, paragraph V, notes 91-92 and corresponding text. The fact that reprisals against neutral States cannot involve the 'use of force' is underlined, among others, by Bothe, *supra* note 1, at p. 207; Schindler, 'Transformations', *supra* note 1, at pp. 381-382.

176 On the modern requirements for reprisals, see generally, the authors quoted *supra*, in note 49 and *infra*, in note 179.

177 See *supra*, paragraph VII, notes 133-134 and corresponding text.

178 See *ibidem*, notes 137-141 and corresponding text.

179 See *ibidem*, note 134. The view that, in general international law, reprisals cannot involve violations of human rights or, at least, of fundamental human rights, is gaining currency: see, for example, F. Lattanzi, *Garanzie dei diritti dell'Uomo nel diritto internazionale generale*, Milan 1989, at p. 241 ff.; Meron, *supra* note 138, at p. 233 ff.; Cassese, *supra* note 103, at pp. 242-244; M. Giuliano, T. Scovazzi, T. Treves, *Diritto internazionale. Parte generale*, Milan 1991, at pp. 444-445; Conforti, *supra* note 55, at pp. 359-360.

180 On practice during the Second World War, see, for example, Oppenheim, *supra* note 8, at pp. 678-679. On practice in the Iran-Iraq war, see, for example: M. Jenkins, 'Air Attacks on Neutral Shipping in the Persian Gulf: the Legality of the Iraqi Exclusion Zone and Iranian Reprisals', 8 *Boston College International and Comparative Law Review* (1985), p. 517 ff.; Boyle, *supra* note 8, at p. 86.

181 On the modern law of belligerent reprisals, see, among others: F. Kalshoven, *Belligerent Reprisals*, Leyden 1971, and *idem*, 'Belligerent Reprisals Revisited', 21 *Netherlands Yearbook of International Law* (1990), p. 43 ff.; R. Bierzanek, 'Reprisals as a Means of Enforcing the Laws of Warfare', in Cassese (ed), *supra* note 40, p. 232 ff.; C. Greenwood, 'The Twilight of the Law of Belligerent Reprisals', 20

of third States, seems rather to bear some resemblance to the very controversial notion of the state of necessity as a circumstance precluding wrongfulness.[182]

Under the traditional law of neutrality, a belligerent was allowed to redress violations of neutrality committed by the enemy: in situations where a neutral State either openly permitted or tacitly acquiesced in the unlawful interference with its rights on the part of one belligerent, the other belligerent could resort to reprisals;[183] where, on the contrary, the neutral State was not guilty of 'unneutral' behaviour, but was unable to prevent violations of its neutrality on the part of one belligerent, the other belligerent could rely, according to some writers, on a state of necessity[184] or, according to other writers, on a specific rule of the law of neutral-

Netherlands Yearbook of International Law (1989), p. 35 ff.
The view that belligerent reprisals cannot excuse direct violations of third States' rights is also taken, among others, by: Guggenheim, *supra* note 8, at p. 517; Verzijl, *supra* note 11, at pp. 36-38 and 253; Ronzitti, *supra* note 9, at p. 48. See also Articles 23 and 24 of the 1939 Harvard Research Draft Convention on Rights and Duties of Neutral States in Naval and Aerial War, *supra* note 5.
182 See, for example, Ronzitti, *supra* note 90 at p. 50. Unlike reprisals, the state of necessity does not presuppose the previous commission of an international wrong by the target State. However, although the 1980 ILC Draft Articles on the Origin of State Responsibility (*infra*, note 193) list the state of necessity among circumstances precluding wrongfulness (Article 33), its operation is subject to various limitations: in particular, a state of necessity may not be invoked in order to excuse violations of *jus cogens* obligations, such as the prohibition on the use of force. Moreover, despite the ILC Draft Articles, the notion of the state of necessity as a general circumstance precluding wrongfulness is still controversial in the literature of international law: suffice it to mention, in this context, Conforti, *supra* note 55, at pp. 341-343.
183 See, for example: Oppenheim, *supra* note 8, at pp. 678-680; Kelsen, *supra* note 10, at pp. 161-162. According to Miele, *supra* note 1, this would be a case of necessity. Other writers took a rather more cautious attitude: see, for example, Stone, *supra* note 8, at pp. 400-401.
184 See, for example: Miele, *supra* note 1, at pp. 242-249.
In this context, it may be necessary to refer to a distinction made by some writers between the state of necessity and the related concept of 'military necessity' ('*Kriegsräson*', '*ragion di guerra*'). Whereas the state of necessity can only be invoked in order to safeguard the existence of the State, or other equally essential interests, against a grave and imminent peril and can never be invoked if the State itself has contributed to its occurrence, the concept of 'military necessity' was often said to have a wider scope: some writers considered it as a general principle limiting the operation of the laws of war, and allowing for violations of the enemy's rights whenever this was necessary for the success of a military operation. Some writers even maintained that the principle of military necessity could excuse violations of third States' rights, provided compensation was paid for damages: see, for example, Balladore Pallieri, *supra* note 8, at pp. 125-130 and 383-387. The better view, however, is that military necessity, as distinct from the state of necessity, is neither a circumstance precluding wrongfulness nor a general 'normative' principle, at least as far as relations between belligerents and neutrals are concerned: it is rather a principle which, like the principle of impartiality (see *supra*, paragraph VI, notes 103-104 and corresponding text), was historically at the basis of the emergence of specific rules of the law of neutrality. Examples of such rules are the one on the right of angary (*supra*, note 121), and, more generally, all the rules granting belligerents certain rights interfering with neutral commerce. From this point of view, there can be no doubt that the concept of military necessity cannot be invoked, *de lege lata*, to justify the exercise of more extensive measures than those allowed for under the law of neutrality: see, especially, G. Sperduti, *Influenza della necessita' nei rapporti fra i belligeranti e i neutrali*, Rome 1939-40.

ity,[185] in order to redress the situation.[186] In modern international law, neither the law of reprisals nor a state of necessity could excuse the 'use of force' – and, more generally, violations of *jus cogens* obligations – against a neutral State;[187] as for specific customary and/or treaty rules of neutrality, any rule conflicting with peremptory norms of international law should be considered as no longer in force.[188] Consequently, inasmuch as a policy of unrestricted economic warfare, involving attacks without warning on merchant vessels, constitutes an act of aggression against the flag State concerned and/or a violation of other *jus cogens* obligations, it should be considered unlawful.[189]

The question arises, in this context, whether the 'non-belligerent' States are in a different position from that of the genuinely neutral States: do these States have to tolerate the exercise on the part of belligerents of more extensive measures of economic warfare than the law of neutrality would allow? As a matter of principle, the answer to this question must be in the negative. Indeed, it must once again be stressed that reprisals cannot be taken against 'non-belligerent' States for the mere fact that their conduct is not in keeping with traditional duties of abstention, prevention or non-discrimination, for the simple reason that those duties are not binding upon them.[190] However, account must be taken of the serious consequences

---

185 See, for example, Sperduti, *supra* note 184, at pp. 27-30.

186 The traditional rule is expressed, in the US 'Annotated Supplement to the Commander's Handbook on the Law of Naval Operations (NWP 9), A. Rev. as follows: 'If the neutral nation is unable or unwilling to enforce effectively its right of inviolability an aggrieved belligerent may resort to acts of hostility in neutral territory against enemy forces, including warships and military aircraft, making unlawful use of that territory'. On the use of force in neutral territory, see also *supra*, note 94 and *infra*, note 189.

187 With reference to the state of necessity, see *supra*, note 182.

188 See also: Schindler, 'Transformations', *supra* note 1, at p. 382.

189 *A fortiori*, acts of hostility by a belligerent on the territory of a neutral State should be considered unlawful, unless such territory has been occupied by the enemy or, possibly, it is otherwise used by the enemy as a base for military operations. Under the principles enshrined in the UN Charter, the use of force against enemy forces in neutral territory would be lawful only if the measures taken could be regarded as necessary and proportionate measures of self-defence: see, for example: D. Schindler, 'L'emploi de la force par un belligerant sur le territoire d'un Etat non belligerant', in *Estudios de derecho internacional. Homenaje al Profesor Miaja de la Muela*, Madrid 1979, p. 847 ff., and *idem*, 'Transformations', *supra* note 1, at p. 382; Greenwood, *supra* note 127, at pp. 277-278; Ronzitti, *supra* note 40, at pp. 34-36. For an examination of recent State practice in this field, see especially: Norton, *supra* note 1, at p. 283 ff. But the question arises, in this connection, of whether, in situations where a neutral State allows the use of its territory as a base for belligerent activities, such State could be accused of an act of aggression against the aggrieved belligerent: on this latter possibility, see *infra*, notes 201-207 and corresponding text.

190 In this sense, see especially: Schindler, 'Transformations', *supra* note 1, at pp. 381-383. Some of the authors who regard 'non-belligerency' as a lawful attitude maintain, at the same time, that the aggrieved belligerent could react by taking 'reprisals': see, especially, H. Lauterpacht, 'Rules of Warfare in an Unlawful War', in *Law and Politics in the World Community. Essays on Hans Kelsen's Pure Theory and Related Problems in International Law*, Berkeley/Los Angeles 1953, p. 89 ff., at p. 111. As Meyrowitz points out (*supra* note 1, at p. 375) this is a contradiction in terms, since reprisals can only be taken against a wrongful act.

that an attitude of 'non-belligerency' may have in situations where the UN system of collective security is ineffectual and where the distinction between the aggressor and the victim of aggression is *prima facie* unclear. As seen above, it is difficult, *de lege lata*, to assert that, in such situations, traditional neutrality obligations are now binding on all States not party to an armed conflict; but where a 'non-belligerent' State supplies a belligerent with arms or war materials, or where it grants loans or subsidies to that belligerent, the aggrieved belligerent may perceive such behaviour as amounting to complicity with the aggressor.[191]

The subject of complicity had not been adequately dealt with in the literature of international law before the UN International Law Commission started its work on the codification of the law of State responsibility.[192] Yet Article 27 of the 1980 Draft Articles on the origin of State responsibility, provisionally adopted by the Commission, states that: 'Aid or assistance by a State to another State, if it is established that it is rendered for the commission of an internationally wrongful act, carried out by the latter, itself constitutes an internationally wrongful act, *even if, taken alone, such aid or assistance would not constitute the breach of an international obligation*'.[193] It is, of course, doubtful whether this provision, framed as it

Of course, the aggrieved belligerent may resort to retorsions, *i.e.* to measures which are not, per se, inconsistent with an international obligation: see, for example, I.F.I. Shihata, 'Destination Embargo of Arab Oil: Its Legality Under International Law', 68 *American Journal of International Law* (1974), p. 591 ff., at pp. 614-615.

191 See *supra*, paragraph VII, notes 113-114 and corresponding text. Of course, the same could be said with respect to States having officially adopted a policy of 'neutrality': for example, according to Boyle, *supra* note 8, at pp. 70-71, the attitude of the United States in the Iran-Iraq war could be considered not only as violating neutrality obligations but also as amounting to complicity in Iraq's 'aggression' against Iran; see also Y. Dinstein, 'Remarks', 82 *Proceedings of the American Society of International Law* (1988), p. 606 ff., at p. 609. It is significant that, during the same conflict, Iran expressly accused 'some States in the area and beyond' of 'backing' the aggressor: see, for example, UN Doc. S/16585, 25 May 1984, rep. in De Guttry, Ronzitti (eds.), *supra* note 31, at p. 28 ff. On United States practice in the Iran-Iraq conflict, see also: S.P. Menefee, 'Commentary', in De Guttry, Ronzitti (eds.), *supra* note 31, p. 99 ff.

192 The question of complicity has often been confused with that of so-called 'indirect responsibility'. According to Ago, the two should be kept distinct since, in the case of complicity, 'the existence of an internationally wrongful act unquestionably commited by a State ... is accompanied by the existence of participation by another State ... in the commission by the first State of its own act'; by contrast, in the case of indirect responsibility, 'the point to be considered is not the part which may in fact be played by a State in the independent commission of an internationally wrongful act by another State, but the existence of a particular relationship between two States' (R. Ago, 'Seventh Report on State Responsibility', *Yearbook of the International Law Commission 1978*, Vol. II, Part One, p. 31 ff., at p. 52).

Among recent studies on complicity, see especially: J. Quigley, 'Complicity in International Law. A New Direction in the Law of State Responsibility', 57 *British Year Book of International Law* (1986), p. 77 ff.; M.L. Padelletti, *Pluralità di Stati nel fatto illecito internazionale*. Milan 1990.

193 The text of the 1980 Draft Articles is in *Yearbook of the International Law Commission 1980*, Vol.II, Part Two, p. 30-34 (emphasis added). Chapter IV of the Draft Articles is entitled 'Implication of a State in the International Wrongful Act of Another State' and contains two articles: Article 27 deals with 'Aid or Assistance by a State to Another State for the Commission of an Internationally Wrongful Act'; Article

is in general terms, corresponds to existing customary law. However, one may detect a tendency in State practice to recognize the unlawfulness of complicity in the violation of customary rules creating *erga omnes* obligations, and, in particular, of the prohibition on the use of force in international relations.[194]

Precisely what consequences may derive from an attitude of complicity is as yet unclear. Complicity with an aggressor may not itself constitute an act of aggression, although, as will be seen shortly, certain kinds of assistance may indeed be qualified as acts of aggression.[195] Where 'unneutral' behaviour, though not constituting in itself an act of aggression, may be seen as amounting to complicity with the aggressor, it may reasonably be assumed that the State acting in self-defence can lawfully take reprisals against the State responsible for such behaviour, provided the modern requirements for reprisals are always respected. Of course, the 'non-belligerent' States concerned will always pretend to be aiding or assisting the victim of aggression; however, where the situation is *prima facie* unclear, they do so at their own risk.

Apart from the law of reprisals, modern practice shows a marked tendency on the part of belligerents to justify unlawful measures against third States' shipping on the basis of the law of self-defence. To give but two examples, during the Falklands conflict, the United Kingdom, claiming a right of self-defence, set up a 'total exclusion zone', involving both enemy and 'neutral' ships, warships included;[196] again, in the recent Iran-Iraq conflict, Iraq's campaign of unrestricted economic warfare was primarily justified on the basis of self-defence.[197] In this connection, however, a plea of self-defence should be rejected. As stated above, it is possible to argue that the modern law of self-defence has influenced the traditional law of neutrality, to the extent that the exercise of belligerent rights is nowadays limited by the requirements of necessity and proportionality; on the other hand, self-defence could not, *per se*, excuse direct violations of third States' rights, *i.e.* it could not justify measures which would otherwise be unlawful *vis-à-vis* a State other than the aggressor.[198] Indeed, State practice in modern armed conflicts confirms the view

---

28, relating to cases of so-called 'indirect responsibility', is entitled 'Responsibility of a State for an Internationally Wrongful Act of Another State'.

194 In this sense, see especially: Padelletti, *supra* note 192, at p. 145 ff.

195 According to Brownlie, cases of 'aid or assistance' may or may not give rise to 'joint responsibility': 'thus the supply of weapons, military aircraft, radar equipment, and so forth, would in certain situations amount to 'aid or assistance' in the commission of an act of aggression but would not give rise to joint responsibility. However, the supply of combat units, vehicles, equipment, and personnel, for the specific purpose of assisting an aggressor, would constitute a joint responsibility' (I. Brownlie, *System of the Law of Nations. State Responsibility*, Part I, Oxford 1983, at p. 191).

196 See, for example: Venturini, *supra* note 128, at p. 210 ff.; T. Oxford, 'Exclusion Zones at Sea: Some Observations on the Conduct of the Falklands War 1982', 2 *Sea Changes* (1985), p. 91 ff.

197 See, for example: Gioia, Ronzitti, *supra* note 31, at p. 236;

198 See *supra*, paragraph VII, notes 127-132 and corresponding text.

that construing self-defence as allowing for direct violations of third States' rights can have very unfortunate practical consequences.[199] In this context, the question should rather be asked of whether there is sometimes a 'right' of self-defence of the neutral State. At least where unlawful measures of warfare also involve interference with neutral States' warships, the States concerned have a right to use force in self-defence.[200]

The question may be asked, in respect of self-defence also, of whether the position of the 'non-belligerent' States is different from that of the strictly neutral

199 As Ronzitti points out, measures which would have been unlawful under the classic rules of neutrality, *a fortiori* would be unlawful under the law of self-defence *supra* note 9, at p. 7). But if one starts from the premiss that self-defence allows for direct violations of third States' rights, then the door is open for a belligerent to invoke self-defence in order to justify otherwise unlawful measures, whenever these are considered as absolutely necessary for its defence and proportionate to the enemy's conduct of hostilities. According to Greenwood, *supra* note 127, at p. 285, 'the traditional law remains useful in setting an upper limit to the rights that may be exercised against neutrals'; it is significant, however, that the same author, while finding it 'difficult to see how the requirements of self-defence could ever justify a use of force more extensive than that permitted by traditional belligerent rights', maintains, at the same time, that the setting up of a 'total exclusion zone' may be lawful 'if adequate warning is given and the danger to neutral shipping is kept to a minimum, so long as the conflict is on a level at which maritime operations on this scale can reasonably be regarded as necessary' (*ibidem*).

The doctrinal debate is further complicated by different views on the concept and scope of self-defence. Thus Greenwood maintains that the view that self-defence can only justify measures against the State guilty of an armed attack is unnecessarily narrow, since even 'the rights of belligerents against neutrals under the classical law of neutrality stemmed from principles of self-defence' *supra* note 9, at pp. 51-52). For our part, we agree with Professor Ago that it is conceptually necessary to distinguish 'cases in which the conduct adopted against a State constitutes a reaction to an internationally wrongful act committed by that State (and to so serious a wrongful act as aggression)' from 'cases in which such conduct is excusable – if excusable at all – solely by reason of the need to ward off a danger that simply originates in the territory of a State, the latter not being guilty of any aggression or of any wrongful act' *supra* note 48, at pp. 61-62). More generally, it is necessary to distinguish between self-defence and the state of necessity, a circumstance in which the target State 'has committed no international wrong against the State taking the action' (*ibidem*, at p. 53). From this point of view, it seems clear that belligerent rights against neutrals under the traditional law of neutrality did *not* derive from 'principles of self-defence': they rather derived from customary rules based on the principle of 'military necessity'. See *supra*, notes 182 and 184.

200 See, for example: R. Lagoni, 'Remarks', 82 *Proceedings of the American Society of International Law* (1988), p. 161 ff., at p. 163; Bothe, *supra* note 1, at pp. 395-396 and *idem*, *supra* note 88, at pp. 207-209.

When attacks on merchant ships are involved, the answer depends on the possibility of qualifying the belligerent's conduct not only as a 'use of force' and as an act of 'aggression' (see *supra*, paragraph VII, notes 137-141 and corresponding text), but also as an 'armed attack' against the flag State concerned within the meaning of Article 51 of the UN Charter. The better view is that at least the use of force against a single or a few private vessels on the high seas is neither an act of aggression nor an armed attack: see, for example, Dinstein, *supra* note 13, at pp. 186-187. For a different view, see, for example: Greenwood, *supra* note 88, at pp. 213-215. The same is true when belligerent ships are caught laying mines in international waters: on this latter question, see, for example, N. Ronzitti, 'La guerre du Golfe, le déminage et la circulation des navires', 33 *Annuaire français de droit international* (1987), p. 647 ff., at pp. 656-658; T. Meron, 'Remarks', 82 *Proceedings of the American Society of International Law* (1988), p. 164 ff.

States. The answer must again be in the negative, as a matter of principle. However, in situations where the UN system of collective security is ineffectual and where the distinction between the aggressor and the victim of aggression is *prima facie* unclear, account must be taken of Article 3(f) of the 1974 Definition of Aggression,[201] which lists among acts constituting aggression 'the action of a State in allowing its territory, which it has placed at the disposal of another State, to be used by that other State for perpetrating an act of aggression against a third State'. Where a 'non-belligerent' State goes as far as allowing its territory to be used by one belligerent as a base for military operations, the aggrieved belligerent may therefore perceive such behaviour as constituting in itself an act of aggression.

Again, the precise consequences of such behaviour are not very clear. Although it is undeniable that the victim of aggression can resort to reprisals, provided the requirements outlined above are respected, it is more doubtful that Article 3(f) of the Definition of Aggression identifies a case of armed attack giving rise to self-defence under Article 51 of the UN Charter:[202] it is, in fact, widely recognized that, under the heading of 'acts of aggression', the 1974 Definition includes acts that do not necessarily all qualify as 'armed attacks'.[203] For example, the 1986 ICJ decision in the Nicaragua case, which determined that the 'substantial involvement' of a State in 'acts of armed force against another State' carried out by 'armed bands, groups, irregulars or mercenaries' (Article 3(g) of the 1974 Definition) does not constitute an 'armed attack' within the meaning of Article 51,[204] would seem to confirm, despite its ambiguities, that cases of 'indirect aggression' cannot give rise to a right of self-defence.[205] But, as far as Article 3(f) is concerned, the situation is far from

---

201 *supra* note 139.

202 The positive view is taken, for example, by: Eustathiadès, *supra* note 139, at p. 87; Bothe, *supra* note 88, at pp. 396-397. Contra, among others: E. Sciso, 'L'aggressione indiretta nella definizione dell'Assemblea Generale delle Nazioni Unite', 66 *Rivista di diritto internazionale* (1983), p. 253 ff. Again, the question arises not only in respect of 'non-belligerent' States but also when States having officially declared themselves neutral are involved: see *supra*, note 189.

203 On this question, see, among others: Lamberti Zanardi, *supra* note 48, at p. 225(n.); Eustathiadès, *supra* note 139, at p. 74 ff.; Ago, *supra* note 47, at p. 68; Sciso, *supra* note 202, at p. 272 ff.

204 See: *ICJ Reports 1986*, at pp. 103-104.

205 On 'indirect aggression', see among others: Bowett, *supra* note 9, at pp. 260-261; Brownlie, *supra* note 13, at pp. 278-279, 325-326, 369-373; Lamberti Zanardi, *supra* note 48, at p. 248 ff., and *idem*, 'Indirect Military Aggression', in Cassese (ed.), *supra* note 40, p. 111 ff.; Sciso, *supra* note 202, *passim* and *idem*, 'Legittima difesa ed aggressione indiretta secondo la Corte internazionale di giustizia', 70 *Rivista di diritto internazionale* (1987), p. 627 ff.; Dinstein, *supra* note 13, at pp. 189-190.

By 'indirect aggression' writers usually intend situations in which, especially in the context of a civil war, a State aids or assists groups of armed individuals, *i.e.* situations covered by Article 3(g) of the 1974 Definition. But the term is quite ambiguous and could be employed to describe other situations listed in Article 3. As suggested by some writers, the term should be avoided: see, for example, Eustathiadès, *supra* note 139, at p. 59 ff.

clear. According to one view, the ICJ decision should not be given too much weight in this context, since it related to a situation of civil war.[206]

As seen above, under the traditional law of neutrality, a violation of neutrality obligations did not automatically make the State concerned a co-belligerent: unless the aggrieved belligerent chose to engage in war with the neutral State, acts of hostility on its part could be seen as acts of reprisal.[207] It has been suggested that, under the modern law of self-defence, armed intervention in order to redress violations of neutrality could only be allowed, in principle, in so far as acts of hostility are confined to enemy forces on neutral territory;[208] *a fortiori*, this should be true where 'non-belligerent' States are concerned, since no violations of neutrality obligations could be attributed to them. But if it is conceded that Article 3(f) of the 1974 Definition of Aggression identifies a case of 'armed attack', then clearly the law of neutrality and/or 'non-belligerency' would play no role: armed hostilities directed against the State responsible for such an armed attack would be allowed both under the law of self-defence and under the *jus in bello*.

Apart from the law of reprisals and the law of self-defence, the question may be asked of whether modern State practice has given birth to new rules of customary international law granting belligerents more extensive rights than they enjoyed under the traditional law of neutrality. If the answer to this question were to be a positive one, the traditional law of neutrality would be, to the extent implied by the new rules, completely superseded: in other words, not only the 'non-belligerent' States but also the strictly neutral States, irrespective of whether or not they were guilty of 'unneutral' behaviour, would have to tolerate the exercise of extensive measures of economic warfare on the part of both belligerents or, as the case may be, on the part of the State acting in self-defence. There is in fact no evidence of a desire on the part of belligerents to distinguish between vessels flying the flag of genuinely neutral States from those belonging to other 'non-belligerent' States.

According to some writers, the traditional rules on immunity of merchant vessels, including neutral vessels, ought to be superseded, in the light of belligerents' practice in the Second World War and in subsequent conflicts, by a more flexible approach whereby merchant vessels that sustain a belligerent's war effort may be seen as military objectives and, therefore, attacked and destroyed; only 'genuine intraneutral shipping', *i.e.* that between third party States, 'which does not in any case directly enhance the economic war strength of one or the other belligerent', would be

---

206 See: Ronzitti, *supra* note 40, at pp. 35-36.
207 See *supra*, notes 91 and 183, and corresponding text.
208 See the authors quoted *supra*, note 189. According to some writers, the same could be said with regard to the traditional law of neutrality: see, especially, Stone, *supra* note 8, at p. 401.

relatively immune from belligerent interference.[209] In other words, an attempt is made to broaden the concept of 'unneutral service' and/or to interpret the expression 'merchant vessel' as excluding all belligerent and neutral vessels that are integrated into the enemy's war effort. According to this view, even a merchant tanker, carrying oil exported from a belligerent State, would constitute a military objective, since the revenue deriving from oil exports could be seen by the other belligerent as essential to the enemy's war effort.

This view undoubtedly reflects one of the trends existing in modern State practice, in particular in the practice of belligerent States: indeed, it seems almost to have been invented in order to justify Iraq's 'tanker war' in the Iran-Iraq conflict.[210] However, it would certainly not be enough to point out that belligerents now behave in a certain way in order to prove the existence, *de lege lata*, of new customary rules binding on all States.[211] Where a belligerent justifies its conduct on the basis of a circumstance precluding wrongfulness, such as self-defence or reprisals, the existing law is not affected, irrespective of whether or not the plea is well-founded. Where, on the other hand, a belligerent invokes the notion of 'changed

---

209 See especially: F.V. Russo, 'Neutrality at Sea in Transition: State Practice in the Gulf War as Emerging Customary Law', 19 *Ocean Development and International Law* (1988), p. 381 ff., and *idem*, 'Targeting Theory in the Law of Armed Conflict at Sea: The Merchant Vessel as Military Objective in the Tanker War', in Dekker, Post (eds.), *supra* note 10, p. 153 ff. See also, with various qualifications: L. Doswald Beck, 'The International Law of Naval Armed Conflicts: The Need for reform', 7 *Italian Yearbook of International Law* (1986-1987), p. 251 ff., and *idem*, 'Remarks', 82 *Proceedings of the American Society of International Law* (1988), p. 599 ff.; R. Grunawalt, 'The Rights of Neutrals and Belligerents', 19 *Ocean Development and International Law* (1988), p. 303 ff.; J.A. Roach, 'Missiles on Target: The Law of Targeting and the Tanker War', 82 *Proceedings of the American Society of International Law* (1988), p. 154 ff.; Fenrick, *supra* note 123, at p. 438 ff., and *idem*, 'Legal Aspects of Targeting in the Law of Naval Warfare', 29 *Canadian Yearbook of International Law* (1991), p. 238 ff. These authors sometimes refer to W.T. Mallisson, *Studies in the Law of Naval Warfare: Submarines in General and Limited Wars* (Naval War College, *International Law Studies 1966*), at p. 129 ff. According to Miele, *supra* note 1, at pp. 218-225, the traditional rules of neutrality would lose their efficacy in cases of 'general conflict', leaving the door open for belligerent measures aiming at the total interruption of neutral trade with the enemy.

210 It may be interesting to recall, in this connection, that, when trying to justify its campaign of economic warfare in the face of Iranian protests, Iraq asserted that 'the term 'neutral mercantile ship' ... is inconsistent with reality, since the activity of the said ships is tantamount, from the point of view of the outcome, to supplying the Iranian military machine and enabling Iran to continue its aggression in violation of the provisions of international law. Accordingly, the said ships forfeit their neutral character since they violate a right unequivocally conferred by international law, and the owners and sailors of those ships and the Iranian regime are all responsible for the consequences entailed by that violation' (UN Doc., S/16972, 20 February 1985, rep. in De Guttry, Ronzitti (eds.), *supra* note 31, at pp. 92-93.

211 A thorough historical analysis would doubtlessly reveal that the 'targeting' theory merely develops claims made by belligerent States from very early times: in a chapter significantly entitled 'No New Thing Under the Sun', P.C. Jessup argued, in 1936, that the recurring arguments of Great Britain - which, as 'mistress of the seas', had had most occasion to assert belligerent claims - were a series of logical deductions from 'some basic principle that a belligerent may prevent a neutral from supplying the enemy with anything useful to it' (Jessup, *supra* note 6, at p. 62).

conditions' in order to bring about a change in the existing law, the attitude taken by the States affected becomes crucial: it is only when the enforcement of a claim on the part of a belligerent is acquiesced in by the States not party to the conflict that the birth of a new customary rule becomes a possibility. But, even leaving aside the old and relatively ambiguous findings of the 1946 Nuremberg judgment,[212] the practice of States not involved in armed conflicts would rather seem to point in the opposite direction.

As seen above, at least the 'non-belligerent' States are not now prepared to tolerate the exercise on the part of belligerents of all their traditional rights: whereas the exercise of a right of visit and search aimed at enforcing the law of contraband seems to have been accepted by most States, the enforcement of a blockade does not seem to have been so accepted unless the UN Security Council has 'authorized' it on the part of States acting in self-defence.[213] In this context, it would be very difficult indeed to prove that third States are prepared to tolerate the exercise of more extensive measures than those allowed by the traditional law of neutrality.[214] To go back to the examples given above, the UK's decision to set up a 'total exclusion zone' in the Falklands conflict raised a number of protests on the part of third States;[215] in the Iran-Iraq conflict, attacks on neutral and 'non-belligerent' shipping by both belligerents were condemned by third States as well as by UN Security Council resolutions.[216] It may be that in major conflicts involving great Powers

212 The Nuremberg Judgment did not address the question of attacks on neutral vessels except in connection with the question of 'war zones' (see *supra*, note 172 and corresponding text). However, since the tribunal found that the sinking of neutral ships without warning when found within such zones was a violation of existing rules of international law, *a fortiori* attacks on ships outside such zones ought to be considered illegal. See: 'International Military Tribunal Nuremberg, Judgment and Sentences, October 1, 1946', 41 *American Journal of International Law* (1947), p. 172 ff., at p. 304.

213 See *supra*, paragraphs VII and VIII.

214 According to Ronzitti, *supra* note 9, at p. 41, the military objective theory 'cannot be based on customary law as it now stands, but has to be founded on new conventional law'. According to Bothe, *supra* note 1, at p. 401, 'measures against neutral shipping going beyond the traditional rights of visit and search, and of seizing of contraband, would require a special enabling resolution by the Security Council'. See also: Heintschel von Heinegg, *supra* note 87, at p. 45.

215 See, for example, Venturini, *supra* note 128, at p. 218 ff.

216 The view has been put forward that 'the Iraqi attacks on third country merchant vessels have not been generally condemned although their definitive appraisal remains largely incomplete', and that 'illustrative of the ambiguous response of the international community to the Iraqi attacks were UN Security Council Resolutions 540(1983), 552(1984) and 582(1986)': these resolutions are said to have been 'silent as to the Iraqi attacks', while 'specifically condemning most of the Irani attacks' (Russo, 'Neutrality at Sea in Transition', *supra* note 209, at p. 157; see also, Roach, *supra* note 209, at p. 158). While debatable reasons of policy may have prevented third States, as well as the UN Security Council, from taking a stronger position, this view seems to overlook that protests were indeed raised against Iraqi attacks and that UN Security Council resolutions deplored 'attacks on neutral shipping' in quite general terms and, as was occasionally made clear in the preceding debates, were intended to refer to attacks by both Iran and Iraq: see Gioia, *supra* note 174, at pp. 71-72; G. Venturini, 'Commentary', in De Guttry, Ronzitti (eds.), *supra* note 31, p. 523 ff., at p. 527.

belligerent States would find it difficult, if not impossible, to abide by the traditional rules of the law of neutrality; however, to say that extensive violations of third States' rights would be rendered lawful by considerations of military necessity alone would be tantamount to saying that international law has no role to play in such situations.

CONCLUSIONS

As a result of the existing rules on the use of force in international relations and of the system of collective security enshrined in the UN Charter, the traditional law of neutrality only plays a marginal role in modern armed conflicts. Traditional neutrality obligations, which were based on a general principle of impartiality towards belligerents, are in fact difficult to reconcile with the need to distinguish between the aggressor and the victim of aggression. This conclusion is independent of the view one may take of the present status of the law of neutrality as a whole and, in particular, of the present conditions for the operation of the law of neutrality.

If the view is taken that the evolution of customary law has not, by itself, abrogated the law of neutrality and that it has not changed the conditions for its operation, then the traditional rules could only come into play in situations where at least one belligerent has recognized, explicitly or by implication, the existence of a 'state of war': in all situations where the parties to an armed conflict do not recognize the existence of a 'state of war' third States are not bound by traditional neutrality obligations. Since modern practice shows a marked tendency on the part of belligerents to avoid recognizing the existence of a formal 'state of war', the result is that the operation of the law of neutrality is now dependent, in most cases, on the intention of each State not party to the conflict: third States may, if they wish, declare themselves neutral, but they have no duty to do so. But even in situations where at least one belligerent has recognized the existence of a formal 'state of war', modern customary law allows third States not wishing to abide by traditional neutrality obligations to discriminate against the State guilty of aggression: individual deviations from neutrality obligations may be justified on the basis of collective self-defence or, possibly, on the basis of the law of countermeasures. Furthermore, even States wishing to remain strictly neutral may be bound to deviate from neutrality obligations as a result of a binding decision of the UN Security Council acting under Article 41 of the UN Charter.

If, on the other hand, the view is taken that the evolution of customary law has indeed changed the conditions for the operation of the law of neutrality, the recognition of a formal 'state of war' on the part of one or both belligerents becomes irrelevant. It is not possible, however, to maintain that the operation of the law of neutrality now depends upon the mere fact of the outbreak of an armed conflict: on the contrary, practice clearly shows that third States do not consider to be bound by all traditional neutrality obligations. Indeed, even the States officially adopting a policy of 'neutrality' do not always abide by all the traditional duties of neutral States. The better view is that strict neutrality has become purely optional in modern international law, irrespective of whether or not a 'state of war' is recognized by belligerents. It is, therefore, theoretically possible to distinguish between 'neutral' States, *i.e.* the States choosing to apply the law of neutrality in its entirety, and 'non-belligerent' States, *i.e.* the States which, while not wishing to enter the conflict on the side of one belligerent, do not, at the same time, choose to abide by all neutrality obligations.

In situations where the Security Council has determined that an act of aggression or a 'breach of the peace' has been committed by one belligerent, and/or has taken enforcement action under Chapter VII of the UN Charter, third States are not bound, in present circumstances, to enter the conflict on the side of the victim of aggression: they may, if they wish, adopt a policy of 'neutrality', but, whether they do it or not, they may be bound to deviate from neutrality obligations if a binding decision is taken by the Security Council under Article 41 of the Charter. States not wishing to adopt a policy of strict neutrality may discriminate against the aggressor irrespective of whether or not a binding decision has been taken by the Security Council. No violations of neutrality could be attributed to them.

In situations where no action has been taken by the UN Security Council, States are free to abide by all traditional neutrality obligations. On the other hand, they are not bound to do so and may discriminate against the aggressor. This situation, however, is open to abuse, since, in the absence of an objective determination by the Security Council, each State is provisionally allowed to decide by itself which belligerent is the aggressor and which is the victim of aggression. In situations where the distinction is *prima facie* unclear, especially where both belligerents claim a 'right' of self-defence, it may be argued that a policy of strict impartiality would still fulfill an important task.[217] *De lege lata*, the better view is probably that a duty to remain neutral in case of uncertainty as to who is the aggressor does not exist. However, where a State supplies the enemy with arms or war materials, or where it grants loans or subsidies to the enemy, the aggrieved belligerent may perceive such conduct as amounting to complicity with the aggressor, and this may lead, at least, to reprisals. Where a State goes as far as allowing its territory to be used by the enemy to carry out military operations, the aggrieved belligerent may even perceive such conduct as amounting, in itself, to an act of aggression. Whether this kind of aggression could give rise to the use of force in self-defence directed against the

217 In this sense, see also, for example: Jessup, *supra* note 6, at pp. 118-213; Bowett, *supra* note 9, at pp. 180-181.

'non-belligerent' State is open to question, inasmuch as it is doubtful that it would constitute an 'armed attack' within the meaning of Article 51 of the UN Charter. Yet, in any case, the law of self-defence would seem to allow for the use of force directed at enemy forces on 'non-belligerent' territory. As for reprisals, it must be stressed that reprisals against States not party to an armed conflict, be they 'neutral' or 'non-belligerent', are to be governed by the law of peace. Therefore, reprisals involving the violation of *jus cogens* obligations are not allowed. In any case, discrimination against one belligerent is undertaken at a State's own risk and may give rise to international responsibility if an authoritative determination is made that assistance was in fact given to the aggressor.

The fact that strict neutrality has become a purely optional attitude does not mean that modern international law does not impose special duties upon States not party to an armed conflict. Some such duties partly correspond to the traditional duties of neutral States. In particular, it is possible to argue, on the basis of recent practice, that all States not party to an armed conflict have to tolerate the exercise, on the part of belligerents, of a right to visit and search merchant vessels flying their flag, in order to ascertain whether they are carrying contraband of war bound for enemy territory. It is more doubtful, however, that third States still have to tolerate the enforcement of a blockade on the part of belligerents. *A fortiori*, it is impossible to agree with those writers who maintain that third States have to tolerate the exercise of more extensive measures on the part of belligerents than the traditional law of neutrality allowed for, such as the setting up of 'total exclusion zones' or the enforcement of a policy of unrestricted economic warfare. Moreover, a duty to tolerate the exercise of belligerent rights on the part of both belligerents only exists in situations where the Security Council has not identified one State as the aggressor, or as the State responsible for a 'breach of the peace': in situations where the Security Council has taken such action and, arguably, in other situations where the distinction between the aggressor and the victim of aggression is clear-cut, only the State acting in self-defence would be allowed to exercise belligerent rights.

Modern practice also shows a tendency to impose on all States not party to an armed conflict certain duties, flowing from principles other than the principle of impartiality, that neutral States did not have under the traditional law of neutrality: for example, as far as the trade in arms and war materials is concerned, it is possible to detect a tendency to impose upon all States a duty to abstain – as well as a duty to prevent private persons – from supplying belligerents with arms the employment of which is prohibited under the *jus in bello*, such as chemical and biological weapons, and from helping belligerents to produce such arms.

My final conclusion would then be that, although a distinction between 'neutrality' and 'non-belligerency' is still theoretically possible, and perhaps also necessary, in present circumstances, international law is clearly evolving towards a situation in which all States not party to an armed conflict will again be placed in the same condition as far as their legal relations with belligerents are concerned. Once this process is completed, the old law of neutrality will be superseded by a new law of 'neutrality' – or, if it is preferred, by a law of 'non-belligerency' or of 'qualified neutrality' – applicable in all situations of international armed conflict. It is possible that some of the rules of the future law of neutrality will still be based on the old principle of impartiality. However, these will only apply in situations where the UN system of collective security is ineffectual and where the distinction between the aggressor and the victim of aggression is *prima facie* unclear.

COMMENTS

Leslie Green[*]

Dr. Gioia has rightly drawn attention to the current 'crisis' in the law of neutrality. The first question that must be considered when facing the issue of 'Neutrality and Non-Belligerency' today is whether there is any legal right of neutrality.

The United Nations consists of some 180 members, that is to say almost the entire complement of states, and if the Security Council decides under Chapter VII that there has been a breach of the Charter or a threat to the maintenance of international peace and security leading to enforcement measures, the question arises whether any member has the right to declare that it is neutral or non-belligerent. This issue does not arise if the Council directs its obligatory decision to named states only. But if the decision is general in character condemning state 'A' as an aggressor, can any member claim to be a neutral? As to non-belligerency, this depends on the extent to which the state concerned is merely non-co-operative, but it is probably no longer open to any member to assert that it would behave towards both the aggressor and its victim in a completely even-handed fashion. However, regardless of the terms of the Charter and the decision of the Security Council there still remains the extent to which such even-handedness is possible after the seventy years that have elapsed since the coming into force of the Briand-Kellogg Pact and the fifty since the Nuremberg Judgment.

During the Gulf War, for example, a number of United Nations members refused to afford any assistance to the Coalition in its military operations against Iraq, but nevertheless recognized the authority of the Security Council in imposing the naval blockade and accepting its realities, pursuing an attitude of non-belligerency rather than neutrality. Others, especially Iran, claimed the right to exercise full neutral rights towards both Iraq and the Coalition, interning the former's aircraft and threatening to do the same to any Coalition aircraft forced to land in Iran. Still others, for example, Jordan, adopted a position which could only be described as benevolent neutrality, maintaining its right to trade with Iraq despite the variety of Security Council condemnatory resolutions. A similar situation has applied with

---

[*] Dr. L.C. Green is Honorary Professor of Law, University of Alberta; he was asked to act as a special commentator to Andrea Gioia's report.

H.H.G. Post (ed.), International Economic Law and Armed Conflict, 111–118.
© 1994 *Martinus Nijhoff Publishers. Printed in the Netherlands.*

regard to the Security Council ban on the supply of arms to all the conflicting parties in Bosnia.

In so far as the Gulf War was concerned, the states refusing to comply either fully or at all with the Security Council Resolutions took refuge in the argument, at least after the commencement of hostilities, that the relevant Resolutions had only authorized action against Iraq and had not decided that such operations were to be embarked upon or conducted under United Nations auspices and command. However, to the extent to which they deviated, in the name of neutrality or non-belligerency, from the economic measures against Iraq ordained by the Council, they were in breach of their obligations as members of the United Nations, even though they might have argued that there was nothing in customary law forbidding their actions. By pursuing such a stance, however, they ignored the impact of the decision of the World Court in the *Wimbledon* case.[1]

To further complicate the 'crisis' in the law of neutrality, not only do we have the problem whether neutrality is still a legal concept, but to such extent as it is, we are faced with the fact that the black-letter law in this field has not changed since 1907. While the Geneva law has been kept relatively up to date by the 1949 Conventions and the Protocols of 1977, and the Hague law has to some extent been modernized by Nuremberg and the Protocols, as Andrea Gioia points out at the beginning of his paper, the law of neutrality to the extent it still exists remains basically customary, modified by the conventions of 1856 and 1907. As if this were not enough, we also have to recognize that, whether we as lawyers like it or not, power plays a major role in the relations between states. As a result we find that, as was shown by the practice of the United States in both World Wars, a powerful state will decide how far it is prepared to assert the rights of a neutral as against a weaker belligerent, or the rights of a belligerent as against a weaker non-participant.

Furthermore, as conflicts become more global in character with virtually every major state, especially maritime powers, involved, there is an unwillingness to acknowledge that those not participating as active belligerents have any rights as neutrals. This is particularly so when a significant number of the belligerents maintain that they are fighting against an aggressor in the name of civilization, an approach evident after World War II when the Soviet Union used such arguments to oppose the admission to the United Nations of pro-western states which had remained neutral during the War. Ideological contentions of this character become even more significant today if action is taken under the authority of a Security Council resolution. In some circumstances, however, the ideology becomes tarnished, as has been seen to some extent in the case of Bosnia, when the United Nations in its efforts to restore peace declares that members of the organization are under an

---

1   The S.S. Wimbledon, PCIJ, Series A, No. 1 (1923).

obligation to pursue a policy of complete neutrality, in the sense that no action may be taken which might assist any belligerent, even though this may result in the type of situation that existed at the time of the Spanish Civil War when a policy of non-intervention was equivalent to one of assisting the rebels as against the legitimate government.

In fact, as has become clear in recent times, if a major power has decided that its policies require action against a particular smaller state, it is prepared, as the United States was during the Cuba missiles crisis, to proclaim its intention to enforce what might only be described as a form of blockade to inhibit any form of trading with its opponent by the rest of the world. When such a blockade is proclaimed under the auspices of a Security Council resolution there is a least some semblance of legal basis which does not exist in the former type of case.

Andrea Gioia states that 'it is possible to argue, with some justice, that the true function of the law of neutrality is to limit the rights of neutrals in order to allow belligerents to wage war relatively undisturbed. It is not surprising, therefore, that the law of neutrality is currently rather 'unpopular''. However, it is equally possible to argue that neutrality is a double-headed coin, whose function is to limit the rights of belligerents to enable those deciding to stay neutral to continue to exercise their rights to the greatest extent possible without unduly interfering with the equal rights of belligerents to conduct their hostilities one against the other. Since 'war', except in self-defence or under the authority of the United Nations, is now outlawed, it may be suggested that belligerency is, in the eyes of the larger part of humanity, at least as unpopular as neutrality has been in the eyes of belligerents.

Andrea Gioia is no doubt correct in reminding us that the mere outbreak of hostilities does not automatically result in bringing about the law of neutrality. It should be remembered, however, that at least prior to 1945 an outbreak of hostilities did not, except as between the parties to the conflict, bring the law of war automatically into operation. From the point of view of third party non-participants recognition of the existence of the conflict as amounting to war was necessary in order for them to claim the rights of neutrals, or for the belligerents to assert the obligations of neutrality against them. A non-participant not recognizing the existence of the 'war' was entitled to treat any assertion of belligerent rights against him as a *casus belli*, while a party to the conflict could exercise its discretion to decide to treat 'non-neutral' activities in the same manner.

It is equally important to bear in mind, as he points out, that nowadays the *jus in bello*, at least as defined in the Geneva Conventions, comes into operation as between belligerents as soon as hostilities begin. It may be questioned, however, whether it is equally true that the law of neutrality only comes into operation when a 'state of war' in the formal sense exists. In the first place, a party to a conflict may be strong enough to assert that some or all third states are obliged to behave as neutrals regardless of their recognition of the 'state of war', while the Security

Council may decide that the 'enforcement measures' authorized by it entail the observance of the strictest type of neutrality by those members of the United Nations which are not active participants in those enforcement measures. At the same time, the Council might recognize that the economic needs of particular members are such that in their case there is no obligation to behave in accordance with strict neutrality. In other words, it may be suggested that while we have witnessed a revival of some sort of 'just war' concept, as was especially witnessed in the Gulf, 'justice' may now be exercised in a dual fashion, recognizing that the justice of the cause for conflict must be tempered by considerations of justice on behalf of some non-participants.

When it is suggested that whether a conflict amounts to war or not entitles third states to discriminate against the aggressor, it does not mean that the aggressor will necessarily recognize the legality of such discrimination, especially if there has not been a condemnatory resolution by the Security Council under Chapter VII. Moreover, it must be accepted that, even in such circumstances, the principle of reciprocity may operate, so that a non-participant denying its obligation to respect the plenitude of the law of neutrality *vis-à-vis* the 'aggressor' may find itself denied the rights pertaining to a neutral insofar as that belligerent is concerned. This is particularly so when the decision whether a 'war' exists is made by an individual state in accordance with its own political predilections and subject to the potential abuse that goes with such political decision-making.

If the Security Council decides that a breach of the peace has taken place and that the state responsible is to be subjected to any form of enforcement measure, a member desiring to remain neutral would now, since the Provisional Measures Order in the Lockerbie case,[2] find that it would have no legal means to ascertain whether it has the right to remain neutral. The ultimate decision, therefore, is now political rather than legal and will be made by the Council itself.

In the event of the Security Council reaching a decision or a recommendation concerning the application of enforcement measures, it may well be true that those complying, whether because the decision is obligatory or out of a desire to give effect to such a recommendation, cannot be considered as a violation of their neutrality allowing for reprisals on the part of the belligerent concerned. However, it is one thing to assert, even though this be true, that obligations under the Charter override those of the traditional law of neutrality, it must be recognized that the mere fact that apparent deviations from neutrality might be legal does not mean that the state against which they are directed will in fact abstain from reprisals, while the geographical position of the complying state may make it impossible for effective aid to be extended to it. In other words, care must be taken not to allow an ideological

---

2   Questions of Interpretation and Application of the Montreal Convention arising from the Aerial Incident at Lockerbie (Libyan Arab Jamahiriya *vs.* United States of America), Provisional Measures, Order of 14 April 1992, ICJ Reports 1992, p. 114.

belief in the power of the law of the Charter to override a realistic approach to international actualities.

Andrea Gioia states that since no agreement envisaged by Article 43 of the Charter has been entered into, if the Security Council decides upon military operations, there is no obligation upon any state to cooperate or even to depart from its neutral status and obligations. In fact, he maintains that such a resolution would be 'illegitimate unless it could properly be placed in the context of Article 51 of the Charter, concerning individual and collective self-defence'. Since the action of the Security Council would be in support of the independence and integrity of the victim of the act of aggression, it is submitted that it follows that every such decision, whether Article 51 is referred to or not, is in fact an act of 'collective self-defence'. Moreover, Article 51 refers to the right of member states acting on their own initiative under the guise of self-defence and there is nothing in the Charter imposing upon the Council an obligation to justify its own decisions in accordance with this Article. As to the right of a state, e.g., Iran in the Gulf War, to declare itself neutral, it is submitted that this possibility only exists to the extent that those involved in carrying out the enforcement measures are prepared to accept such an attitude.

Dr. Gioia suggests that in the absence of a Council resolution, states are able to decide whether they will apply the full rigours of neutrality or claim a status of 'non-belligerency' deviating to some extent from the traditional role of a neutral, though this may result in the state discriminated against regarding the *soi-disant* non-belligerent as an ally of its adverse party. It is submitted, however, that since the Briand-Kellogg Pact and the interpretation thereof by the Nuremberg Tribunal it may be argued that states are more or less expected to adopt such a policy of benevolence towards the victim of an aggressive attack. Today, should there be a decision by the Council and a member wishes merely to stand aside from active enforcement while participating in some measure of economic blockade, the difference between 'neutrality' and 'non-belligerency' – or to use another nomenclature 'benevolent neutrality' – becomes somewhat semantic.

In the event of an armed conflict occurring and the Security Council not making a definitive finding as to the party responsible for the breach of the peace or calling upon member states to adopt a policy of absolute non-intervention, economic or otherwise, members would remain entitled to adopt a policy of strict neutrality, to trade with both belligerents on equal terms, to continue to favour one party as if peace still prevailed, or to make a unilateral decision as to the identity of the aggressor and to assist the victim. Theoretically, at least, there remains the possibility that at some time the Council or *opinio juris* might *ex post facto* define an aggressor and conclude that the act of a discriminating non-party was in breach of the traditional law of neutrality or was incompatible with obligations under the Briand-Kellogg Pact, in which case the party aggrieved might seek some judicial or other remedy.

Andrea Gioia suggests that the right of self-defence may only be exercised against the aggressor, so that 'neutral' rights cannot be claimed by the victim against third states. It is submitted, however, that this is incompatible with the Briand-Kellogg Pact and the Charter, and ignores the reality that 'self-defence' will almost always involve a claim to be entitled to inhibit any action by any third state which might assist the aggressor. It follows, therefore, that the state resorting to legitimate self-defence must be able to claim from third states the obligation to remain neutral or to exercise benevolent neutrality on its behalf. Moreover, in practice it is likely that the Security Council will have been called upon to decide whether there has been a legitimate resort to self-defence under Article 51, in which case the obligations of non-belligerents are those normally consequent upon such a Council decision.

As regards Andrea Gioia's comments referring to particular treaty obligations banning certain weapons or resolutions forbidding their supply to parties to a conflict, these may be regarded as part of the *lex specialis* and would clearly override any provisions in the *lex generalis* of neutrality. Should any such provision harden into customary international law it will of necessity itself become part of the law of neutrality merely extending the obligations borne by a neutral.

It is always dangerous to draw general conclusions from isolated acts which might not be in accordance with traditionally accepted law. There is some doubt in fact whether neutral warships do have a right to convoy neutral merchant ships to evade their being subjected to visit and search by parties to a conflict. That this was successful during the Iran-Iraq war does not in fact mean that 'under modern international law, belligerents cannot attack vessels travelling under 'non-belligerent' convoy,' even though it may suggest that this will serve as a precedent for the future when some non-belligerents are powerful enough to ensure that the belligerents find it advisable to acquiesce in such activities. It may thus be considered as customary law *in nascendi*.

This commentator finds it difficult to apply the provisions of Article 2(4) of the Charter and even less so of Article 3(d) of the non-binding definition of aggression, both of which are directed at states, as applying to the Security Council. If the Security Council decides on action in accordance with Article 41 of the Charter, it is submitted that measures amounting to a blockade against a state condemned by the Council are certainly justifiable. Moreover, in accordance with the World Court's Provisional Measures Order in the Lockerbie case[3] there is no judicial body able to rule upon the lawfulness of Security Council decisions. Nor is it possible to agree with the suggestion, particularly in the light of practice, that the Council is unable to 'delegate' its powers of enforcement to individual members whether by calling upon them by name or, as in the Gulf War, authorizing such measures as are necess-

3   *Ibid.*

ary to ensure compliance with Council decisions, and this is so regardless of the relevance of Article 51.

While it may appear to be a strict interpretation of the Charter to suggest that 'it would be very difficult to admit that belligerents could enforce a blockade in situations where economic sanctions have not been recommended or decided by the Security Council and, even more so, where the distinction between aggressor and victim remains unclear', in practice it remains true that, as may be seen from the United States 'quarantine' against Cuba, whether such a blockade may be established and enforced or not will depend entirely on the strength of the blockading power and the compliance of third states.

Since international law, including the law of armed conflict, is essentially the product of state practice, the tendency to 'comply' with such things as 'long-distance blockades', extensive and somewhat non-traditional lists of contraband, the proclamation of exclusion zones and similar departures from the formerly accepted law of neutrality suggests that what used to be the customary law has given way to a new neutrality regime wherein the rights of neutrals are determined primarily by the extent to which the belligerents are prepared to recognize them.

Andrea Gioia points out that the traditional means of replying to unlawful breaches of neutrality was by a declaration of war or reprisals. As he indicates, today war may only, subject to arguments relating to preventive or anticipatory action, be declared against an unlawful attacker, but is it not a little dogmatic to suggest that reprisals by way of armed force within the meaning of Article 2(4) are forbidden? Perhaps if the use of force is clearly proportionate to the wrongful act by or against the alleged neutral, and not directed against the state's territorial integrity or political independence, it would not be in breach of the Charter or an unlawful reprisal.

Since the law of neutrality involves *ipso facto* some interference with the non-participant's legitimate rights, it is difficult to accept Andrea Gioia's argument that if the reprisals taken against third states as a response to the enemy's prior resort to similar measures involve direct, as distinct from incidental violations of the rights of such states they are 'always considered unlawful'. Nor is it easy to accept the contention that economic 'reprisals cannot be taken against 'non-belligerent' States for the mere fact that their conduct is not in keeping with traditional rules of abstention, prevention or non-discrimination, *for the simple reason that those duties are not binding upon them*'. One is inclined to ask 'why not', and by what rule of law, other than the Briand-Kellogg Pact or the Charter, or by seeking to invoke some so-called obligation arising from the General Assembly's definition of aggression, is a belligerent expected to acquiesce in this one-sidedness? After all, even he recognizes that 'where a 'non-belligerent' State supplies a belligerent with arms or war materials, or where it grants it loans or subsidies, the aggrieved belligerent may perceive such behaviour as amounting to complicity with the aggressor', as in normal circumstances he is fully entitled to do, especially in the absence of any decision of the Security Council under Chapter VII.

In view of what has been suggested above that the recent practice of states, accompanied by the general acquiescence in such practices by third states may be responsible for the development of a customary law of neutrality more in keeping with current needs than was the traditional law, it does not mean that the law of neutrality or concerning the rights of 'non-belligerent' states has been superseded. It merely means that when looking at the law of neutrality today attention must be paid to the actual practice of the most powerful belligerent powers, for they will determine how far non-participants are permitted to continue trading with an adverse party. Regard must equally be accorded to the extent that those non-participants submit to or fail to protest such claims. On the basis of such practice and acquiescence will rest the modern law of economic warfare in so far as it relates to neutrality and non-belligerency. The fact that some non-participants protest, or are temporarily excluded from the full effect of such practices, does not alter this contention. Similarly, it should not be forgotten that when the Security Council condemns 'attacks on neutral and 'non-belligerent' shipping by both belligerents', such condemnation is only possible because it has been decided upon by the most powerful members of the United Nations determined in the particular circumstances not to tolerate any interference with their shipping or that of states upon which their own economies depend.

COMMENTS

Ove Bring[*]

Andrea Gioia's Report is extremely useful and I have no objections to his conclusions on the law of neutrality. The remarks I would like to make relate to his treatment of the law of the UN Charter.

Dr. Gioia 'shares the view' that a resolution of the Security Council authorizing the use of force on the part of individual member states, leaving such states in command of military operations, 'would be illegitimate unless it could be properly placed in the context of Article 51 of the Charter, dealing with individual and collective self-defence' (p. 73). I do not agree with this statement. With regard to the latest Gulf War and Security Council Resolution 678 on the liberation of Kuwait, the following should be said:

Although no specific provision in the Charter could be referred to as the basis for Resolution 678, that does not imply that the Security Council was wrong in referring to Chapter VII in general as the legal ground for its mandate to authorize the use of force. It is true that no agreements with Member States have been concluded on the scope of military contributions (as provided for in Article 43), but this should not prevent the Security Council from taking decisions to fulfil its 'primary responsibility for the maintenance of international peace and security' (as provided for in Article 24). It is also true that the command of the coalition forces was not under UN leadership (as foreseen by Article 42), but the Council must be free to look for politically realistic solutions in fulfilling its primary duty to uphold the principle of collective security.

The fact that, in practice, the United Nations is finding new avenues and procedures which differ from those which were envisaged in 1945 does not in itself mean that such innovations are unlawful or inappropriate. The parties to a multilateral treaty regime (like the UN Charter) can develop and amend it informally by instituting new practices which become generally accepted. During the Korean War the Acheson Plan, adopted by the General Assembly as the 'Uniting for Peace' resolution, extended the authority of the General Assembly, contrary to the wording of Article 11 of the Charter. At the time, this was regarded as a *de facto* revision of

[*] Dr. O.E. Bring is Special Legal Adviser, Ministry for Foreign Affairs, Stockholm.

the Charter. In November 1950, the Swedish Foreign Minister, Mr Undon, declared in the United Nations that the adoption of the Acheson Plan should be seen as 'a happy circumstance for our organization, whose Charter, in common with every other written constitution, should be developed organically so as not to become a dead letter'. The late Secretary-General Dag Hammarskjöld considered that the Acheson Plan was a deviation from the letter of the Charter, but not from its spirit.

In the same way, today, with Resolution 678 in mind, we can speak of an innovation within the spirit of the Charter, a new supplementary procedure adapted to current political realities, which does not exclude the possibility that the procedure prescribed in the Charter can still be applied at a later date. The procedure which was introduced during the Gulf war is clearly regarded as lawful by a majority of the member states of the United Nations and this gives it *de facto* legitimacy as an extension of the Charter (perhaps a new Article 41 1/2).

Andrea Gioia asserts that inasmuch 'as states do not have a duty to join in military operations undertaken or 'authorized' by the United Nations, they are free to declare themselves neutral and to end their neutral status'. I do not agree with this statement. Article 2(5) of the UN Charter has the following wording:

'5.   All Members shall give the United Nations every assistance in any action it takes in accordance with the present Charter, and shall refrain from giving assistance to any state against which the United Nations is taking preventive or enforcement action.'

Against this normative background and considering the Security Council's decisions on economic and other sanctions against Saddam Hussein's Iraq, Iran had no right to declare itself neutral during the Gulf war (as Gioia seems to imply). After the coalition legitimized by the UN started its air operations against Iraq, the Swedish Foreign Minister, Mr Andersson, made clear that although Sweden was a non-belligerent in the conflict, 'we are not neutral'. The UN Charter prevailed over the Swedish policy of neutrality.

COMMENTS

Dietrich Schindler[*]

Dr. Gioia's paper gives an excellent interpretation of the present-day situation of neutrality and non-belligerency in international law. I will not comment on any details of it but rather raise a more general question: Is it correct and appropriate to maintain the sharp distinction between neutrality and non-belligerency as it is made in the title of Andrea Gioia's report? I believe that this distinction has lost much of its importance. I may note first that the use of the term 'non-belligerency' seems rather unfortunate to me in present-day circumstances. This term was used in World War II for States which assisted a belligerent by supplying him with war materials or by placing military bases at his disposal. Non-belligerency often was the first step in entering the war. It was qualified as a violation of the law of neutrality. Another term, used in the period of the League of Nations, the term 'qualified' or 'differential' neutrality, would correspond better with the present-day situation. It was used for States which, while refraining from taking part in military operations, applied economic sanctions against a State which had resorted to war in disregard of the League Covenant. All members of the League, including Switzerland, were automatically bound by the Covenant to apply sanctions against any aggressor. No particular decision by the League Council was required therefore. Absolute neutrality was not admissible under the Covenant. In the years immediately preceding World War II several European neutrals, especially Switzerland and the Nordic States, returned to absolute or integral neutrality, thereby excluding participation in sanctions. After World War II, however, absolute neutrality was no longer practised by any States except a few European neutrals, particularly Switzerland and Austria. Andrea Gioia points to States which at the occasion of specific armed conflicts since 1945 declared that they would remain neutral. I doubt, however, that any of these States had the intention to become thereby bound by the law of neutrality. Their behaviour rather permits to think that they simply wanted to state that, for the time being, they would not assist either side. They hardly ever referred to the law of neutrality. Most States considered the law of neutrality as having become irrelevant.

---

[*]   Dr. D. Schindler is Professor Emeritus of Law at the University of Zürich.

Even the newly independent States which adopted an attitude of non-alignment did not show any interest in it. When Laos in 1962 and Malta in 1980 assumed a status of permanent neutrality no reference was made to the law of neutrality.

It was only the first Gulf War which gave rise to a new interest in the law of neutrality. But this interest was restricted to neutrality in naval warfare. It became apparent that neutrality in naval warfare forms a part of international law which is largely independent of the rest of the law of neutrality. It had historically developed earlier than the other parts of that law. Belligerent States which interfered with the commerce of non-belligerents in former centuries distinguished between enemy and non-belligerent ships and goods but - apart from particular treaty relations - not between different categories of non-belligerents. It therefore seems quite natural that belligerent restrictions on neutral trade since World War II were also applied to 'neutrals' and 'non-belligerents' alike. This was the practice with regard to the Egyptian belligerent measures in the Arab-Israeli War and again in the first Gulf War. It appears that some parts of the law of neutrality, especially the duties of acquiescence and the so-called rights of neutrals, apply to all non-belligerents without regard to whether or not these States comply with all the duties of neutrals according to the classical law of neutrality. It will have to be examined more closely whether all the rules of neutrality in naval war fall into this category.

Neutrality in its strict sense - as practiced so far by Switzerland and Austria - has not experienced any revival as a consequence of the new interest in neutrality in sea warfare. On the contrary, the permanently neutral States of Europe, in view of their probable adherence to the European Community, are on the way to reduce their neutrality to a pure non-participation in armed conflicts. A study group instituted by the Swiss government proposed last year to reduce Swiss neutrality to its military core, *i.e.* to non-participation in armed conflicts. That would mean that Switzerland would henceforth take part in economic sanctions against aggressors. The Swiss government has already acted in that way by participating in all the economic sanctions adopted by the Security Council since 1990. All the neutrals joining the EC will almost inevitably restrict their neutrality to a pure non-participation in armed conflicts and in military alliances. Neutrality thus seems to become more and more identical with 'non-belligerency'. Some of the rules of the law of neutrality will remain applicable to all States not party to an armed conflict while others seem to lose - or have already lost - their binding force. International lawyers should therefore turn to the question of what rules apply to all States not participating in armed conflicts rather than to the vanishing distinction between 'neutrals' and non-belligerents'. This does not preclude the possible development of new duties of abstention, especially with regard to the delivery of war materials, for all non-belligerent States, as Andrea Gioia suggests. States will also have the possibility to maintain or develop individual policies of neutrality, as they have done in the past, but this will not be a question of the law of neutrality, but an aspect of foreign policy.

THE USE OF ECONOMIC SANCTIONS BY
THE UN SECURITY COUNCIL:
AN INTERNATIONAL LAW PERSPECTIVE

Nico Schrijver*

If any Member of the League breaks or ignores these promises with regard to arbitration and discussions, what happens, War? No, not War but something more tremendous than war. Apply this economic, peaceful, silent, deadly remedy and there will be no need for force. The boycott is what is substituted for war. A nation that is boycotted is a nation that is in sight of surrender.

President Woodrow Wilson, 1919.

INTRODUCTION

At 1 January 1994, there were eight cases of collective sanctions against Iraq, Libya, Somalia, South Africa, former Yugoslavia (especially Serbia and Montenegro), Liberia, Haiti and the territory of Angola not controlled by its Government but by UNITA. Prior to August 1990, the Security Council had imposed sanctions only twice, against Southern Rhodesia (1966-79) and South Africa (from 1977 onwards). The sanctions in these nine cases vary widely in scope and actual purpose. As regards the scope, they range from mere arms embargoes (South Africa 1977, former Yugoslavia 1991, Somalia 1992, Liberia 1992), through an arms and air embargo (Libya, 1992) and an arms and oil embargo (Haiti 1993, UNITA/Angola 1993), to comprehensive packages of economic and financial sanctions (Iraq 1990, rump Yugoslavia 1992). Some of these sanctions are (were) meant as an alternative to war, most notably in the initial phase of the Kuwait crisis and in the Libyan case. In the

* Dr. N.J. Schrijver is Senior Lecturer in International Law and International Institutions at the Institute of Social Studies, The Hague. In 1990-91, he served as Legal Officer in the Office of the Legal Counsel, Office of Legal Affairs, United Nations, New York. The research for this report was completed in January 1994. The author gratefully acknowledges the useful comments and helpful suggestions made by Vera Gowlland-Debbas (special commentator on this chapter), Karin Arts, Hans-Peter Gasser, Joann Hinrichs, Johan Kaufmann, Karel Wellens as well as the editor of this volume.

H.H.G. Post (ed.), International Economic Law and Armed Conflict, 123–161.
© 1994 *Martinus Nijhoff Publishers. Printed in the Netherlands.*

Yugoslavian, Somalian, Liberian, Haitian and Angolan cases the sanctions are meant to pressurize (factions of) the governments concerned, or (irregular) entities within a State's territory, to stop violent action. The sanctions against Southern Rhodesia and South Africa had the ambitious goal of contributing to the dismantling of the white minority régime and the apartheid régime, respectively, and thus to changing the status quo in these countries. Consequently, some sanctions are peace time instruments and belong to the *jus pacis*, while others are employed during armed conflict.

Collective sanctions involve far-reaching reactions of the international community against unlawful or unacceptable behaviour of States in international relations. Though they aim to obtain compliance with international obligations, they cannot but override other principles and rules of international law such as non-interference in internal affairs, sovereignty, the duty to co-operate, non-discrimination and freedom of trade and navigation. The 1992 Libya-Lockerbie case demonstrated the scope of the Security Council's discretion in determining the policy goals for which sanctions can be used.[1] This raises important questions as to the legal status and legal effects of Security Council resolutions, a discussion to which the International Court of Justice made an important contribution in both its 1971 Namibia advisory opinion and its order made in the Libya-Lockerbie case on 14 April 1992.[2]

These and other issues relating to collective sanctions are discussed in this report. The first part is devoted to some general issues, including terminology, background and the constitutional framework for economic sanctions under the UN Charter. The second part reviews the practice of the UN Security Council with respect to imposing economic sanctions. Nine cases are discussed.[3] In the third part these nine cases are compared by examining such issues as the legal foundation, objectives, scope, addressees and implementation of the sanctions. An assessment and comparison of their effectiveness would be beyond the limits of this paper.[4] Finally, some comparative and more general conclusions are drawn.

---

1   See for critical comments Th. M. Franck, 'The Powers of 'Appreciation': Who is the Ultimate Guardian of UN Legality?', in 86 *AJIL* (1992), pp. 519-523 and P.H. Kooijmans, 'Zwijgt het recht als de Veiligheidsraad spreekt?', in *Nederlands Juristenblad*, No. 27, 16 July 1992, pp. 847-851.
2   *Cf. ICJ Reports 1971*, pp. 51-53 and *ICJ Reports 1992*, pp. 123-126.
3   See for a survey of these nine cases the Appendix.
4   There is a wealth of literature on this issue. For a review and analysis, P.A.G. van Bergeijk, *Economic Diplomacy, Trade and Commercial Policy: Positive and Negative Sanctions in a New World Order*, Edward Elgar: Cheltenham, 1994. See also R.H. Dehejia and B. Wood, 'Economic Sanctions and Econometric Policy Evaluation: A Cautionary Note', in 26 *Journal of World Trade* (1992), pp. 73-84.

I. BACKGROUND AND CONSTITUTIONAL FRAMEWORK

1. Concept and Possible Functions of Collective Sanctions

The use of economic sanctions to achieve political ends is not new. Throughout history, States have often resorted to economic sanctions for a wide variety of reasons. In ancient Greece, Athens instituted sanctions against Megara because of the latter's expansionist policy and kidnapping of three women. In the 20th century, Hufbauer *et al.* identified as many as 116 cases[5] which indicate the widespread use of unilateral sanctions, counter-measures, reprisals and retorsions in international relations.[6]

Relatively new, however, is the concept of collective sanctions which for the purposes of this chapter can be defined as collective measures imposed by organs representing the international community, in response to perceived unlawful or unacceptable conduct by one of its members and meant to uphold standards of behaviour required by international law. This concept of collective sanctions is closely linked to schemes for collective security and measures for the prevention or containment of armed conflicts as well as the enforcement of international law. These issues lie at the heart of the debate on the effectiveness of the United Nations system and of international law.[7]

The phrase 'collective sanctions' as such has not (yet) a well-defined status in international law. On various occasions, the International Law Commission (ILC) examined the question of sanctions when discussing its Draft Articles on State Responsibility. In 1979 the Commission rejected Professor Ago's proposal to declare in Draft Article 30, which deals with counter-measures with respect to an internationally wrongful act, that the wrongfulness of an international act is precluded when it is committed 'as the legitimate application of a sanction...in consequence of an internationally wrongful act'.[8] Several members of the Commission objected to the use of the word 'sanction'. Ultimately, Ago recommended the term 'counter-

---

5   G.C. Hufbauer, J.J. Schott, and K.A. Elliott, *Economic Sanctions Reconsidered: History and Current Policy*, 2nd. ed., two vols., Washington DC 1990. See also Lisa L. Martin, *Coercive Cooperation. Explaining Multilateral Economic Sanctions*, Princeton 1992.
6   Recent examples include sanctions by the United States and members of the European Community against Iran during the hostage crisis in 1980, against the USSR in the aftermath of the Soviet invasion in Afghanistan in 1980, and by the United States against the European Community in 1992 to press the latter to accept reform of its agricultural policy during the GATT Uruguay Round.
7   *Cf. Oppenheim's International Law*, ed. by Sir Robert Jennings & Sir Arthur Watts, vol. I PEACE, 9th. ed., Dordrecht 1992, pp. 10-11 and Oscar Schachter, *International Law in Theory and Practice*, Dordrecht 1991, Chapter XI.
8   *Yearbook International Law Commission 1979*, vol. II (Part One), pp. 39-47.

measures' instead of 'sanctions'.[9] Draft Article 30 now reads as follows: 'The wrongfulness of an act of a State not in conformity with an obligation of that State towards another State is precluded if the act constitutes a measure legitimate under international law against that other State, in consequence of an internationally wrongful act of that other State.' One may thus conclude that in principle collective sanctions imposed by the UN Security Council are subsumed in the word 'counter-measures' as in the heading of Draft Article 30 and in the word 'measure' as used in its text. Furthermore, from the ILC's commentary it also follows that there is a clear link between collective sanctions as a ground for the legitimate application of countermeasures and Draft Article 19 which deals with 'international crimes and international delicts'. In this connection, the ILC pointed out that sanctions were to be considered as:

'reactive measures applied by virtue of a decision taken by an international organization following a breach of an international obligation having serious consequences for the international community as a whole, and in particular for certain measures which the United Nations is empowered to adopt, under the system established by the Charter, with a view to the maintenance of international peace and security.'[10]

The Commission defined counter-measures as 'measures the object of which is...to inflict punishment or to secure performance – measures which, under different conditions, would infringe a valid and subjective right of the subject against which the measures are applied'.[11]

Collective sanctions can be adopted to serve a variety of functions. As with 'punishment' in national criminal law, one can distinguish two main functions of such sanctions: (a) a form of punishment and retaliation for unlawful or unacceptable behaviour; and (b) a method of persuading or forcing a change of policy. They can also have the additional function of deterrence and dissuasion as well as expressing strong condemnation.

2. The League of Nations

The Covenant of the League of Nations (1918) included an article relating to collective measures of an economic or military nature. Had any Member of the

---

9   Cf. O.Y. Elagab, *The Legality of Non-Forcible Counter-Measures in International Law*, Oxford 1988, pp. 2-5 and 84-85.

10   *Yearbook of the International Law Commission 1979*, vol. II (Part Two), p. 121.

11   *Ibid.*, p. 116.

League resorted to war in violation of its international obligations, the Covenant provided that the aggressor State would be immediately subjected to, among other measures, 'the severance of all trade or financial relations' (Article 16).[12] In the 1920s, the League successfully used the threat of sanctions against Yugoslavia should it remain unwilling to withdraw its troops from disputed territory in Albania. Similarly, Greece was compelled to renounce territorial claims on Bulgarian territory. The Chaco War between Paraguay and Bolivia (1928-38) led the Council to adopt a recommendation for an embargo on the sale of arms to both sides. But only Mussolini's military attack on and subsequent conquest of Abyssinia in October 1935 gave rise to the mobilization of the machinery of Article 16. The League instituted economic sanctions against Italy including an arms embargo, a restriction on financial dealings with the Italian government and private enterprises, the prohibition of most imports from Italy, and a ban on the exportation of mules (sic!), rubber and important minerals.[13] However, the sanctions were not mandatory and did *not* include what might have been really effective: an oil embargo and an interruption of communications, including a closure of the Suez Canal and an air embargo in North Eastern Africa. While some 50 League members joined the sanctions, some important non-member States did not, including the United States. Moreover, France and the United Kingdom adopted a half-hearted attitude towards Italy and the League's sanctions, arguing that they did not want to drive Mussolini into Hitler's arms and subsequently to war with themselves. As early as June 1936, Chamberlain reportedly declared as the 'very midsummer of madness'[14] the idea that continuation of sanctions would save Ethiopia. Consequently, the sanctions against Italy were not very effective and were lifted in July 1936.

Yet, the sanctions against Italy were the first and the last attempt to enforce the rules of the League against a major power. After Japan attacked China in Manchuria, Japan itself could veto a resolution calling for a cease-fire and the League's Council took no further action beyond the sending of a commission of enquiry. Similarly, the League remained passive *vis-à-vis* the German re-armament and reoccupation of the Rhineland (1936) in violation of the Treaty of Versailles and the Locarno Treaties, as well as towards the annexation of Austria (1938) and invasion of other countries in the late 1930s. These failures to respond to serious breaches of the Covenant of

---

12 See on the drafting and 'parliamentary' history of Article 16, Sir Anton Bertram, 'The Economic Weapon as a Form of Peaceful Pressure', in *Transactions of the Grotius Society*, vol. 17 (1932), pp. 139-174.
13 For a review see Margaret Doxey, *International Sanctions in Contemporary Perspective*, London 1987, Chapter 3.
14 Doxey, *ibid.*, p. 27.

the League of Nations undoubtedly contributed to its withering away as a force in international politics.[15]

3. The Charter of the United Nations

The Charter of the United Nations built on the League's Article 16[16] and provided a more elaborate and centralized system of collective measures in Chapter VII, including measures not involving the use of armed force (Art. 41) and – as *ultimum remedium* – military action (Art. 42). In order to be able to take measures under Article 41, the Security Council is firstly, under Article 39, required to determine 'the existence of any threat to the peace, breach of the peace or act of aggression'. The Council can either recommend or command collective measures under Chapter VII. Article 41 provides that such measures may include 'complete or partial interruption of economic relations and of rail, sea, air, postal, telegraphic, radio, and other means of communication, and the severance of diplomatic relations'. Before resorting to sanctions and enforcement action, the Council can call upon the parties to comply with provisional measures such as a cease-fire and negotiations between the parties (Art. 40).

In empowering the Security Council to command collective economic sanctions and to take military enforcement measures which all members are obligated to accept and to carry out, the Charter has gone far beyond the system of the League Covenant.

While Article 41 is often associated with economic sanctions only, its actual scope is obviously wider. Apart from *economic measures*, it may also include restriction or complete interruption of *communications*, as detailed in Article 41 itself; of *cultural exchanges* such as academic exchanges and sporting links; and severance of *diplomatic and political relations, e.g.* cancellation of official visits, suspension of negotiations on treaties and reduction of level and scale of diplomatic representation. As can be inferred from its text ('may include'), the list of sanctions in Article 41 is not meant to be exhaustive. Moreover, all of them may, but need not be, resorted to. Thus, the Security Council has a wide discretion.

Economic sanctions can amount to a wide-ranging package[17] which may include the following:

---

15 *Cf.* F.P. Walters, *A History of the League of Nations*, 1952, vol. II; G. Scott, *The Rise and Fall of the League of Nations*, 1974.

16 *Cf.* P.M. Eisemann, 'Article 41', in J.P. Cot et A. Pellet (ed.), *La Charte des Nations Unies. Commentaire article par article*, 2e éd., Paris 1991, pp. 691-704.

17 Doxey identifies an extensive list of financial, commercial and technical measures. *Supra* note 13, pp. 11-12.

- partial or complete embargo on imports;
- partial or complete embargo on exports;
- denial of most-favoured nation treatment and suspension or cancellation of trade agreements;
- reduction or suspension of technical assistance programmes in the context of international institutions;
- complete or selective blocking of transportation;
- ban on credit facilities, interest payments and other transfer payments;
- ban on any capital movements;
- no international funding of any assistance programmes and no rescheduling of debt repayments;
- freezing or confiscation of financial assets of the target State.

II. PRACTICE OF THE UN SECURITY COUNCIL UNDER ARTICLE 41

4. Practice of the Security Council under Chapter VII Prior to August 1990

Until August 1990, the use of collective economic sanctions was limited. In debates by the Security Council there was frequent speculation, quite often after repeated urging by the UN General Assembly, over the imposition of economic sanctions, for example against Spain in 1946, against Belgium in 1961, against South Africa in 1963, and against Portugal in 1965. It was, however, only in 1966 that the Security Council used its power under Article 41 for the first time, namely in the Southern Rhodesian case.

Southern Rhodesia.[18] After the white minority régime of Ian Smith proclaimed the Unilateral Declaration of Independence (UDI) on 11 November 1965, the Security Council met in a series of emergency sessions. As early as 12 November, the Council condemned this declaration and called on all States not to recognize 'this illegal racist minority régime in Southern Rhodesia and to refrain from rendering any assistance to this illegal régime' (S/RES/216, 1965). Eight days later the Council adopted a further resolution (S/RES/217, 1965) in which it hinted for the first time at measures under Chapter VII: it determined that 'the situation resulting from the proclamation of independence by the illegal authorities in Southern Rhodesia is extremely grave' and that 'its continuance in time constitutes a threat to international peace and security'. All States were called upon not to entertain economic relations

---

18 See on this case Ralph Zacklin, *The United Nations and Rhodesia. A Study in International Law*, New York 1974; P.J. Kuyper, *The Implementation of International Sanctions. The Netherlands and Rhodesia*, Alphen aan den Rijn 1978; Vera Gowlland-Debbas, *Collective Responses to Illegal Acts in International Law. United Nations Action in the Question of Southern Rhodesia*, Dordrecht 1990.

with Southern Rhodesia, in particular not to deliver any arms, oil and petroleum products to the Smith régime. Legally, Rhodesia was (and remained till 1979) a self-governing colony of the United Kingdom. In 1965, the United Kingdom and 28 other member States imposed sanctions against Southern Rhodesia. In its Resolution 217(1965) the Council called on the United Kingdom, the former colonial power, to 'quell this rebellion of the racist minority' and to take all appropriate measures to bring it to 'an immediate end', thus opening the possibility of the use of force if necessary. On 9 April 1966, the Security Council reaffirmed the voluntary arms and oil embargo and expressed grave concern about the impendent delivery of substantial supplies of oil by the tanker the Joanna V through Beira to Southern Rhodesia. It led to a very remarkable resolution: S/RES/221(1966).[19] The Council determined that the situation resulting from such oil deliveries constituted 'a threat to the peace', and called upon the Portuguese Government not to pump or receive oil destined for Southern Rhodesia at Beira, and upon the United Kingdom 'to prevent, by the use of force if necessary, the arrival at Beira of vessels reasonably believed to be carrying oil destined for Southern Rhodesia'. While there was only a voluntary arms and oil embargo in place, the Council thus authorized a particular member State to enforce its implementation on the high seas, if necessary by the use of armed force.

Only eight months later, the Council labelled the situation in Rhodesia 'a threat to international peace and security' and imposed selective mandatory economic sanctions against the illegal minority-régime in Southern Rhodesia (S/RES/232, 1966). In doing so, the Council explicitly referred to Articles 39 and 41. In 1968, the Security Council finally launched a fully-fledged trade and financial embargo and severance of diplomatic relations, with exceptions provided for medical supplies, educational materials and, in special humanitarian circumstances, foodstuffs (S/RES/253, 1968). Moreover, the Council established a monitoring committee, commonly known as the 'Watchdog Committee', to supervise the implementation of the sanctions. On various occasions the sanctions were refined.[20] Yet, these measures did not result in a complete end to all trade with the illegal régime. It proved to be difficult indeed to fully control the activities of multinational corporations. In addition, Portugal in the initial phase and South Africa throughout the whole period continued intensive trading with Southern Rhodesia despite the sanctions. Other States, including the United States, France and even the United Kingdom itself, did not observe the sanctions as scrupulously as required. The sanctions were maintained up to 1979, when the Lancaster House Agreement led to the long-awaited independence of Zimbabwe on the basis of black majority rule. Sanctions were lifted in Resolution 460 of 21 December 1979.[21]

---

19 For a detailed discussion, see Vera Gowlland-Debbas, *supra* note 18) pp. 400-421.
20 *Cf.* Security Council Resolutions 277(1970), 386(1976) and 409(1977).
21 Adopted by 13 votes to none, with 2 abstentions (Czechoslovakia and USSR).

South Africa. Hardly any other question has caused such heated UN debates as *apartheid* in South Africa. Ever since the Sharpville massacre in 1960 the Council has been gripped by this matter. In Resolution 134(1960) the Council described the situation as 'one that has led to international friction and if continued might endanger international peace and security'. On 7 August 1963, the Council, being convinced that 'the situation in South Africa is seriously disturbing international peace and security', called on all States to observe a voluntary arms embargo, *i.e.* 'to cease forthwith the sale and shipment of arms, ammunition of all types and military vehicles to South Africa' (S/RES/181, 1963). Subsequently, various other resolutions were adopted condemning the apartheid policies and re-affirming the voluntary arms embargo, but it proved to be impossible to go beyond this.

From the mid-1960s onwards the UN General Assembly adopted a series of resolutions on South Africa's apartheid policy, calling it 'a threat to international peace and security'.[22] Conventions were adopted in which the policy of apartheid was labelled as 'a crime against humanity'.[23] There was widespread fear for a racial war in South Africa and there were rumours that South Africa might be capable of 'going nuclear'. Therefore, the Security Council determined that 'the constant build-up of the South African military and police forces' constitutes 'a potential threat to international peace and security' and 'a real threat to the security and sovereignty of independent African States' (S/RES/282, 1970). However, it took another seven years before the Council was willing to determine, explicitly acting under Chapter VII, that 'the acquisition by South Africa of arms and related *matériel* constitutes a threat to the maintenance of international peace and security' (S/RES/418, 4 November 1977).[24] It is striking that the Council did not label the situation itself, but the acquisition of arms, as a threat to peace; this was a compromise proposed by the Indian presidency of the Council in an effort to break the stalemate. It was the second time that the Council had instituted an embargo under Chapter VII, but it was the first time that it was against a member State of the United Nations! The sanctions included a prohibition to deliver arms and other military materials to South Africa as well as a ban on licensing and servicing arrangements for the manufacture and maintenance thereof. In addition, all co-operation with South Africa in the manufacture and development of nuclear weapons was prohibited. By its Resolution 421(1977) the Council established a commission of the Council to monitor the sanctions. Despite repeated proposals from African and other non-aligned countries,

---

22 See for example GA Res. 2202 (XXI), 3324 E (XXIX) and 37/69 A.

23 *E.g.*, the 1965 Convention of all Forms of Racial Discrimination and the 1973 Convention on the Suppression and Punishment of the Crime of Apartheid. *Cf.* K.C. Wellens, '*Apartheid*, an international crime', in L. Heyde *et al.*, *Begrensde Vrijheid* (Liber Scheltens), Zwolle 1989, pp. 288-311.

24 The negotiations leading to this Security Council resolution have been described in Johan Kaufmann, *United Nations Decision-making*, Dordrecht 1980, pp. 46-49.

the Council could never agree on extending the range of the mandatory sanctions beyond this arms embargo. By July 1985, the Council was only prepared to encourage UN members to impose voluntary economic sanctions, including a suspension of all new investment in South Africa and prohibition of the sale of krugerrands.[25] Yet, this Resolution was not adopted under Chapter VII: a proposal to that effect was vetoed by the United Kingdom and the United States, with France abstaining. Later proposals faced a similar fate.[26] No doubt this was related to the important economic and business links between South Africa and the Western States, particularly the United States, the United Kingdom and France. Following a Dutch initiative in 1984, the Security Council requested (on a voluntary basis) that States refrain from importing arms, ammunition of all types and military vehicles produced in South Africa; the mandatory arms embargo was thus complemented with a voluntary arms boycott (S/RES/558, 1984). In the context of the UN General Assembly more far-reaching (but voluntary) economic sanctions were imposed, including an oil embargo and trade, financial and investment measures. These were lifted on 8 October 1993, in anticipation of the transition process from apartheid to a non-racial democracy during which apartheid was to be officially dismantled with the first non-racial multiparty elections scheduled for April 1994.[27] The mandatory sanctions relating to arms and nuclear weapons remained in place, pending the formation of a new government after the elections. Yet, opinions differ whether the South African régime experienced any significantly negative effects from these sanctions.[28]

5. The Use of Sanctions during the 1990-1991 Gulf Crisis[29]

Breach of the peace. In the early morning of 2 August 1990, the Security Council met at the urgent request of Kuwait and the United States to discuss the invasion of Kuwait by military forces of Iraq. Within hours, this led to the adoption of

25 *Cf.* S/RES/569(1985), adopted by 13 to none, with 2 abstentions (United Kingdom and United States).
26 *E.g.*, draft resolution contained in *UN Doc.* S/18785. See 'Text calling for comprehensive mandatory sanctions against South Africa vetoed after discussions in eight meetings', in *UN Chronicle*, vol. 24, No. 3, August 1987, pp. 22-25.
27 A/RES/48/1.
28 See W.H. Kaempfer, A.D. Lowenberg, H.N. Mocan and K. Topyan, 'International sanctions and anti-apartheid policies in South Africa: An empirical investigation', in *The Use of Economic Sanctions in Trade and Environmental Policy*, OCfBE, Research Centre for Economic Policy, Erasmus University Rotterdam, Research Memorandum, No. 9307, 1993, pp. 1-36. *Cf.* also Peter A.G. van Bergeijk, *supra* note 4, Hufbauer *et al.*, *supra* note 5, and Doxey, *supra* note 13.
29 This section is based on Nico Schrijver, 'The United Nations and the Use of Sanctions During the Gulf Crisis', in 22 *Georgia Journal of International and Comparative Law* (1992), No.1, pp. 40-53. See also Oscar Schachter, 'United Nations Law in the Gulf Conflict', in 85 *American Journal of International Law* (1991), pp. 452-473, at pp. 454-457.

Resolution 660(1990). The Council immediately used one of the key phrases to open the door to the mandatory Chapter VII, namely that there existed 'a breach of international peace and security'. Acting under Articles 39 and 40, the only occasion during the Gulf crisis on which the Council explicitly indicated the legal foundation of its action, the Council demanded that Iraq withdraw all its forces from Kuwait immediately and unconditionally. It called upon Iraq and Kuwait to begin 'immediately intensive negotiations for the resolution of their differences' and supported all efforts in this regard, especially those of the League of Arab States. However, Iraq was unwilling to comply and the conflict escalated.

Mandatory Sanctions Against Iraq and Occupied Kuwait. On 6 August 1990, only four days after the adoption of Resolution 660(1990), the Security Council determined that Iraq had so far failed to comply with the demands of this resolution. The Council decided thereupon to impose comprehensive economic and financial sanctions against Iraq and occupied Kuwait, which are contained in Resolution 661(1990). It thus applied Article 41, measures not involving the use of force. Never before had the United Nations imposed such far-reaching sanctions against one of its member States. A Sanctions Committee was established to monitor the sanctions régime. The sanctions régime of Resolution 661(1990) has been refined and completed in later resolutions. On 25 August 1990, the Security Council adopted Resolution 665(1990); this called upon member States which were co-operating with the Government of Kuwait and deploying maritime forces to the area to halt maritime shipping in order to ensure strict implementation of the trade embargo contained in Resolution 661(1990). It was understood that, if necessary, a limited use of force would be allowed to intercept the ships. This was the first time, during the Gulf crisis, that the Security Council opened up the option of a limited use of force.

At the initiative of the USSR, the Security Council decided on 25 September 1990 to supplement the trade and financial embargo with a cargo-related air embargo: Resolution 670(1990). This provided, subject to certain exceptions, for States to deny permission to any aircraft to take off from their territory if the aircraft was carrying cargo to or from Iraq or occupied Kuwait. It also provided that overflight countries would have the duty to deny any aircraft destined to land in Iraq or Kuwait permission to fly over their territory, unless (a) the aircraft in question landed at an airfield outside Iraq or Kuwait for inspection, to ensure that there was no cargo on board in violation of the trade embargo; (b) the particular flight had been approved by the Sanctions Committee; or (c) the flight was solely for the purposes of UNIIMOG.[30]

'Use of all necessary means'. By the autumn of 1990, scepticism was growing as to whether the unanimous stand of the world community against the Iraqi

---

30 United Nations Iran-Iraq Military Observer Group.

aggression and the economic sanctions would prove to be sufficient to pressurize the Hussein régime into withdrawing its forces from Kuwait and freeing the hostages held as 'human shields'. It became obvious that in the short run the Iraqi people, rather than the Iraqi régime and army, were being seriously affected by the embargo, especially by the shortage of food and medicine and the loss of income.

In British and American political circles, especially, voices were heard from September 1990 that a military solution of the crisis would be inevitable and that the main questions were when and how. In continental Europe and in Third World countries there was an inclination to maintain the embargo in the expectation that Iraq would finally give in. On 29 November 1990 a compromise was found in the form of Resolution 678(1990) which granted authorization, unless Iraq withdrew from Kuwait on or before 15 January 1991, to 'use all necessary means'. Iraq was thus given a grace period of 47 days. However, the Hussein régime refused to comply: a six weeks modern war ensued, in which the American-led coalition force of 30 countries defeated Iraq in its 'mother of all battles'.

Sanctions continued. After the cease-fire in March 1991, the sanctions remained in force, although those with respect to foodstuffs and supplies for 'essential civilian needs' and financial payments related thereto were relaxed (Resolution 687, 1991). On various occasions the Iraqi Government and members of the Security Council such as Cuba and Yemen claimed that the sanctions should be lifted now that Iraq had withdrawn from Kuwait and had complied with most of the demands contained in Resolution 687. However, in 1991 they agreed on a UN controlled export programme under which Iraq would be allowed to pump and export oil and other States were authorized to import oil and oil products from Iraq up to an amount of 1.6 billion US dollars, each purchase to be approved by the Security Council's Sanctions Committee. Payments for these products would be made to a special account of the United Nations, administered by the UN Secretary-General (S/RES/706 and 712, 1991). Thirty percent of this fund, *i.e.* 480 million US dollars, would be allocated to the UN Compensation Fund to meet claims against Iraq. The remaining part of the money would be used for such varying purposes as payments for food, medicines and supplies to meet essential civilian needs of the Iraqi population; full cost of the UN supervised return of all Kuwaiti property; half of the costs of the Boundary Demarcation Commission; and costs arising from the removal and destruction of Iraqi biological and chemical weapons as well as from inspecting nuclear materials in Iraq. Iraq considered these resolutions and related arrangements as an infringement of its sovereignty and thus as unacceptable: up to the present day (December 1993) it has proved impossible to agree on a modification of the sanctions régime. A majority of the members of the Security Council, including most if not all permanent members, wanted to maintain the sanctions until the time that Iraq had complied with *all* elements of Resolution 687, including the destruction of all its biological and chemical weapons, the return of all Kuwaiti property seized by Iraq and acceptance of the arrangements of the demarcation of the boundary. In the view of the Council only then could peace and security in the region be restored. After intensive informal consultations in November 1992, the President of the Security Council stated that the Council regretted the lack of any indication of how Iraq intends to comply with the resolutions of the Council. It also rejected *in toto* 'the baseless threats, allegations and attacks' of Iraq against the Council, the Special Commission (for the weapons inspection), the IAEA, the Iraq-Kuwait Boundary Demarcation Commission and the Sanctions Committee. Consequently, on 24 November 1992 the Council gave the following verdict: 'In the view of the Security Council, while there have been some positive steps, the Government of Iraq has not yet complied fully and unconditionally with its obligations, must do so and must immediately take the appropriate actions in this regard.'[31] Thus the sanctions régime was fully maintained, a situation which did not change during 1993.

6. Six New Cases of Sanctions by the United Nations

(a) *Yugoslavia*. In July 1991 heavy fighting broke out in various parts of the Republic of Yugoslavia. After violation of various cease-fires and in view of the deteriorating situation, the Security Council decided unanimously on 25 September 1991 that all States should immediately implement a general and complete embargo on all deliveries of weapons and military equipment to Yugoslavia (S/RES/713, 1991). In doing so, the Security Council acceded to a request from the minister of Foreign Affairs of Yugoslavia, the target country of the sanctions. This element is certainly a *novum* in the history of UN sanctions. In the minister's view Yugoslavia was in a serious crisis with itself: 'Yugoslavia can no longer be simply repaired. It should be redefined'.[32] Although in the initial phase the conflict itself was domestic, the Council was very much concerned that the continuation of the fighting would have consequences for the countries of the region, in particular for the border areas of neighbouring countries. The Council, therefore, stated that the continuation of this situation constituted 'a threat to international peace and security'. In adopting the arms embargo by Resolution 713(1991), the Council acted under Chapter VII. Despite intensive mediation by various organizations including the European Community and the United Nations, cease-fires continued to be broken and peace could not be maintained. On 21 February 1992, the Council established a United Nations Protection Force (UNPROFOR), once again through a unanimous vote.[33] On 30 May 1992, the Council took a major step forward with the sanctions régime.

---

31 *UN Doc.* S/24839, 24 November 1992.
32 As quoted in XXVIII *UN Chronicle*, December 1991, No. 4, p. 35.
33 S/RES/743 (1992).

It adopted Resolution 757(1992) by 13 votes to none with two abstentions (China and Zimbabwe), which established wide-ranging sanctions against the Federal Republic of Yugoslavia (Serbia and Montenegro). In this Resolution the Council determined that the situation in Bosnia and Hercegovina and in other parts of the former Socialist Federal Republic constitutes 'a threat to international peace and security'. The sanctions are modelled upon the Rhodesian and Iraqi sanctions but also go beyond these to some extent. They include a full ban on imports from and exports to Yugoslavia (Serbia and Montenegro), a cut-off of financial relations, reduction of diplomatic representation, a suspension of sporting contacts, of scientific and technical co-operation and cultural exchanges. Exemptions are provided for the sale or supply of 'commodities and products for essential humanitarian need'.[34] The Council later also authorized the enforcement of the sanctions at sea (S/RES/787 (1992) of 16 November 1992). In the same vein a Security Council Committee was established to monitor the sanctions régime (Resolution 724, 1991). Faced with continued refusal of the Bosnian Serb party to accept the Vance-Owen peace plan, the Security Council tightened the sanctions régime considerably by way of Resolution 820(1993) of 17 April 1993. Effective as of April 26, 1993, this included the closing of border crossings to and from the areas in Croatia and Bosnia and Hercegovina under control of Bosnian Serb forces, and bringing all transport to and from these areas under the strict control of these two States; preventing diversion of commodities and products to Serbia and Montenegro. It also included close monitoring of all river traffic along the Danube; prohibition of all commercial maritime traffic, both on the Danube and through the territorial sea; the impounding and detaining of all Yugoslavian vessels, freight vehicles and aircraft, as well as the forfeiture of these means of transportation and of their cargoes in case they were used in violation of the sanctions resolutions. Furthermore, Resolution 820 compelled the freezing of all overseas financial assets of Yugoslavia. The new sanctions régime is the toughest ever adopted by the Security Council.

(b) *Somalia.* In recent years there has been extensive fighting between Somalian war lords, resulting in a collapse of the Somalian administration and in mass migration and starvation of ordinary people. Initially, none of the great powers took a serious interest in these events: in the immediate post-Cold War era the Horn of Africa was no longer an area of very much (strategic) concern. Neither did the Organization of African Unity or the United Nations show much interest. Yet the situation in Somalia culminated in such a drama that no one could claim any longer to be ignorant and indifferent. After the failure of various resolutions calling for a cease-fire and negotiations, the Security Council decided, unanimously and acting

---

34 The exemption clauses of Security Council Resolution 757(1992) are elaborated in Resolution 760 of 18 June 1992.

under Chapter VII, to establish 'a general and complete embargo on all deliveries of weapons and military equipment to Somalia' (S/RES/733, of 23 January 1992). After mediation by the UN Secretary-General's personal envoy to Somalia, James Jonah, a cease-fire was established between the two main fighting parties in Somalia in March 1992. Various reports of the Secretary-General and resolutions followed; a monitoring commission and later a peace-keeping operation (the United Nations Operation in Somalia, UNOSOM) were mounted to observe the cease-fire (S/RES/746 and 775, 1992); other resolutions called for co-operation in facilitating delivery of humanitarian assistance (S/RES/751 and 767, 1992). Yet, when fighting continued at the heavy cost of human life and disintegration of the country, the Security Council on 3 December 1992 authorized the Secretary-General and member States 'to use all necessary means to establish as soon as possible a secure environment for humanitarian relief operations in Somalia' (S/RES/794, 1992). This resulted in a military operation under the unified command of the United States (Unified Task Force, UNITAF) with contingents from, among other countries, the United States, the United Kingdom, France, Belgium, Egypt and Pakistan. It is interesting that Resolution 794(1992) also contains a particular clause relating to the enforcement of the arms embargo:

'[The Security Council, ...]
Acting under Chapters VII and VIII of the Charter, *calls upon* States, nationally or through regional agencies or arrangements, to use such measures as may be necessary to ensure strict implementation of paragraph 5 of resolution 733 (1992).'

By Resolution 814(1993), the Security Council aimed at regulating the phased take-over of UNITAF by an expanded UNOSOM, UNOSOM II, the first UN-peace-keeping operation authorized to use force under the collective security provisions of Chapter VII of the UN Charter. Apart from 'the facilitation of humanitarian assistance and the restoration of law and order, and of national reconciliation in a free and democratic and sovereign Somalia', UNOSOM II's mandate came to include the implementation of the arms embargo within Somalia.[35]

(c) *Libya*. After intensive investigations the Lord Advocate of Scotland and the US District Court for the District of Columbia brought charges against two Libyan nationals for their alleged involvement in the bombing of Pan Am flight 103 on 21 December 1988 over Lockerbie, Scotland. This crash resulted in 270 deaths; among them the UN Commissioner for Namibia, Berndt Carlsson. In addition, France

---

35 See paragraph 10 of Resolution 814, unanimously adopted on 26 March 1993. See also Resolution 856(1993) of 22 September 1993 (also unanimously adopted).

accused Libya of involvement in the crash of Union de transports aériens (UTA) Flight 772 above the Sahara on 19 September 1989, which resulted in 160 deaths. The United Kingdom and the United States demanded that Libya surrender its two nationals so that the suspects could be brought to trial in the places where the charges were brought against them. Libya refused to comply, since constitutional provisions prevented it from handing over Libyan citizens in the absence of an extradition treaty. At this point, the two Western countries brought the case before the Security Council which unanimously adopted Resolution 731 on 21 January 1992. In this resolution the Council condemned the destruction of the two civilian aircraft and the resultant losses of human lives. It also strongly deplored the fact that Libya had not responded to requests for co-operation in establishing responsibility for those 'terrorist acts'. Therefore, the Council urged Libya to provide immediately 'a full and effective response to those requests so as to contribute to the elimination of international terrorism'. On 3 March 1992, Libya took a challenging counter-offensive: at the International Court of Justice it instituted separate proceedings against the United Kingdom and the United States since the latter two countries had rejected Libya's efforts 'to resolve the matter within the framework of international law', including the 1971 Montreal Convention for the Suppression of Unlawful Acts Against the Safety of Civil Aviation. Libya also requested provisional measures under Article 41 of the Court's Statute in order to protect Libya against the 'immense pressure' by the United Kingdom and the United States, including the threat to use force, to surrender its two nationals. From 26 to 28 March 1992, the Court organized public hearings between the parties with respect to Libya's request for provisional measures. While the Court was considering its decision on this matter, the Security Council took further action by adopting Resolution 748 on 31 March 1992. In this resolution the Council 'reaffirms that, in accordance with the principle in Article 2, paragraph 4, of the Charter of the United Nations, every State has the duty to refrain from organizing, instigating, assisting or participating in terrorist action in another State or acquiescing in organized activities within its territory towards the commission of such acts, when such acts involve a threat or use of force'. Thus the Security Council brought its concern over acts of international terrorism under the ban of force article of the Charter and within the realm of Chapter VII. The Council also determined that the Libyan refusal to implement Resolution 731 constituted 'a threat to international peace and security'. In this way the Council paved the way for a decision, acting under Chapter VII, to impose an air and arms embargo against Libya to become effective on 15 April 1992, unless before or on that date Libya provided a 'full and effective response' to requests by France, the United Kingdom and the United States to co-operate fully in establishing responsibility for the bombings of the aircraft in question. The embargo would include the prohibition of the sale or supply of any aircraft or aircraft components to Libya, and of engineering and maintenance service of Libyan aircraft or components. Apart from this conditional air and arms embargo, the Council also demanded that all States reduce their diplomatic relations with Libya. On 14 April 1992, one day before the deadline, the Court ruled by a vote of 11 to 5 that 'the circumstances of the case are not such as to require the exercise of its power under Article 41 of the Statute to indicate provisional measures'.[36] A main argument of the Court's judgment was that Security Council Resolution 748 was adopted under Chapter VII of the UN Charter and that according to Articles 25 and 103 of the UN Charter obligations under this Charter prevail above other obligations, including those arising from the Montreal Convention. It is expected that a judgment on the merits of the case itself may take several years. In the meantime the sanctions as contained in Resolution 748(1992) are fully in place, since consultations on the surrender of the two suspects or their trial in a third country (*e.g.* in Geneva or The Hague) remained unsuccessful. In order to exert further psychological pressure, the sanctions were tightened by the Council, in a vote of 11 to none with 4 abstentions, on 11 November 1993. Although they still do not contain an oil embargo, they have targeted three further key areas: the freezing of Libyan assets abroad (but with exceptions for revenues accrued from the sale of oil, natural gas and agricultural products), a ban on exports to Libya of equipment for the downstream oil and gas sectors, and further restrictions on the Libyan aviation industry (S/RES/883, 1993).

(d) *Liberia.* As from 1989, a tragedy unfolded itself in Liberia as a result of the armed struggle for political power between the National Patriotic Front of Liberia (NPLF) and the United Liberation Movement in Liberia (ULIMO). The warring parties undermined the domestic order in Liberia to such an extent that civil war broke out. Moreover, it quickly became a source of destabilisation in the West African subregion and thus a threat to international peace and security. The civilian population suffered considerably and hundreds of thousands of refugees – reportedly more than a third of the population of Liberia – scattered around the various neighbouring countries or became displaced within the country. Since May 1990, the Economic Community of West African States (ECOWAS)[37] took various initiatives for a peaceful settlement of the Liberian conflict. For example, in an early stage it established a Mediation Committee, negotiated a cease-fire and deployed the Economic Community Monitoring Group (ECOMOG) to observe its compliance. A series of peace conferences took place to develop a comprehensive ECOWAS' peace plan, finally resulting in the Yamoussoukro IV Agreement of 30 October 1991. This entailed, *inter alia*, the encampment and disarmament of the combatants under

36 See 'Questions of Interpretation and Application of the 1971 Montreal Convention arising from the Aerial Incident at Lockerbie', *ICJ Reports 1992*, pp. 114-128, at p. 127.
37 The Treaty of the Economic Community of West African States was signed at Lagos, Nigeria, on 28 May 1975 and entered into force on 20 June 1975; text in 14 *ILM* (1975), p. 1200. At present ECOWAS has 16 member countries.

ECOMOG supervision, the establishment of an Electoral Commission and an Ad Hoc Supreme Court to which appeals arising from electoral disputes could be referred, the formation of a transitional government and the conduct of free and fair elections under international supervision. This process was to be completed by April 1992. Yet, the protagonist parties proved to have their own different agenda's. Hostilities continued and in October 1992 things further deteriorated when some ECOMOG peace-keepers protecting Liberia's capital Monrovia were murdered, while some others were disarmed and held hostage. In November 1992, a ministerial committee of nine ECOWAS countries[38] approached the Security Council and requested endorsement of its decision to impose comprehensive sanctions so as to ensure broad international compliance for the pressurizing of the belligerent Liberian parties to respect ECOWAS' peace plan.[39] It was not the first time the Security Council dealt with the situation in Liberia. Earlier it had issued presidential statements[40] in which it expressed its concern for the deterioration of the conflict and had called on all parties to co-operate fully in implementing the Yamoussoukro IV accord as the best possible framework for a peaceful solution of the Liberian conflict. Furthermore, in 1990, 1991 and 1992 the UN General Assembly expressed its deep concern about the devastating effects of the Liberian conflict and called for emergency aid and assistance for the rehabilitation and reconstruction of Liberia.[41]

On 19 November 1992, the Security Council unanimously adopted Resolution 788(1992), in which it first of all commended ECOWAS for its efforts to restore peace, security and stability in Liberia. Secondly, the Council reaffirmed its belief that the Yamoussoukro IV Accord offered the best possible framework for a peaceful resolution of the Liberian conflict by creating the necessary conditions for free and fair elections in Liberia. Thirdly, in its preamble the Council determined that the deterioration of the situation in Liberia constitutes a threat to international peace and security, particularly in West Africa as a whole. This finding paved the way, fourthly, for the imposition of a mandatory embargo on all shipments of weapons and military equipment to the parties to the conflict, as requested by the nine visiting ECOWAS Ministers of foreign affairs. The Liberian Minister of Foreign Affairs fully supported this. Recalling that in 1990 international opinion on Liberia was divided 'between the imperatives for humanitarian intervention, on the one hand, and the value of reaffirming classical conception of sovereignty, however anachronistic, on the other', he now pointed out to the Security Council:

---

38   Benin, Burkina Faso, Ivory Coast, Gambia, Ghana, Guinea, Nigeria, Senegal and Togo.
39   *Cf. UN Doc.* S/24725 and S/24812. In these documents ECOWAS requested Security Council support for sanctions against Liberia, which would consist of a blockade of all points of entry to Liberia – by land, air and sea – in order to prevent the parties to the conflict from having access to war *matériel* and from exporting products from the zones they control in the country.
40   *UN Doc.* S/22133, 22 January 1991 and S/23886, 7 May 1992.
41   GA Resolutions 45/232, 46/147 and 47/153, all adopted without a vote.

'We are here because peace is not possible in Liberia unless these belligerent parties are divested of the prospect of acquiring additional arms. Peace is not achievable unless their capacity to wage war is curtailed...The Liberian situation has all the makings of one that could degenerate into a wider configuration in West Africa. By its spill-over effects, it is already a clear and present danger to neighbouring Sierra Leone; it is slowly transforming West Africa into an arms market.'[42]

Exception has been made for weapons and military equipment delivered for the sole use of the peace-keeping forces of ECOWAS in Liberia. The Resolution also calls on all parties to the conflict and all others concerned to respect strictly the provisions of international humanitarian law. Finally, it requested the Secretary-General to dispatch urgently a Special Representative to Liberia to evaluate the situation.

In July 1993, the NPLF, ULIMO and the Interim Government of National Unity of Liberia signed a peace agreement in Cotonou, Benin. Thereupon, on 22 September 1993, the Security Council established the UN Observer Mission in Liberia (UNOMIL) to monitor the cease-fire established by the July 1993 agreement, observe elections scheduled for February/March 1994 and co-ordinate humanitarian aid (S/RES/866, 1993). UNOMIL will closely co-operate with ECOMOG, but each of them will remain independent and responsible to its own Organization. As such Resolutions 788(1992) and 866(1993) provide a relevant example of supplementary peace-keeping and peace-making efforts simultaneously undertaken by the United Nations and a regional institution, as envisaged in Chapter VIII of the UN Charter.

(e) *Haiti*. In 1990 the United Nations acceded to the request of Haiti's military-backed provisional Government to supervise the electoral process, including assistance in maintaining public order. This gave rise to an extensive debate within the United Nations as to the competence of the Organization to become involved in a situation with no clear international dimension. Ultimately, in October 1990 the General Assembly authorized the creation of UNOVEH, the UN Observer Group for the Verification of Elections in Haiti.[43] The mission did not involve military peace-keepers, but only electoral experts and election monitors, and public security advisers and observers. On 16 December 1990 the Haitian people, by an overwhelming majority, elected Father Jean-Bertrand Aristide; the United Nations certified that 'the elections were conducted freely and fairly, with exemplary participation by political parties and the electorate in a historical break with a past of electoral fraud'.[44] However, it was not granted to Haiti to enjoy its newly-won democracy and a military Government under the leadership of Lieutenant-General Raoul Cédras,

---

42 S/PV.3138, p. 18 (19 November 1992).
43 GA Res. 45/21, 10 October 1990.
44 UN Press Release SG/SM/4531.

Commander-in-Chief of the Haitian Armed Forces, took power. Intensive diplomatic efforts followed aimed at the return of President Aristide and the resumption of the democratic process in Haiti, but so far without result.

In order to exert maximum pressure on the military Government, the Security Council decided to impose an oil and arms embargo under Resolution 841, unanimously adopted on 16 June 1993. On 3 July 1993 an Agreement to resolve the political crisis in Haiti was reached between all involved at Governors Island in New York, with the assistance of mediators of the United Nations and the Organization of American States.[45] Among other things, it provided for a six-month political truce to enable the Haitian Parliament to resume its normal functioning and the selection of a new Prime Minister. In August this process seemed well under way and therefore the Security Council decided to suspend the oil and arms embargo (S/RES/861, 1993). However, soon the Secretary-General had to report that the Haitian military authorities were found to be 'in serious and consistent non-compliance' with the Governors Island Agreement. Thereupon, the Security Council decided to reimpose the sanctions on 13 October 1993 (S/RES/873, 1993) and, after the assassination of the Minister of Justice on 14 October, tightened them three days later in Resolution 875.[46] The initial sanctions had prevented the sale of petroleum, petroleum products, arms or related *matériel*, including military vehicles, police equipment or spare parts, to any perseon or body in Haiti, and had frozen all overseas assets controlled, directly or indirectly, by the *de facto* authorities of that country. A Security Council Committee was authorized 'on an exceptional case-by-case basis under a no-objection procedure', to decide on the importation to Haiti of petroleum products and propane cooking gas 'in non-commercial quantities and only in barrels or bottles' for verified essential humanitarian needs. In Resolution 875 member States were called upon to ensure strict implementation of the embargo against Haiti, and in particular to halt ships travelling to Haiti, in order to inspect and verify their cargoes and destinations. The Council reaffirmed that, in 'these unique and exceptional circumstances' the failure of the military authorities in Haiti to fulfil their obligations under the Agreement, constituted a threat to peace and security in the region.

(f) *UNITA/Angola*. Following the signing of peace accords, 'Acordos de Paz' between the two main rival Angolan parties, the MPLA-government party and the opposition movement UNITA,[47] in Bicesse, near Lisbon in Portugal on 30 May 1991, the Security Council established in June 1991 the UN Angola Verification

---

45 See *UN Chronicle*, vol. XXX, September 1993, No. 3, pp. 8-9.
46 See *UN Chronicle*, vol. XXX, December 1993, No. 4, pp. 20-22.
47 MPLA is the acronym for the Popular Movement for the Liberation of Angola, while UNITA stands for the National Union for the Total Independence of Angola.

Mission II (UNAVEM II)[48] to monitor the cease-fire and to observe and verify elections. These elections were held in September 1992 and were verified by the United Nations as 'generally free and fair'. In the parliamentary elections, the MPLA achieved 53.74 per cent and UNITA 34.1 per cent. In the presidential elections Angolan President Dos Santos received 49.57 per cent of the votes, while UNITA's President Savimbi got 40.07 per cent. Although a second round was now necessary (a 50% victory is required), UNITA questioned the validity of the results and new fighting broke out. Ever since, UNAVEM II in particular and the United Nations in general have sought to help the two sides to solve the post-electoral crisis and to restore peace. In various resolutions the UN Security Council demanded that UNITA accept unreservedly the results of the 1992 democratic elections and abide by the Acordos de Paz. When UNITA refused to do so, the Council urged, firstly, all States in Resolution 834(1993) to refrain from providing any form of military assistance or other support to UNITA and, secondly, it expressed its willingness to impose a mandatory arms embargo (S/RES/851, 1993).

Ultimately, the Security Council decided on 15 September 1993 that an arms and oil embargo would come into force in 10 days time unless an effective cease-fire had been implemented in accordance with the peace-agreements (S/RES/864, 1993). Since this was not the case, the embargo became effective on 25 September 1993 and entailed a prohibition on the sale or supply of arms and related *matériel* and military assistance, as well as petroleum and petroleum products, to the territory not controlled by the Government. The Council announced that it was ready to consider further measures, including trade measures against UNITA and restrictions on the travel by UNITA personnel, should UNITA continue to fail to co-operate.

In a sense, this is a historic resolution since it was for the first time that the Security Council imposed sanctions against a rebellious faction controlling part of the territory of a State. Earlier, in 1992, the Council acted in Resolution 792(1992) against the *Khmer Rouge* in Cambodia, but the specific wording was 'moratorium' and in adopting this Resolution the Council was not acting under Chapter VII. Moreover, in the latter resolution there was no finding under Article 39, while in the Angolan case the Council determined that, as a result of UNITA's military actions, the situation in Angola constituted a threat to international peace and security.

---

48 Originally, UNAVEM was established to oversee withdrawal of Cuban troops from Angola, as part of the package agreement which led to the independence of Namibia in 1990.

III. COMPARING THE NINE SANCTIONS CASES

7. Legal Foundation of the Sanctions

In nearly all main sanctions resolutions adopted for the cases under review it is explicitly pointed out that the Security Council is 'acting under Chapter VII of the Charter of the United Nations'. The only exception is Security Council Resolution 232(1966), which imposed mandatory economic sanctions against Southern Rhodesia. However, this resolution is the only one which contains an explicit reference to Article 41.

In all cases the Council made a decision under Article 39 of the UN Charter. In eight cases the Council determined that 'a threat to international peace and security' existed. Only in the case of the Iraqi invasion of Kuwait did the Council state that a 'breach of the peace' existed. This consistent practice emphasizes that sanctions under Article 41 can only be instituted after a prior determination of the Security Council under Article 39.

In nearly all cases some pre-mandatory resolutions contain phrases such as 'the consequences of which threaten international peace and security in the region' (*e.g.*, S/RES/217, 1965), 'its continuance in time constitutes a threat to international peace and security' (*e.g.*, S/RES/132, 1960 and S/RES/182, 1963), or 'seriously disturbs international peace and security' (S/RES/311 and 393, 1972). As regards the protection of the Kurdish people, the Council in its Resolution 688 of 5 April 1991 did not go beyond the phrase 'the consequences of which threaten international peace and security'. Neither did it indicate that it was 'acting under Chapter VII'. Such resolutions fall short of Article 39 of Chapter VII and can only be interpreted as hints that the Security Council might be willing to consider placing future action under Chapter VII.

8. Objectives of Sanctions Resolutions

The Security Council has ample discretion in determining the objective of sanctions measures; the first sentence of Article 41 of the Charter only provides that they should be employed 'to give effect to its decisions'. The objectives of the sanctions resolutions in the nine cases under review are multifarious indeed. In only two cases (Iraq, Yugoslavia in the later phase), they are clearly meant to serve the 'classical' case of the Chapter VII machinery, *i.e.* to halt aggression of one State against another and thus to maintain the international *status quo*. In six cases (Southern Rhodesia, South Africa, Somalia, Liberia, Haiti and Angola) the true objective rather seems to be to enforce a change of the *status quo* at domestic level. The Libyan case, finally, is a rather special one in so far as the main objective of the sanctions is to compel

Libya to surrender two Libyan nationals allegedly involved in acts of international terrorism and to demonstrate by concrete actions its unambiguous renunciation of terrorism (cf. S/RES/731 and 748, 1992).

In the case of Iraq, the objectives of the sanctions as indicated in particular in Security Council Resolutions 660(1990) and 662(1990), include:

i)   to bring the invasion and occupation of Kuwait by Iraq to an end;

ii) to restore the sovereignty, independence and territorial integrity of Kuwait;

iii) to restore the authority of the legitimate Government of Kuwait;

iv) to protect the assets of the legitimate Government of Kuwait.

In a later stage, after the defeat of the Iraqi army in February 1991 (Operation Desert Storm), additional objectives of the sanctions were formulated in the mandatory peace-package as contained in Security Council Resolution 687(1991) of 3 April 1991. Although the four objectives as summarized above were basically achieved, the Security Council decided to continue the sanctions régime in order to compel Iraq to comply with all elements of what has been called 'the mother of all resolutions' (Resolution 687), including acceptance of the demarcation of the boundary between Iraq and Kuwait, the destruction of all Iraqi chemical and biological weapons and the inspection of nuclear materials in Iraq. Paragraph 28 provides that at least once in the 120 days the Security Council has to assess Iraq's compliance with Resolution 687(1991) as well as the general progress towards the control of armaments in the region. On the basis of this assessment the Council has to decide whether or not the sanctions will be lifted (or relaxed). As discussed above, the Security Council has so far refused to do so.

Also in the Yugoslavian case things have become somewhat complicated. In the initial phase the arms embargo was imposed 'for the purposes of establishing peace and stability in Yugoslavia', in order thus to contribute to a halt in the fighting in Yugoslavia and to maintaining a cease-fire. When Yugoslavia started to fall apart and newly independent States emerged, the Security Council decided to impose a fully-fledged trade embargo against the remaining part of the Republic of Yugoslavia (Serbia and Montenegro) with the declared objective of compelling it to stop fighting against and interfering in the affairs of Bosnia and Herzegovina (S/RES/752 and 757, 1992) and to put pressure on the Bosnian Serb party to cease military attacks and to sign and implement the comprehensive peace plan for Bosnia and Herzegovina (S/RES/820, 1993). What initially mainly was meant as involvement with domestic strife thus became an effort to establish peace and stability between neighbouring States as well.

The cases relating to Southern Rhodesia, South Africa, Somalia, Liberia and Haiti, respectively, embody efforts on the part of the international community to effectuate radical changes in the domestic policies of the target States in question. In the first two cases and in the Haitian case these efforts were clearly directed towards the régimes in power, and in the Somalian and Liberian cases also other actors ('the war lords', and opposition movements) were involved as power factors.[49] In the Angolan case sanctions were imposed to compel the UNITA-rebel movement to comply with the cease-fire and the peace agreements established in 1991.

Finally, the Libyan case is rather peculiar. The objective of the sanctions can be traced from Resolutions 731 and 748(1992) and include the surrender of the two suspected Libyan nationals and an unambiguous renunciation by Libya of terrorism. Yet, it seems obvious that an additional motive was 'to teach colonel Khadaffi a lesson' and it is therefore rather uncertain whether the sanctions would be lifted immediately if Libya surrendered its two nationals.

With the exception of the Libyan and perhaps the Iraqi case, the sanctions were thus intended not so much to punish or repress the target State, but rather to coerce it to put an end to unlawful policies. In other words, they were meant to serve as collective measures to redress an international wrongful act and to restore legality.

9. Scope of the Sanctions

In three of the nine cases under review the Security Council imposed comprehensive packages of economic and financial sanctions, namely against Southern Rhodesia, Iraq and Yugoslavia (Serbia and Montenegro). The sanctions as contained in the resolutions concerning these three cases, namely Security Council Resolutions 253(1968), 661(1990), and 757(1992) and 820(1993), include the prohibition of:
- the import of all commodities and products originating in the target State in question;
- the sale or supply of any commodities or products, including weapons or any other equipment to any person or body in that State;
- any activities by the nationals of States which would promote or could be calculated to promote the export or transshipment of any commodities or products from or to the State in question;
- any transfer of funds or other financial or economic resources to the target State.

Not prohibited is the transfer of funds from the target State to third parties and States. There is, consequently, no complete truncation of financial relations in theory. In all three cases exceptions to the prohibitions include supplies intended strictly for medical purposes, and, in humanitarian circumstances, foodstuffs. States are called upon to comply with the sanctions 'notwithstanding any contract entered into or licenses granted' before the date of the adoption of the sanctions resolutions, by which the sanctions to a certain extent are given a retroactive character. In the

---

49 *E.g.*, in paragraph 1 of S/RES/794(1992) the Council addresses itself to 'all parties, movements and factions in Somalia'.

Rhodesian case the sanctions were complemented with severe diplomatic measures in the sense of a full ban on any diplomatic relations with the 'rebellious régime'. They also included an air embargo for all flights, which was also instituted in the Yugoslavian and Libyan cases. In the Iraqi case, only cargo related flights are prohibited. In general, flights which do not engage in activities contrary to the trade embargo are allowed to continue. In all air embargo-related resolutions exceptions are provided for some particular categories of flights, including:

a) flights for shipments of medical supplies and foodstuffs, if authorized by the Sanctions Committees in humanitarian circumstances;

b) particular flights approved by the Sanctions Committees, for example for the purpose of evacuating foreign nationals, or VIP flights;

c) flights certified by the United Nations as solely for the purpose of a UN peace-keeping operation, *e.g.* UNIIMOG and UNPROFOR, or for mediation or monitoring activities such as those in the context of the Conference on Yugoslavia or the European Community.

Against Libya both an arms and an air embargo have been instituted; against Haiti and arms, oil and financial embargo; and in the cases of South Africa, Somalia and Liberia arms embargoes only. Basically, these relate to all deliveries of weapons and military equipment. The exact scope of the arms embargoes has been specified in the South African, Iraqi and Libyan, Haitian and Angolan cases,[50] but so far not for Yugoslavia, Somalia and Liberia.

The sanctions régime in the Yugoslavian case is the toughest. Resolution 820(1993) considerably tightened it by including the prohibition of services (with exceptions for telecommunications, postal services and legal services), transshipments over land, sea and through the Danube and impounding and detaining of all means of transportation (vessels, trucks, aircraft) and even their forfeiture as well that of their cargoes in case they were found to be used in violation of the sanctions.

10. Addressees

The Security Council resolutions which embody the sanctions, are addressed to 'all States', including member States and non-member States of the United Nations such as Switzerland.[51] The sanctions resolutions contain phrases such as 'all States shall

---

50 *Cf.* S/RES/591(1986); S/RES/687(1991), para. 21; and S/RES/748(1992).

51 Article 2, paragraph 6 of the UN Charter provides for such a wide power of the United Nations: 'The Organization shall ensure that states which are not members of the United Nations act in accordance with these Principles so far as may be necessary for the maintenance of international peace and security'. Yet, the question whether non-members of the United Nations have indeed obligations pursuant to binding

prevent', 'all States shall not make available', and 'calls upon all States'. This implies that the primary responsibility for the implementation of the sanctions rests with *States* and that they are obliged to introduce the sanctions in their national legislation and domestic legal order, for which no uniform practice exists. Indirectly, the sanctions resolutions also address commercial companies. Yet, it is through their home States and not through the United Nations that their compliance with the sanctions has to be ensured. In the Rhodesian case the evasion of the sanctions by multinational corporations was a major issue.

Apart from this the question has arisen on various occasions as to what the effect of the sanctions would be on activities of United Nations organs and international organizations. In view of Article 48, paragraph 2 of the Charter and in view of the relationship agreements between the United Nations and the various specialized agencies,[52] it seems obvious that those of their activities which are export- or import-related would be covered by the sanctions. In the Iraqi case, the Security Council affirmed, indeed, in Resolution 670 of 25 September 1990, that 'the United Nations Organization, its specialized agencies and other international organizations in the United Nations system are required to take such measures as may be necessary to give effect' to the sanctions (S/RES/670(1990), para. 11). In the sanctions resolutions concerning Yugoslavia (Serbia and Montenegro), Libya, Haiti and UNITA/Angola, the Council explicitly called on all international organizations to act strictly in accordance with the sanctions régimes.

11. Special Economic Problems for Third Countries Resulting from the Sanctions

Article 50 of the United Nations Charter provides:

'If preventive or enforcement measures against any state are taken by the Security Council, any other state, whether a Member of the United Nations or not, which finds itself confronted with special economic problems arising

resolutions of the Security Council remains a bone of contention. For example, while Switzerland declared its willingness to implement sanctions against Iraq in response to a note of the Secretary-General, it stated: 'As a non-member of the United Nations, Switzerland is not in fact legally bound by the decisions of the Security Council nor, in this case, by resolution 661 (1990)'.

52 Under these agreements most specialized agencies are obliged to render 'such assistance to the Security Council as that Council may request, including assistance in carrying out decisions of the Security Council for the maintenance of international peace and security'. *Cf.* D.W. Bowett, *The Law of International Institutions*, 4th ed., London 1982, pp. 65-69; H.G. Schermers, *International Institutional Law*, Alphen aan den Rijn 1980, pp. 837-842.

from the carrying out of those measures shall have the right to consult the Security Council with regard to a solution of those problems.'

In practice, actions by the Security Council under this Charter Article have been limited. During the Rhodesia sanctions this Article was invoked by Malawi, Zambia, Mozambique and Botswana. However, it only led to some hortatory resolutions appealing to all States and international organizations to provide assistance to the countries in question.[53]

During the Gulf crisis it soon became obvious that after the Iraqi invasion of Kuwait in August 1990 a whole network of trade, financial and human relationships had become seriously affected. One should make a distinction between special economic problems directly arising from the carrying out of the sanctions (to which Article 50 applies) and those indirectly resulting from the international crisis, such as the impact of the sudden rise of oil prices, lost business opportunities, the stopping of aid and of the flow of oil at concessional prices from Iraq or Kuwait. The latter problems, however, are not within the scope of Article 50 of the United Nations Charter.

In 1990-91, twenty-one countries invoked Article 50 because of special economic problems due to the economic sanctions against Iraq and occupied Kuwait. Roughly, they consisted of three groups:

a) neighbouring countries with close economic relationships with Iraq and Kuwait, such as Lebanon, Jordan and Yemen;

b) Asian States with many migrant labourers in the Gulf region whose economies are partly dependent on their remittances, including such countries as Sri Lanka, Bangladesh, India, Vietnam and the Philippines;

c) countries with strong economic and political relationships with Iraq such as some North African and Eastern European States.

The Sanctions Committee established a Working Group with the task of examining requests for assistance under the provisions of Article 50 and of making appropriate recommendations to the President of the Security Council (*cf.* also S/RES/669, 1990). From November 1990 on, the Working Group convened a series of meetings during which representatives of the affected States were heard and during which their special economic problems were identified.[54] Their main problems include the losses resulting from undelivered products to the Gulf area and undelivered oil shipments from Iraq and Kuwait as well as loss of workers' remittances and costs associated with repatriation and rehabilitation of their nationals returning from Iraq and Kuwait. The Working Group has made recommendations to,

---

53 For a discussion of the relevant resolutions see Gowlland-Debbas, *supra* note 18, pp. 633-639.
54 See the reports and recommendations by the Sanctions Committee, *UN Doc.* S/21786, S/22021 and Add.1 and 2.

among others, the President of the Security Council to appeal to all States on an urgent basis to provide immediate technical and financial assistance to the countries concerned and to invite international organizations and development institutions to review and upgrade their assistance programmes in these countries. With a few exceptions, no substantial relief as compensation has been offered.[55]

It is interesting to note that the main sanctions resolutions concerning both Libya (S/RES/748, 1992) and Yugoslavia (S/RES/757, 1992) contain a reference to Article 50 in the following paragraph of the preamble:

> '*Recalling* the right of States, under Article 50 of the Charter, to consult the Security Council where they find themselves confronted with special economic problems arising from the carrying out of preventive or enforcement measures ...'

Obviously, the inclusion of such a paragraph in the main sanctions resolutions is a result of the experience of severe economic consequences for third States arising from the sanctions against Iraq. So far, the Security Council has not yet dealt with special economic problems of States due to the sanctions against Libya. In the Yugoslavian case it received, as of 31 December 1993, communications under Article 50 from eight States[56] and established a procedure for dealing with such requests (S/RES/843, 1993). The Sanctions Committee concerning Yugoslavia made recommendations for relief and assistance similar to those adopted in the Iraqi sanctions case.[57]

In his *An Agenda for Peace* (1992), Secretary-General Boutros Boutros-Ghali advocated that States confronted with special economic problems should not only have the right to consult the Security Council regarding such problems, but also have a realistic possibility of having their problems addressed: 'I recommend that the Security Council devise a set of measures involving financial institutions and other components of the United Nations system that can be put in place to insulate States from such difficulties. Such measures would be a matter of equity and a means of encouraging States to co-operate with decisions of the Council.'[58] So far, little progress could be achieved in this regard.

55 *Cf.* Johan Kaufmann, Dick Leurdijk, Nico Schrijver, *The World in Turmoil: Testing the UN's Capacity*, Academic Council on the United Nations, Reports 1991-4, pp. 29-31.
56 Albania, Bulgaria, Hungary, Romenia, the former Yugoslav Republic of Macedonia, Uganda, Ukraine and Slovakia.
57 *UN Doc.* S/26040 and Add. 1 and 2.
58 Boutros Boutros-Ghali, *An Agenda for Peace*, United Nations, New York 1992, p. 24.

12. Implementation, Supervision and Enforcement of the Sanctions

Monitoring. States have frequently reported to the United Nations, as requested under the relevant resolutions, on the way they were carrying out the sanctions.[59] In addition, the Secretary-General has regularly sent out notes to all States informing them of their obligations under the Security Council resolutions as well as questionnaires soliciting information on action taken at national level concerning the implementation of the sanctions.[60] In the Iraqi case, for example, by 16 January 1991 (the day Operation Desert Storm was launched), replies had been received from 121 member States and four non-member States to the *note verbale* of the Secretary-General concerning Resolution 661(1990). By the same date 80 States had sent in replies to the questionnaire, a rather high score for UN standards.

The Sanctions Committees. With the exception of the Liberian case, in all other cases the Security Council decided to establish a Committee consisting of all members of the Council, commonly known as the Sanctions Committees. All these committees take their decisions by consensus only, which often proves to be far from easy. The mandate of these Sanctions Committees includes in general:

– to examine the progress reports, submitted by the Secretary-General, on the implementation of the sanctions resolutions;
– to seek from all States further information regarding the action taken by them concerning the effective implementation of the sanctions;
– to consider any information brought to its attention by States concerning violations of the sanctions and, in that context, to make recommendations to the Council on ways to increase their effectiveness.

In the Iraqi case the Security Council charged its Sanctions Committee with specific responsibilities as regards the impact of the trade embargo on the food situation in Iraq, an issue which received wide attention in the immediate aftermath of the war. These specific responsibilities included:

– constantly reviewing the availability of food in Iraq (and occupied Kuwait) in order to determine whether or not circumstances have arisen in which there would be an urgent humanitarian need to supply foodstuffs to Iraq (and occupied Kuwait) to relieve human suffering (S/RES/666, 1990); and
– approving the sale or supply to Iraq of 'materials and supplies for essential civilian needs' as well as the export and international sale of oil by Iraq in order to enable it to pay for these imports (S/RES/687, 1991).

---

59 As regards the Iraqi case, a wealth of information on this can be found in E. Lauterpacht *et al.* (eds), *The Kuwait Crisis: Sanctions and Their Economic Consequences*, Part I and II, Cambridge 1991.
60 See Gilberto B. Schlittler, 'Sanctions Procedures at the United Nations', in *Proceedings of the American Society of International Law*, Washington DC 1991, pp. 175-183.

The Committees in the Yugoslavian and Haitian cases have similar responsibilities.

In the cases of the sanctions against Iraq, Yugoslavia and Libya, the responsibilities of the Sanctions Committees in question include the competence to approve
particular flights on humanitarian grounds, such as for evacuating (foreign) nationals
or providing medical or food supplies. For example, between 25 September 1990, the
date air embargo-Resolution 670 was adopted, and 16 January 1991, the date that the
deadline of Resolution 678(1990) passed, the Sanctions Committee in the Iraqi case
dealt with 198 flights to and from Iraq and Kuwait. An interesting practice emerged.
If the Committee approved a particular flight, the aircraft in question did not have
to land in overflight countries to allow inspection as provided for in paragraph 4 of
the resolution, but it was often stipulated that the aircraft should be inspected before
departure to and upon arrival from Baghdad by the customs authorities of the country
where the flight originated or ended, in the presence of representatives of the United
Nations or an appropriate international humanitarian agency, such as the International
Organization for Migration. In this way a kind of international surveillance of the
aircraft in question evolved.

A rather new element of international enforcement of sanctions is introduced in
the Somalian case. In Resolution 814(1993) the Council requests the Secretary-
General to arrange support from the peace-keeping force UNOSOM II for the
implementation of the arms embargo within Somalia.

Enforcement at sea. Occasionally, the Security Council has authorized naval
enforcement of the trade embargo. An early but rather odd example was Resolution
221(1966), in which the Council addressed the problem of continued oil supplies to
Southern Rhodesia despite its call upon all States to apply an oil embargo. In this
Resolution 221 of 9 April 1966 the Council called upon the Portuguese Government
not to permit oil to be pumped through the pipeline from Beira to South Rhodesia,
and upon the British Government 'to prevent, by *the use of force* (my emphasis) if
necessary, the arrival at Beira of vessels reasonably believed to be carrying oil
destined for Southern Rhodesia'. It is rather striking that the Security Council went
that far at a time when mandatory sanctions had not yet been imposed. In the Iraqi
case, by Resolution 665(1990) the Security Council called upon those member States
co-operating with the Government of Kuwait which were deploying maritime forces
in the area to halt all inward and outward maritime shipping in order to inspect and
verify their cargoes and destinations. The Council requested the States addressed to
co-ordinate their action, using as appropriate the Military Staff Committee (*cf.* Article
47 of the UN Charter). This was a concession to the USSR which in that particular
phase of the conflict took pains to advocate an active overall role for the United
Nations in managing the Gulf crisis, including a re-animation of the Military Staff
Committee which is composed of the Chiefs of Staff of the Permanent Five and

which was convened several times during the first months of the Gulf crisis.[61] In the Yugoslavian case, too, the Security Council took similar action. On 16 November 1992, the Council expressed its deep concern about reports of violations of the sanctions against Yugoslavia, particularly the diverting of exports meant for neighbouring States to Yugoslavia (Serbia and Montenegro). It then decided to tighten the sanctions régime by prohibiting the transshipment through Yugoslavia of a series of materials including energy and transport-related products and goods, and by authorizing States, acting nationally or through regional agencies or arrangements (such as the Western European Union), 'to use such measures commensurate with the specific circumstances as may be necessary under the authority of the Security Council to halt all inward and outward maritime shipping in order to inspect and verify their cargoes and destinations and to ensure strict implementation of the provisions of Resolutions 713(1991) and 757(1992)'.[62] This was further elaborated and extended with respect to transshipments over the Danube and *in* (sic) the territorial sea of Yugoslavia (Serbia and Montenegro) in Resolution 820(1993). Also in the Somalian case, the Security Council called upon States 'to use such measures as may be necessary to ensure strict implementation' of the arms embargo (S/RES/794, 1992). In the Haitian case a Resolution (S/RES/875, 1993) was adopted which calls upon the member States, in terms nearly identical to Resolution 665(1990) in the Iraqi case, to interrupt maritime shipping as necessary to inspect and verify their cargoes and destinations. In these various ways third state participation was foreseen in monitoring compliance and, if necessary, enforcement of the sanctions.[63]

From a constitutional point of view, these paragraphs of Resolutions 665(1990), 787 and 794(1992) present some ambiguities. Resolution 665 does not indicate the Chapter or articles of the Charter under which the Council acted. In contrast, the relevant paragraphs concerned of Resolutions 787 and 794(1992) contain explicit references to Chapters VII and VIII of the UN Charter. Although the phrase 'use of force' does not appear in so many words in the texts, it follows from the object and purposes of these resolutions as well as from the Council's debate,[64] that they certainly leave open the possibility for a limited use of military force, if necessary, to halt maritime shipping in order to inspect their cargoes and destinations. Would

---

61 See Johan Kaufmann, Dick Leurdijk and Nico Schrijver, *supra* note 55, Chapter I, p. 15.
62 S/RES/787, 16 November 1992.
63 See Captain J.F.T. Bayliss, 'The Law and Practice of Maritime Embargoes and Blockades in the Context of UN Security Council Enforcement Measures', in *Contemporary International Law Issues: Opportunity at the time of momentous change. Proceedings 1993 Joint Conference of the American Society of International Law and Netherlands International Law Association*, Dordrecht 1994, pp. 339-342.
64 In the case of Resolution 665(1990), among the Members of the Council, only China clearly stated that it had voted in favour of the draft resolution on the understanding that it did not imply the use of force.

this and the reference to 'under the authority of the Security Council' (and in the case of Resolution 665 to the Military Staff Committee as well, which is an integral component of the enforcement machinery foreseen in Chapter VII), imply that these resolutions have been adopted under Article 42 of the Charter? The answer is no. The paragraphs concerned of Resolutions 665(1990), 787 and 794(1992) certainly do not envisage a United Nations operation for the purpose of enforcing the embargoes; they only empower certain member States to take measures which in specific circumstances may require a limited use of force. The measures provided for by Article 42 have a broad scope and their application is based upon the condition that the Security Council considers that 'measures provided for in Article 41 would be inadequate or have proved to be inadequate'. The Security Council, however, did not make such a decision. The provisions of these resolutions are instead meant to supplement the economic sanctions imposed under Resolutions 661(1990), 733 and 757(1992), respectively, with the objective of ensuring strict implementation of the provisions thereof. While under specific circumstances it can go beyond the 'measures not involving the use of force' provided for in Article 41, these resolutions cannot be positioned under Article 42. It seems to be a rather innovative use of the powers of the Council under Chapter VII, bringing about the option of a last resort measure which falls – if the connoisseurs wish to hear – somewhere between Articles 41 and 42.[65]

SOME FINAL OBSERVATIONS AND GENERAL CONCLUSIONS

Although Article 41 of the UN Charter is not an original piece of international law-making (it is built on Article 16 of the Covenant of the League of Nations), the innovative element is that it is part of a comprehensive system for collective security. This is laid down in Chapters VI and VII of the UN Charter and bestows the Security Council with major discretionary powers, which – in contrast to the League's Council – can be exercised by a qualified majority.

The League's discussions on sanctions and their actual imposition against Italy, related to territorial disputes only. The sanctions against Italy in 1935-36, because of its invasion of Ethiopia, were the first collective sanctions experiment, but they were a complete failure. In 1945, the use of sanctions was foreseen as part of the collective security system to keep the 'negative peace', *i.e.* to prevent the use of force in international relations, particularly to protect States against military attacks from other States. The Chapter VII machinery, including Article 41, was originally

65 *Cf.* Ralph Zacklin, 'Les Nations-Unies et la crise du Golfe', in Brigitte Stern (ed.), *Proceedings of Colloque sur les aspects juridiques de la Crise et de la 'Guerre' du Golfe*, Paris 1991, p. 68.

meant to maintain the international status quo. It is, therefore, rather striking that the two first, and for a long time only sanctions cases, *i.e.* those against Southern Rhodesia (1966-1979) and South Africa (from 1977), were ordered in situations not foreseen in 1945. Due to developments in international law relating to self-determination, decolonization and racial discrimination the UN General Assembly and in its track the Security Council, albeit reluctantly, took the view that the existing situation in these two countries had become intolerable. Sanctions were instituted as part of the effort to change the status quo, which in the perception of the Security Council disturbed the maintenance of international peace and security and thus constituted a threat to peace.[66]

In all nine cases reviewed in this report the Security Council positioned the economic and other measures it took squarely under Chapter VII. In the relevant sanctions resolutions there was a prior determination under Article 39 of the Charter (see the Appendix). All of them can be situated under Article 41 and all sanctions are of a mandatory nature. This Article as such is of a wide ranging nature. The Security Council is vested with broad discretionary powers to decide if, when and which measures will be applied and whether they will be of a mandatory or voluntary nature. Within the UN system, the Security Council is the only organ competent to impose mandatory economic sanctions.[67] Those instituted by the General Assembly, for example against Northern Korea and China in 1951,[68] can only have a voluntary character. Sometimes the Security Council only recommends the imposition of economic sanctions. A recent and rather peculiar example is Resolution 792(1992), by which the Council supported the decision of Cambodia's Supreme National Council to set a moratorium on the export of logs from Cambodia in order to protect Cambodia's natural resources. As additional measures, the Security Council suggested a similar moratorium on the export of minerals and gems as well as the freezing of the assets held by the Parti Démocratique Kampuchea (PDK, *i.e.* the Khmer Rouge) outside Cambodia should it obstruct the implementation of the peace plan.[69]

This report illustrates that in the post-Cold War era collective economic sanctions are more easily applied than in the past and seem to have become a major policy tool of the United Nations.[70] This coincides with renewed interest in and a considerably

---

66   *Cf.* B.V.A. Röling, *Volkenrecht en Vrede*, 3rd rev.ed., Deventer 1985, p. 45. *Cf.* also his 'International law and the maintenance of peace', in IV *Netherlands Yearbook of International Law* (1973), pp. 1-103, at p. 25.

67   *Cf.* the ICJ in its Advisory Opinion on Certain Expenses of the United Nations, *ICJ Reports 1962*, p. 163.

68   GA Res. 500 (V), 18 May 1951.

69   *Cf.* paragraphs 11, 13 and 14 of Security Council Resolution 792 (1992).

70   See also Report of the Twenty-Fourth United Nations Issues Conference of the Stanley Foundation, *Political Symbol or Policy Tool? Making Sanctions Work*, Muscatine 1993.

more assertive role of the United Nations. This is not to say that sanctions have become very effective instruments to restore peace and stability and to return to legality. But apart from their official goals, sanctions can serve a host of other purposes, including serving as instruments to express strong disapproval, to reaffirm certain norms, to outlaw certain policies, and to satisfy domestic public demands. These collective functions of sanctions should not be underestimated. Under Article 41 only 'negative' obligations can be imposed on States, in the sense that they should refrain from doing something, *e.g.* from conducting trade and entertaining diplomatic relations with the target State. Yet the cutting off of relations, whether commercial or diplomatic, may also eliminate opportunities for dialogue and public pressure. One may therefore wonder whether sometimes certain rewards and, if appropriate, a policy of sticks *and* carrots, may not be equally efficient.

Generally, sanctions are intended to change a target country's behaviour and to influence its further policy decisions by inflicting or threatening to inflict economic pain. The goals are thus punishment and coercion. The pain can result from a wide variety of measures such as imports and exports barriers to goods and restrictions on financial relations, communications and transportations. However, the experience with imposing economic sanctions learns of a lot of suffering by the civilian population while those in power remain relatively untouched. It poses the dilemma of how long the international community should impose punishment on the citizens of a country whose leaders prove to be beyond its control. This also raises pertinent questions as regards the applicability of international humanitarian law and its relationship to obligations under binding Security Council resolutions.[71] The Fourth Geneva Convention Relative to the Protection of Civilian Persons in War is of special relevance here, the very purpose of which is to protect civilians and to provide relief to severe human suffering. Enforcement action should find its limit where the survival of the civilian population is at stake.[72] Therefore, it would be incorrect indeed if the Security Council as a political organ vests itself with the right to completely block the efforts of humanitarian organizations such as the International Committee of the Red Cross and Médecins sans Frontières. This calls for checks and balances between the United Nations as a political organization and these humanitarian agencies.[73]

The primary responsibility for the implementation of the sanctions rests with *States*; they are obliged to introduce the sanctions in their national legislation and

---

71 *Cf.* Article 103 of the UN Charter but see also Article 60, para. 5 of the 1969 Vienna Convention on the Law of Treaties.

72 *Cf.* Report to the Secretary-General dated 15 July 1991 on humanitarian needs in Iraq prepared by a mission led by Sadruddin Aga Khan, Executive Delegate of the Secretary-General, *UN Doc.* S/22799, a mission in which the present author participated.

73 See the interesting comments on this chapter made by H.P. Gasser, legal adviser to the International Committee of the Red Cross in Geneva, in this volume.

domestic legal order[74] for which no uniform practice exists, not even in the context of the European Union.[75] Binding decisions of international institutions are in only a few States 'directly applicable', in the sense that they can have direct legal effects without an intermediate legal step by a national authority. More uniform transformation procedures will most likely result in better compliance with Security Council measures. Based on the recent experiences with multilateral sanctions, co-ordination and harmonization of domestic sanctions legislation would be very appropriate by, for example, drafting a model law of wide application to give effect to Security Council resolutions.[76] Maybe such a task could be taken up in the context of the International Law Commission or the International Law Association.

The capabilities of the UN Secretariat should be strengthened for the purposes of option assessment, intelligence analysis and actual monitoring. UN monitors including well-trained customs officials could be posted at critical points along the borders of target countries in order to assure that sanctions are complied with. Of course, the actual interdiction and enforcement operations would remain the responsibility of local authorities. The international Sanctions Assistance Missions (SAM) and the appointment of the Sanctions Coordinator by the Conference on Security and Co-operation in Europe (CSCE) provide useful precedents. It would be beneficial to improve the co-operation between the United Nations and regional arrangements such as the European Community, CSCE, the Organization of African Unity and the Organization of American States.

By now 'Sanctions Committees' have become a permanent feature of the organizational structure of the Security Council. These committees have an important task in monitoring the implementation of the sanctions, clarifying the scope and implications of the sanctions resolutions, and approving the use of their exception clauses. Yet an analysis of the relevant paragraphs of the sanctions resolutions clearly shows that they have hardly any powers. They do not have the power either to receive information from any source or to investigate alleged violations by inspections *in situ* or surveillance at the border of the target State, let alone powers to enforce the sanctions resolutions. Communication with non-State entities, whether humanitarian NGOs or the business community, is far from easy. The Sanctions

---

74 See, *e.g.*, Hazel Fox, and C. Wrickremasinghe, 'UK Implementation of UN Economic Sanctions', in 42 *International and Comparative Law Quarterly* (1993), pp. 945-970. For data on the Netherlands implementing legislation of the sanctions against Iraq (and occupied Kuwait), see P.C. Tange, 'Netherlands municipal legislation involving questions of public international law 1990', in XXII *Netherlands Yearbook of International Law* (1991), pp. 370-371.

75 See P.J. Kuyper, 'Trade Sanctions, Security and Human Rights', in Marc Marescau (ed.), *The European Community's Commercial Policy after 1992: The Legal Dimension*, Dordrecht 1983, pp. 387-422, at pp. 421-422. S. Bohr, 'Sanctions by the United Nations Security Council and the European Community', in 4 *European Journal of International Law* (1993), pp. 256-268.

76 *Cf.* P.J. Kuyper, *supra* note 18, pp. 240-245; J.P. Carver, in *Proceedings of the 85th Annual Meeting of the American Society of International Law*, Washington DC 1991, p. 183.

Committees have to take their decisions by consensus, which often is very difficult. Therefore, wider powers for the Sanctions Committees would be recommendable as well as decision-making by qualified majority, but with some defined supervision by the Security Council itself. In view of the proliferation of sanctions, it could also be appropriate to establish a Standing Committee of the Security Council which has the competence to deal with all sanctions cases of the Security Council as well as with some general issues such as improving the effectiveness of sanctions and coping with the special economic problems of third States as a result of collective sanctions.

In today's interdependent world effective sanctions cut deep in all kinds of relations (trade, financial and human), probably much deeper than foreseen in 1945 at the time of drafting the Charter. The founding fathers of the United Nations already foresaw that such a situation would call for an equitable sharing of the burden, both politically (Articles 48 and 49) and economically (Article 50 of the Charter). They did not and could not, however, foresee that our world would become so interdependent that the imposition of sanctions against one or two particular countries would result in so many unintended shifts in trade and financial flows, to the benefit of a few countries and to the detriment of many others. These 'spillover effects' came to the fore in particular during the sanctions against Iraq, which gave rise to severe economic problems for a large group of third States as well as for tens of thousands of migrant workers. If the international community wishes to maintain the imposition of collective economic sanctions as a major 'weapon' to combat aggressors, it has to substantially improve the Article 50 machinery, for example by devising measures involving the international financial institutions and trade arrangements to assist these countries and people in overcoming their special economic problems.[77]

The frequent resort to the imposition of collective sanctions in recent years testifies not only to the increasing use of the United Nations as an instrument of foreign policy, but also emphasizes the more general trend in international relations towards narrowing the scope of State sovereignty and expanding the realm of international law. This comes particularly to the fore in the large number of sanctions cases where the dispute at stake is essentially of a domestic nature. In view of recent experiences in Iraq, Somalia, Liberia, Haiti and Angola, it seems premature to predict that the concept of full State sovereignty will be replaced by a 'use it responsibly or lose it' approach.[78] Yet, there can be little doubt that under modern international law State sovereignty is increasingly embedded in a web of international responsibilities and obligations which governments cannot afford to ignore.

---

77 See also Margaret Doxey, 'Sanctions in an Unstable International Environment: Lessons from the Gulf Conflict', in 2 *Diplomacy & Statecraft* (1991), pp. 207-225, at p. 212 and pp. 216-221.
78 *Cf.* Thomas G. Weiss and Larry Minear (eds.), *Humanitarism Across Borders. Sustaining Civilians in Times of War*, Boulder and London 1993, p. 61.

Appendix
Survey of mandatory collective economic UN Security Council sanctions (1946-93)

Target country	Main sanctions resolutions and date of adoption	Voting record (in favour - against - abstention)	Article 39 qualification
Southern Rhodesia (1966-79)	S/RES/232(1966), 16 December 1966 S/RES/253(1968), 29 May 1968	11 - 0 - 4 Adopted unanimously	Threat to international peace and security
South Africa (1977 up to the present)	S/RES/418(1977), 14 November 1977	Adopted unanimously	Threat to international peace and security
Iraq (and occupied Kuwait) (1990 up to the present)	S/RES/661(1990), 6 August 1990 S/RES/670(1990), 25 September 1990 S/RES/687(1991), 3 April 1991	13 - 0 - 2 (Cuba and Yemen) 14 - 1 (Cuba) - 0 12 - 1 (Cuba) - 2 (Ecuador and Yemen)	Breach of international peace and security
All successor States to former Yugoslavia (1991 up to the present) Yugoslavia (Serbia and Montenegro) (1992 up to the present)	S/RES/713(1991), 25 September 1991 S/RES/757(1992), 30 May 1992	Adopted unanimously 13 - 0 - 2 (China and Zimbabwe)	Threat to international peace and security
Somalia (1992 up to the present)	S/RES/733(1992), 23 January 1992	Adopted unanimously	Threat to international peace and security
Libya (1992 up to the present)	S/RES/748(1992), 31 March 1992 S/RES/883(1993), 11 November 1993	10 - 0 - 5 (China, Cape Verde, India, Morocco and Zimbabwe) 11 - 0 - 4	Threat to international peace and security
Liberia (1992 up to the present)	S/RES/788(1992), 19 November 1992	Adopted unanimously	Threat to international peace and security
Haiti (1993 up to the present)	S/RES/841(1993) 18 June 1993 S/RES/873(1993) 13 October 1993	Adopted unanimously Adopted unanimously	Threat to international peace and security
UNITA/Angola (1993 up to the present)	S/RES/864(1993) 15 September 1993	Adopted unanimously	Threat to international peace and security

Survey of mandatory collective economic UN Security Council sanctions (1946-93)

Main nature of the conflict	Type of sanctions	Main objectives of the sanctions	Exception clauses for:
Domestic	Selective economic sanctions Trade, financial and air embargo	To bring to an end the rebellion in Southern Rhodesia	Medical supplies and educational materials. Foodstuffs in special humanitarian circumstances
Domestic	Arms embargo	To end violence against the African people and neighbouring States	None
International	Trade and financial embargo + Cargo related air embargo Continuation of sanctions with exceptions for humanitarian supplies	To restore the sovereignty and territorial integrity of Kuwait To enforce compliance by Iraq with all elements of S/RES/687 (1991)	Medical supplies and, in humanitarian circumstances, foodstuffs Humanitarian and UNIIMOG flights Medicines, health supplies, foodstuffs and supplies for essential civilian needs
Domestic and International	Arms embargo Trade, financial and air embargo	To establish peace and security in former Yugoslavia To stop fighting and interference in Bosnia and Hercegovina	None Medical supplies and foodstuffs
Domestic	Arms embargo	To establish peace and stability in Somalia	None
International	Arms and air embargo Specified financial and trade measures	To surrender two Libyan nationals suspected of terrorism and to renounce all forms of terrorrist action	Humanitarian flights
Domestic	Arms embargo	To establish peace and security in Liberia	Arms for the sole use of the ECOWAS peace keeping force
Domestic	Arms and oil embargo and freeze of funds	To restore the legitimate Aristide Government to power	Non-commercial supplies of oil for verified essential humanitarian needs
Domestic	Arms and oil embargo	To establish an effective ceasefire and to implement the 'Acordos de Paz' and relevant SC resolutions	None

COMMENTS

Vera Gowlland-Debbas[*]

The increasing resort to economic sanctions by the UN Security Council presents complex problems of implementation having far-reaching legal consequences. Whilst it is of course necessary to examine the validity of these measures from the point of view of their constitutional legitimacy, I would like to address certain questions which go beyond the constitutional framework of the UN and which relate to the relationship between Charter law and the international legal order. In my view, moreover, enforcement action by the Security Council and more generally the Charter, should be interpreted against the backdrop of the evolution of international law since 1945.

I. THE LINK BETWEEN UN COLLECTIVE MEASURES AND STATE RESPONSIBILITY

The definition given by Nico Schrijver of collective sanctions as 'collective measures imposed by organs representing the international community in response to unlawful conduct by one of its members' establishes a link between Charter mechanisms for peace maintenance and state responsibility. It should be emphasized, however, that this definition is of relatively recent origin, for unlike the League system, Chapter VII measures were not originally intended to be limited in their application to cases of non-compliance with international obligations. Kelsen had concluded that 'the purpose of the enforcement action under Article 39 is not: to maintain or restore the law, but to maintain, or restore peace, which is not necessarily identical with the law'.[1] This is borne out by the wide discretion the Council has in making determinations under Article 39 which do not require attribution of guilt or of responsibility.

* Dr. V. Gowlland-Debbas is a Research Fellow at the Geneva Graduate Institute of International Studies and Adjunct Professor of International Law at Webster University in Geneva.
1   H. Kelsen, *The Law of the United Nations*, London 1950, p. 294.

H.H.G. Post (ed.), International Economic Law and Armed Conflict, 163–173.
© 1994 *Martinus Nijhoff Publishers. Printed in the Netherlands.*

It is in its practice, however, that the Council has linked determinations under Article 39 to determinations of the illegality, and in some cases the nullity,[2] of certain unilateral acts of states or non-state entities. Moreover, what is involved is not just any unlawful conduct, as Nico Schrijver suggests, but breaches of a particularly serious character, since they constitute alleged violations of norms of a fundamental nature, related to such concepts as *jus cogens, erga omnes* obligations, or international crimes.[3] In particular, the Security Council in its resolutions adopted on the basis of Article 41, Chapter VII, has singled out the right to self-determination, and the prohibition of the threat or use of force, with references, *inter alia,* to apartheid, humanitarian law, the practice of 'ethnic cleansing', and international terrorism, which are, however, linked to the first two basic norms, violations of which are said to incur state responsibility.[4]

This perception of collective measures as legal sanctions has been the approach adopted in the ongoing codification work of the International Law Commission, which in its commentary has indeed reserved the term sanctions for 'reactive measures applied by virtue of a decision taken by an international organization following a breach of an international obligation *having serious consequences for the international community as a whole*'.[5]

Such collective responses, though quite evidently neither automatic nor impartial since emanating from a political organ, may be viewed therefore as having an important law-enforcement function.

II THE EFFECTS OF ECONOMIC SANCTIONS ON THE INTERNATIONAL LEGAL ORDER

Measures adopted under Article 41 are mandatory and under Article 25, states have an obligation to 'accept and carry out the decisions of the Security Council in accordance with the present Charter'. Since universality of implementation is essential for effectiveness, no state can be dispensed, notwithstanding the fact that the cost to some may be, in some cases, far greater than to the targeted state itself, that

---

2   For example, Resolutions 216 and 217(1965) relating to the illegality and invalidity of the Unilateral Declaration of Independence of Southern Rhodesia and Resolutions 662 and 664(1990) relating to the nullity of Iraq's purported annexation of Kuwait.
3   See Articles 53 and 64 of the 1969 Vienna Convention on the Law of Treaties; *Barcelona Traction, Light and Power Co. Ltd., Second Phase, ICJ Reports 1970*, p. 32; Article 19 of Part I of the International Law Commission's Draft Articles on State Responsibility, respectively.
4   For an elaboration of these ideas, see V. Gowlland-Debbas, 'Security Council Enforcement Action and Issues of State Responsibility, 43 *International and Comparative Law Quarterly* (1994), pp. 55-98.
5   *Yearbook of the International Law Commission* 1979, vol. II (Part Two), p. 121 (italics added).

the burden is far from being equally distributed, and that recourse to Article 50 is not a remedy in itself, as has been pointed out on numerous occasions.

However, as has been so rightly stated in Nico Schrijver's report, such measures cannot but override other legal principles and rules. I would like to elaborate on this by focussing on the effects of UN economic sanctions on the international legal order from the viewpoint of three sets of relationships which touch on fundamental questions relating to concepts of a hierarchy in international law. These are: 1) the relationship between the Charter and the internal legal order of states, for implementation entails encroachment on private legal and economic relations; 2) the relationship between the Charter and the conventional legal order insofar as states have an obligation under Article 103 of the Charter to implement collective measures notwithstanding any conflicts that may arise 'under any other international agreement'; finally, 3) the relationship between the Charter and international public policy in the form it has taken since 1945, particularly in relation to human rights and humanitarian law, which poses the problem of resolution of conflicts between the Charter, so far considered to represent the constitutional law of the international community, and other norms of a non-derogable nature.

Economic sanctions and the domestic legal order

Economic sanctions adopted by the Security Council under Article 41, may be assimilated to non-self-executing treaty obligations;[6] as such they require domestic implementation. Unlike measures taken at the official level, such as the severance of diplomatic relations, they affect private rights and require control of the activities of private parties, which may be at variance with the constitutional or general legal order of the member state concerned. This is illustrated by: 1) the fate of contracts and 2) the requirement of extraterritorial application.

1) The common provision in Resolutions 232(1966) and 253(1968) on Southern Rhodesia, 661(1990) on Iraq, and 670(1990) on Yugoslavia, that the prohibitions against sale or supply of commodities or products and financial transactions related thereto shall apply 'notwithstanding any contract entered into or any licence granted before the date of the resolution', poses complex problems relating to the determination of its scope, as the debates in the respective Sanctions Committees have revealed. For this directly affects a whole variety of private acts covering diverse commercial transactions, such as contracts relating to sales, services, leasings,

---

6   See *Sei Fujii v. State of California,* 19 *International Law Reports* (1952), p. 312; and *Diggs v. Dent,* 14 *International Legal Materials* (1975), p. 797.

franchising, promotional and sub-contracting activities. It also raises, in relation to existing contracts, the question of their nullity or suspension, and the problem of retroactivity.[7] A quick perusal of the reports concerning state implementation is sufficient to show the disparate solutions which have been brought to these problems.

At the same time, compensation at the international level for losses arising from unfulfilled contracts as a result of the trade embargo has not been envisaged, the Compensation Commission on Iraq having decided on the basis of Resolution 687(1990) which deals with Iraq's responsibility, that only direct losses resulting from Iraq's unlawful invasion and occupation of Kuwait were eligible.[8] The Security Council also excluded any possibility of claims from the targeted state in connection with transactions affected by the trade embargo.[9]

2) In seeking also to enforce sanctions against violations by multinationals operating world wide, Security Council Resolutions clearly require states to adopt legislation with extraterritorial reach. States are to prohibit, *inter alia*, any activities that promote or are calculated to promote the sale or supply of prohibited items 'by their nationals or from their territories'; and the 'shipment in vessels or aircraft of their registration or under charter to their nationals' (Res. 232(1966) and 661(1990)), or in aircraft 'operated by an operator having his principal place of business or permanent residence' in their territory (Res. 670(1990)).[10] The resolutions, however, do not spell out the scope of this prescriptive jurisdiction nor do they explicitly require states to adopt penal sanctions.

Now in the past, not only has extraterritorial application of laws not been considered a duty on states, but extensive extraterritorial claims by states in application of unilateral economic policies have been met by accusations of intervention in domestic jurisdiction, as the 'Siberian pipelines' case shows.[11] Whilst the exercise of extraterritorial jurisdiction to give effect to multilateral treaty

---

7   See generally B. Grelon and C.-E. Gudin, 'Contrats et crise du Golfe', 118 *Journal du droit international* (1991), pp. 633-677; V. Gowlland-Debbas, *Collective Responses to Illegal Acts in International Law. United Nations Action in the Question of Southern Rhodesia,* Dordrecht/Boston/London 1990, pp. 600-605.

8   For example Decision taken by the Governing Council of the United Nations Compensation Commission, 6 March 1992 (S/AC.26/1992/9).

9   Security Council Resolutions 687(1991) and 757(1992).

10   See also Res. 757(1992) on Yugoslavia. it is interesting to note that the Security Council extends the criteria for the determination of the nationality of ships of the Federal Republic of Yugoslavia to 'any vessel in which a majority or controlling interest is held by a person or undertaking in or operating from the Federal Republic of Yugoslavia regardless of the flag under which the vessel sails'.

11   Export Administration Regulations as amended (47 Fed. Reg. (5 January, 1982), pp. 141-145) relating to exports to the USSR of oil and gas equipment, which extends to juridical bodies wherever organized or doing business that are owned or controlled by citizens or residents of the US, or persons actually within the US. See also reaction of the United Kingdom, and Statement of the Foreign Ministers of the European Community of June 23, 1982, in 21 *International Legal Materials* (1982), pp. 851 and 891.

obligations in theory would appear to pose a different *problématique*, since by definition, this no longer falls 'essentially within domestic jurisdiction'[12] (and moreover, such a duty has been incorporated in Article VII of the recently adopted Chemical Weapons Convention),[13] it would appear, however, that states are somewhat more reluctant to extend their jurisdiction in such cases. The United States, for example, with respect to the application of sanctions against Southern Rhodesia, had refused to extend its jurisdiction over the foreign subsidiaries of US corporations abroad, though it has not hesitated to do so on other occasions.[14] Switzerland had also claimed at the time that it could not proceed in law against Swiss registered companies insofar as their transactions had been conducted outside Swiss territory. This position, however, was subsequently challenged in a memorandum by the UN Legal Council dated May 8, 1973,[15] which referred to case law, *e.g.* the famous *Lotus* case, and to examples of state practice, such as the UK Trading with the Enemy Act of 1939. Legislation implementing UN sanctions has, moreover, in some cases, made provision for extraterritorial jurisdiction, e.g. the measures adopted by the European Community in the case of sanctions against Iraq.[16]

In short, implementation of economic sanctions illustrates the uneasy relationship between international and municipal law, underlining the weakness of an international law which is dependent for its execution on domestic processes escaping its ambit and control: state reports on such implementation reveal, *inter alia*, the dirth of enabling legislation for the implementation of UN decisions, time-lags in domestic execution and differences in interpretation in the range of sanctioned goods.

Moreover, such implementation raises the problem of the solution of conflicts arising between international law and domestic law. Whilst the Charter is silent with respect to the internal law of member states, since Article 103 relates to international

---

12 V. Gowlland-Debbas, *State Responsibility and Jurisdiction to Enforce*, Paper presented to the Colloquium on State Responsibilitty for Extraterritorial Acts of Corporations Involving Arms Control Issues, Geneva, March 6-7, 1992.

13 1993 Convention on the Prohibition of the Development, Production, Stockpiling and Use of Chemical Weapons and on their Destruction, which calls on each state Party, in Article VII, sub-para.(c), 'to extend its penal legislation ... to any activity prohibited under the Convention undertaken anywhere by natural persons possessing its nationality, in conformity with international law'.

14 See *South Africa US Policy and the Role of US Corporations.* Hearings before Subcommittee on Africa of Senate Committee on Foreign Relations, 94th Congress, 2nd sess. (Sept.8-30, 1976), pp. 257-419, refering to the activities of Mobil South Africa in Southern Rhodesia. On this topic A.F. Lowenfeld, *Trade Controls for Political Ends,* New York 1983, 2nd ed.

15 S/11178/Rev.l. Gowlland-Debbas, *supra* note 7, pp. 596-600.

16 Council Regulation (EEC) No. 2340/90 of August 8, 1990. These measures are reproduced in E. Lauterpacht and D. Bethlehem (eds.), *The Kuwait Crisis: Sanctions and their Economic Consequences,* Part I, Cambridge 1991.

agreements,[17] a number of judicial and arbitral decisions, from the 1872 *Alabama Claims* Arbitration[18] to the 1988 *PLO Missions Case*[19] have affirmed the well-established rule of the primacy of international law, which naturally includes Charter law, over domestic law. Of course, domestic courts bound by their own rules may not always uphold this principle as is illustrated by the case of *Diggs v. Shultz* arising from resumption by the United States of importation of chrome from Rhodesia under the umbrella of the Byrd amendment.[20]

But implementation of collective sanctions also entails what is a novel element in international law: the introduction of a duty – and not only, as traditionally was the case, a right – to exercise state control over private activities both at home and abroad. Moreover, when imposed in a situation of armed conflict, this goes beyond the traditional duties of neutral states, which were not bound to prevent their subjects from furnishing supplies, including military supplies, to belligerents in the way of ordinary commerce.[21]

Economic sanctions and Article 103 of the Charter

The implementation of economic sanctions has the effect of modifying the legal position of states under other international agreements, or for that matter, general international law. I will give in this respect one example for the unusual aspects it presents: the enforcement of economic sanctions at sea. The interesting problem of the compatibility between collective measures and a status of permanent neutrality, which also arises in this context, will not be examined, since neutrality has already been the subject of discussion at this symposium.[22]

Plainly, the provisions in Resolutions 221(1966) on Southern Rhodesia, 665(1990) on Iraq and 787(1992) on Yugoslavia, relating to the enforcement of the economic embargo at sea, which imply, and in the case of Rhodesia explicitly refer to, the use of a limited amount of force, call for measures which in the absence of a Charter basis, depart from member states' international law obligations both in time of peace and with respect to the *jus in bello*.

---

17 See discussions at San Francisco in relation to this question, 13 *UNCIO DOCS.*, No. 527, and C. Cadoux, 'La supériorité du droit des Nations Unies sur le droit des Etats membres', 63 *Revue général de droit international public* (1959), pp. 649-680.
18 I. Moore, *International Arbitrations*, p. 656.
19 *Applicability of the Obligation to Arbitrate under Section 21 of the United Nations Headquarters Agreement of 26 June 1947, ICJ Reports 1988*, pp. 34-35.
20 11 *International Legal Materials* (1972), p. 1258. See Gowlland-Debbas, *supra* note 7, pp. 500-514.
21 Oppenheim/Lauterpacht, *International Law*, vol. II, London 1952, 7th ed., p. 739.
22 See Gowlland-Debbas, *supra* note 7, pp. 514-526, for a discussion of this topic.

Whilst Great Britain as the administering authority could have exercised certain rights of surveillance and control over trade with Southern Rhodesia, the interception, forcible search and eventual arrest called for by Resolution 221 of third-party ships on the high seas in time of peace, would have been contrary to the law of the sea relating to freedom of navigation.[23] Nor could this have been justified even under the traditional rules relating to a pacific blockade (now prohibited by Article 2(4) of the Charter), which, in contrast to blockades in time of war, could not be directed against the shipping of third States.

In the case of the armed conflict between Iraq and Kuwait, or the on-going conflict in former Yugoslavia, the exercise of such measures by an unspecified number of States[24] all technically non-belligerents, though possibly not neutrals, against one of the belligerents, as well as against all other non-belligerent or neutral third-party ships, involving naval operations over an ill-defined geographical area[25] could have been claimed only with difficulty to constitute the exercise of traditional belligerent rights (leaving aside the controversy as to whether such rights can only be exercised during a state of war as opposed to an armed conflict).

The justification in the Iraq-Kuwait crisis of naval operations under the umbrella of collective self-defence (Article 51 is explicitly referred to in Resolution 661(1990) and implicitly recalled in Resolution 665(1990)),is tenuous, since that right is closely conditioned, as the Court's decision in the *Nicaragua* case[26] has shown. Moreover, any ambiguity arising from Resolution 665 is removed by the total absence to any reference to Article 51 in any of the other resolutions relating to enforcement of economic sanctions.

That the enforcement at sea of economic sanctions is contrary to international law and requires specific authorization by the Security Council which cannot be implied from Article 41 itself, is underlined by the precedents. The UK had called for the adoption of Resolution 221, since without the authority of the Security Council 'the United Kingdom Government has to face defiance of the United Nations with its hands tied ...', Lord Caradon had stated, for it could 'not risk acting in breach of the law of nations ...'.[27]

---

23 This well-established rule is reflected in Articles 87 and 110 of the 1982 United Nations Convention on the Law of the Sea.
24 Resolution 221(1966) calls on only one state – the United Kingdom; Resolution 665(1990) calls on all States 'cooperating with the government of Kuwait'; Resolution 787(1992) on Yugoslavia calls upon 'States, acting nationally or through regional agencies or arrangements ...', *i.e.* literally any state, member of the UN or not.
25 See intervention by Cuba in SCOR (1990), 2938th meeting, para. II. On this issue see G. Guillaume, 'La crise du Golfe et son développement jusqu'au 15 janvier 1991', in B. Stern (ed.), *Les Aspects juridiques de la crise et de la guerre du golfe*, Paris 1991, pp. 123-130.
26 *Military and Paramilitary Activities in and Against Nicaragua (Merits), ICJ Reports 1986.*
27 SCOR, 21st year, 1276th meeting, para. 21.

Again, despite the initial position of the United States and the UK that measures of visit and search of Iraqi and other vessels had been adopted in response to a request from the Kuwaiti government in exile, it was again nonetheless considered necessary to seek authorization from the Council.

Article 103 of the Charter of course ensures that 'in the event of a conflict between the obligations of the Members of the United Nations ... and their obligations under any other international agreement' their Charter obligations prevail. It is interesting to note, in that connection, that Resolution 670 on Iraq relating to the cargo-related air embargo, specifically refers to that article, in view of the likelihood of conflicts between the Charter and the Chicago Convention or other agreements regulating air traffic, though both this resolution and a similarly worded one on Yugoslavia, refer also to 'rights' in addition to the obligations stipulated by Article 103.[28]

However, the question that is posed with respect to enforcement at sea, is the extent to which the Security Council can by means of a resolution *not governed by Article 25 of the UN Charter* override, under Article 103, the obligations of member states under international law. For in none of these resolutions is the call to enforce the economic embargo made mandatory.

The portent of this was underlined by Arthur Goldberg, then US Ambassador to the UN, when he characterized Resolution 221 as: 'one of the gravest and most far-reaching proposals that has been made to this Council ... we are asked ... to put our sanction upon what will be a rule of international law – that when this Council acts vessels on the high seas can be arrested and detained in the interest of the international law which we will be making here today ...'.[29]

If indeed such 'calls' on states are seen as authorizations for states to resort to measures ordinarily prohibited by international law, the lack of an express Charter provision empowering the Security Council to authorize action as distinct from a recommendation or a decision, results in a certain ambiguity.

This question has its importance in the framework of state responsibility and has been addressed in passing by the International Law Commission, which has stated: 'Sanctions applied in conformity with the provisions of the Charter would certainly not be wrongful in the legal system of the United Nations, even though they might

---

28 See also *Case concerning Questions of Interpretation and Application of the 1971 Montreal Convention Arising from the Aerial Incident at Lockerbie (Libyan Arab Jamahiriya v. United States of America)* and *ibid., (Libyan Arab Jamahiriya v. United Kingdom), ICJ Reports 1992*, Requests for the Indication of Provisional Measures (Orders of 14 April 1992), dissenting opinion of Judge Bedjaoui, common para. 29: 'That Article (103), is aimed at 'obligations' – whereas we are dealing with (Libya's) alleged 'rights' ... and, in addition, does not cover such rights as may have other than conventional sources and be derived from general international law.'

29 SCOR, 21st year, 1276th meeting, paras. 68 and 69.

conflict with other treaty obligations incumbent upon the State applying them ...
(even) where the taking of such measures is merely recommended.'[30]

Economic sanctions and non-derogable rights

The exception noted by Nico Schrijver in Resolution 661 on Iraq relating to the
provision of foodstuffs,in humanitarian circumstances, has aroused a certain degree
of controversy.

Quite apart from the scope of the provision, the authority to determine when the
exception applies, and the practical difficulties involved in its implementation, many
commentators have expressed concern in respect of its compatibility with peacetime
human rights as well as humanitarian law.[31]

Such concern over the incompatibility of certain measures with constitutional and
international human rights law had already been expressed at the time of the adoption
of the Southern Rhodesian sanctions. It will be noted that these sanctions resolutions
carried broader exceptions than those on Iraq and Yugoslavia, since they also
encompassed educational equipment, publications, and news material (Res.
253(1968)). Moreover, the severance of 'postal, telegraphic, and radio communications', a measure clearly provided for by Article 41, was not resorted to on the basis
that this would run counter to the free flow of information and would be contrary to
the fulfilment of essential human needs.

Finally, the barring of entry into states' territories of certain categories of
Southern Rhodesian residents (Res. 253(1968)), whilst adopted as a measure, had
been considered by some representatives to be contrary to individual freedom of
movement, including those of nationals.[32]

This debate gathered force in the Sanctions Committee on Iraq with respect to the
exception relating to foodstuffs. Cuba and Yemen, for instance,wished to see a
general exemption for foodstuffs, stating that they could never accept any definition
which would allow the supply of foodstuffs only to avert famine, since this would
be in direct violation of the international human right to food.[33]

With respect to the incompatibility of this provision with the provisions of the
1949 Geneva Conventions protecting the civilian population of Iraq and occupied

---

30 *Yearbook of the International Law Commission* 1979, Vol. II (Part Two), p. 119; *ibid.*, Vol. II (Part
One), pp. 43-44. See also a question raised by a member of the ILC in *ibid.*, 1979, Vol. I, p. 57.
31 See L. Condorelli, 'Le droit humanitaire dans la crise et la 'Guerre' du Golfe', in *Les aspects
juridiques de la crise et de la Guerre du Golfe*, *supra* note 25, pp. 195-197; J.-P. Lavoyer, 'Le CICR et
le conflit du Golfe – quelques aspects juridiques', in *ibid.*, p. 201.
32 See Gowlland-Debbas, *supra* note 7, pp. 437-441 and 459-460.
33 See interventions by Cuba in the Sanctions Committee, reproduced in Lauterpacht and Bethlehem,
supra note 16, Part II, pp. 778 and 793.

Kuwait, it has been pointed out[34] that the wording of Resolution 661 is more restrictive than that provided for in Article 23 of the Fourth Convention, which relates to the free passage, subject to certain conditions, of consignments, *inter alia,* of medical supplies, essential foodstuffs and clothing.

This consciousness of the need to bring Chapter VII measures in line with humanitarian law, is reflected in Resolution 666, which in singling out the need to pay particular attention to the more vulnerable categories of civilians, *i.e.* children under 15 years of age, expectant mothers, maternity cases, the sick and the elderly, comes closer to fulfilling the requirements of humanitarian law. Yet it was only after the shattering report of the UN mission headed by the executive delegate of the Secretary-General, Martii Ahtissari,[35] which concluded on the serious nutritional and health situation of the Iraqi civilian population, that the Council eased the sanctions regime by excluding materials and supplies for essential civilian needs, though with the prior approval of the Sanctions Committee (Res. 687(1991)).[36]

The essential question remains whether Article 103 can operate where member states' obligations under other instruments or under customary law arise from norms which are non-derogable.

It is generally agreed that the protective norms of the Geneva Conventions belong to the realm of peremptory norms which represent the superior interests of the international community.[37] This is attested to by several provisions ensuring their application in all circumstances, above all common Article 1, in which the High Contracting Parties undertake to respect and to ensure respect for the Convention in all circumstances. Moreover, Article 60, para. 5 of the Vienna Convention on the Law of Treaties specifically provides that provisions in treaties of a humanitarian character relating to the protection of the human person cannot be terminated or suspended.

It should be pointed out that in its *Namibia Opinion* the International Court of Justice did indeed draw the outer parameters of the interpretation of Security Council

---

34   T. Meron, 'Prisoners of War, Civilians and Diplomats in the Gulf Crisis', 85 *AJIL* (1991), pp. 104-109, at pp. 107-108.

35   UN Doc. S/2236, 20 March, 1991. *Report to the Secretary-General on humanitarian needs in Kuwait and Iraq in the immediate post-crisis environment by a mission to the area led by Mr. Martti Ahitisaari, Under Secretary-General for Administration and Management.* The report states, *inter alia,* 'The mission noted that Iraq has been heavily dependent on food imports which have amounted to at least 70 per cent of consumption needs .... Sanctions decided upon by the Security Council had already adversely affected the country's ability to feed its people', p. 6.

36   Resolution 757(1992) on Yugoslavia is more broadly worded in exempting supplies 'intended strictly for medical purposes and *foodstuffs notified to the* (Sanctions) *Committee* ...' (italics added).

37   See G. Abi-Saab, 'The Specificities of Humanitarian Law', in *Studies and Essays on International Humanitarian Law and Red Cross Principles,* C. Swinarski (ed.), Geneva/The Hague 1984, pp. 265-280; L. Condorelli and L. Boisson De Chazournes, 'Quelques remarques à propos de l'obligation des Etats de 'respecter et faire respecter' le droit international humanitaire 'en toutes circonstances'', in *ibid.,* pp. 17-35.

Resolutions. Interpreting paragraph 2 of Resolution 276(1970), the Court held that the obligation on States not to enter into treaty relations with South Africa could not be applied to certain general conventions such as those of a humanitarian character, the non-performance of which might adversely affect the people of Namibia. Again it stated that the duty of non-recognition imposed by Resolution 276 of South Africa's administration of the territory should not result in depriving the people of Namibia of any advantage derived from international co-operation.[38]

The controversy which has arisen over the scope of sanctions measures therefore lies at the heart of the debate on an international public policy, for surely the Charter should be read in the light of the evolution of human rights law since 1945, and of international efforts since World War I to extend the protection afforded to the civilian population in time of armed conflict?

I would like to conclude by quoting the Court's views in the *Namibia Opinion*, admitting of an evolutionary approach to Charter interpretation. The Court, though taking into account 'the necessity of interpreting an instrument in accordance with the intentions of the parties at the time of its conclusion', considered that certain concepts embodied in a treaty – in the case before it, the concepts of Article 22 of the Covenant relating to the 'sacred trust' – were not static but evolutionary concepts and that it must have been the intention of the parties at the time to have accepted them as such. The Court went further in holding also that 'an international instrument has to be interpreted and applied within the framework of the entire legal system prevailing at the time of the interpretation'.[39]

COMMENTS

Hans-Peter Gasser[*]

As rapporteur Nice Schrijver correctly writes in his paper (p. 145): 'In all three cases [Southern Rhodesia, Iraq and Yugoslavia (Serbia and Montenegro)] exceptions to the prohibitions include supplies intended strictly for medical purposes and, in humanitarian circumstances, foodstuffs.' The purpose of my comment is to clarify what is meant by a 'humanitarian exception' to economic sanctions and to discuss some of the lessons to be learned, in particular from the Second Gulf War.

1. With its Resolution 661 (of 6 August 1990) the Security Council decided to take economic sanctions against a State – Iraq – which at that moment was involved in a war. The norms of international humanitarian law applicable to international armed conflict applied to this conflict. Iraq and the members of the Coalition were therefore bound to respect in particular the four 1949 Geneva Conventions and relevant customary law. (Additional Protocol I of 8 June 1977 was not applicable as neither Iraq nor the major Coalition powers had acceded to it.) The Security Council had to take these treaty obligations into account when deciding on the embargo under Chapter VII of the United Nations Charter.

Article 103 of the Charter presumes the powers of the Security Council to override treaty obligations of States. The purpose here is not to discuss the implications of this rule. Suffice it to say that in adopting a resolution under Chapter VII, the Security Council may be presumed to have no intention of infringing upon treaty obligations which otherwise bind Member States. Therefore, such a resolution must be construed in a way which avoids collision with such other obligations. This seems particularly true in the case of multilateral treaties of a humanitarian character which are universally accepted - such as the 1949 Geneva Conventions. They carry a weight which the Security Council acting under Chapter VII must take into account.

2. Any decision on economic sanctions against a State involved in an armed conflict must therefore heed in particular Article 23 of the Fourth Geneva Convention relative

---

[*]   Dr. H.-P. Gasser is Legal Adviser at the International Committee of the Red Cross in Geneva.

H.H.G. Post (ed.), International Economic Law and Armed Conflict, 175–179.

to the protection of civilian persons in war (of 12 August 1949). According to this provision a party to an international armed conflict has the right to receive relief for its civilian population as follows:

a) consignments of medical and hospital stores and objects necessary for religious worship, for the benefit of the civilian population in general, and

b) consignments of essential foodstuffs, clothing and tonics, for the benefit of children under fifteen, pregnant women and mothers with small children.

All States, *i.e.* both adversary and neutral ones, are under an obligation to allow the free passage of such relief consignments. This holds true whether they are bound for the adverse party's own population or for the inhabitants of occupied territory.

The passage of such relief consignments may be made subject to the following conditions or arrangements (Article 23 paras. 2 and 3):

a) that there be adequate assurance that the goods are not diverted to other use;

b) that there be effective control over the operation;

c) that no definite advantage can be derived by the embargoed State through substitution;

d) that distribution of the goods be made under the supervision of the Protecting Power or the International Committee of the Red Cross.

Additional Protocol I of 8 June 1977, while confirming the law of 1949, has also widened the basis for international relief for war victims. Under the heading 'Relief Actions', its Article 70 specifies that relief operations 'which are humanitarian and impartial in character and conducted without any adverse distinction' shall be undertaken if the civilian population is not adequately provided with the goods essential for its survival. In addition to food and medical supplies, the Protocol mentions *inter alia* clothing, bedding and means of shelter. It also stipulates that relief operations shall be undertaken 'subject to the agreement of the Parties concerned'. Under 'parties concerned' are comprised the State party to an armed conflict on whose territory the needs have arisen, the adverse party which may have physical control over access to that territory, and third-party States, normally neutrals, through which relief would have to be shipped. These States are under an obligation to give their consent to such an operation if the absence of assistance would amount to exposing the population concerned to starvation. Indeed, Protocol I has not only strengthened the international rules on relief assistance but its Article 54 has reiterated a basic rule of humanitarian law: 'Starvation of civilians as a method of warfare is prohibited.'

Although Protocol I was not applicable to the Gulf War, a case can be made for considering that the prohibition of starvation as embodied in its Article 54 is part of customary law. As such, the rule had to be respected by parties to the conflict ... and by the Security Council as well.

To sum up this short analysis of the applicable international rules, international law requires that relief must reach civilians in need of assistance, even though economic sanctions may have interrupted the flow of goods into that country. That means that international humanitarian law does not permit a total ban on the shipment of goods into an embargoed country. Exceptions have to be granted: those are the 'humanitarian exceptions'.

3. Did the Security Council heed these provisions when imposing economic sanctions on Iraq? An exception from the ban on all imports of goods into Iraq is made by Resolution 661 (of 6 August 1990), in its para. 3c), for 'supplies intended strictly for medical purposes and, in humanitarian circumstances, foodstuffs'. This means that supplies for medical purposes are totally excluded from the embargo. The delivery of foodstuffs, however, needs be authorized only 'in humanitarian circumstances'. With such broad wording of the exception Resolution 661 goes beyond Article 23 of the Fourth Convention, in which the obligation to bring relief is limited to children, pregnant women and mothers with small children. Resolution 661 extends the right to relief to the population at large in conformity with Article 70 of Protocol I. This is a highly commendable step towards taking into account the needs of all sections of the population. The same Resolution establishes a committee of the Security Council – the 'Sanctions Committee' – with the task of supervising the implementation of the sanctions.

According to Resolution 661 supplies of foodstuffs for civilians have to be exempted from the embargo only if 'humanitarian circumstances' so require. This is a vague wording which contrasts with the more specific guideline given by Article 70 of Protocol I: 'If the civilian population ... is not adequately provided with the supplies mentioned in ....' The Security Council had two options for making the notion of 'humanitarian circumstances' operational: either to render its wording more specific or to set up procedures to determine its meaning in any specific case. The Council chose the second course and, without modifying the substantive provisions of Resolution 661, Resolution 666 (of 13 September 1990) established procedures under which the Sanctions Committee has to grant permission for importing foodstuffs into Iraq.

Under Resolution 666, the Secretary General was given the task of monitoring the availability of foodstuffs in Iraq and the then occupied Kuwait and reporting his findings to the Sanctions Committee. As the resolution specifically mentions, special attention has to be given to the situation of children, expectant mothers, maternity cases, the sick and the elderly (implied reference to Article 23 of the Fourth Convention!). The Secretary General is requested to seek information from UN agencies and, in particular, from humanitarian organizations. Furthermore, relief goods should be transferred to Iraq or Kuwait through the United Nations, in cooperation with the ICRC and other humanitarian organizations, and distributed by them. Resolution 666 thereby acknowledges the mandate of the ICRC, whose delegates were present in Iraq for the whole duration of the war and have been on the spot ever since. They are particularly well qualified to make surveys of the nutritional and medical situation and to evaluate the needs. ICRC delegates were also in a position to monitor the distribution of relief supplies to persons in need and, to a certain extent, to prevent relief goods from falling into wrong hands.

4. How did the sanctions against Iraq affect assistance to Iraqi civilians? How did the ICRC cope with these – for the ICRC – unusual potential constraints on its assistance activity? The following comment is confined to ICRC operations in Iraq as its delegates had no access to occupied Kuwait.

Delegates determined the needs of those parts of the Iraqi population to which they had access, *i.e.* during the war mainly the people in the Baghdad area, and of stranded foreigners. Their reports were assessed at headquarters in Geneva. The ICRC then informed the Sanctions Committee of the Security Council about its planned operation, giving all details of the proposed shipment. Strictly speaking, the ICRC did not ask the Sanctions Committee for permission to go ahead with the relief operation. In its view, the Geneva Conventions give the ICRC full authority to act as a neutral intermediary for the benefit of the victims of war, subject only to the applicable standards set out in the humanitarian law treaties.

The Sanctions Committee delivered the necessary documents without delay. A quick and acceptable answer sometimes had to be found in difficult instances, such as the request to import spare parts for water pumps or chemicals for the purification of water. Both items could also be used for less peaceful purposes. Shipments were always open to inspection. Through its delegates on the spot who monitored distribution of the relief goods the ICRC was able to offer an adequate guarantee for the destination of the goods. The ICRC's open and forthright approach meant that working relations between the UN Sanctions Committee and the ICRC were good. It seems that the neutral and impartial character of the ICRC, combined with its capacity to monitor the distribution of the relief goods through physical presence of its delegates in the war zone, convinced the members of the Sanctions Committee – and through it the Security Council (of which the major Coalition powers were members) – that the International Committee had a necessary and beneficial role to play in the context of the economic sanctions against Iraq, namely to make the 'humanitarian exception' in favour of the civilian population work.

5. With Resolution 757 (of 30 May 1992) the Security Council decided to impose economic sanctions on Yugoslavia (Serbia and Montenegro). The 'humanitarian exception' as established by this resolution is broader than the one allowed for in Resolution 666 on Iraq: all medical supplies and foodstuffs are exempted from the sanctions.

6. To conclude this short comment on humanitarian exceptions to economic sanctions, it should be noted that although under present-day international law economic sanctions are permitted instruments of warfare, economic sanctions must not place an intolerable strain upon the civilian population, and in particular its especially vulnerable groups. Humanitarian law, above all the Fourth Geneva Convention and Additional Protocol I, make 'humanitarian exceptions' to the sanctions obligatory. As a neutral and impartial institution mandated by the community of States to work on behalf of all groups of war victims, the ICRC is well equipped to implement such exceptions.

COMMENTS

Karel Wellens[*]

Professor Bothe and Dr. Gioia[1] both indicated the impact of binding Security Council resolutions on the principle and practice of neutrality. I would like to draw the attention to recommendatory resolutions of the Security Council, frequently used in the period preceding the adoption of a binding resolution – 'calling upon States not to ...'. In these cases the choice of staying neutral is just simply taken away from Member States by the Security Council.

In paragraph I of his paper Nico Schrijver gives a definition of sanctions. I would like to point out that the necessary link between peace and security and the imposition of sanctions becomes more and more questionable in certain cases. On the one hand the Security Council inevitably has to go through the qualification under Article 39 before it can even recommend or impose sanctions. On the other hand, the Council considers the hindrance of delivery of humanitarian assistance also under the same umbrella. The decision in the *Lockerbie* case[2] has demonstrated the difficulty in this approach when the Security Council is confronted with alleged violations of international law, even serious ones, but the Council then has to classify them as threats to international peace and security in order to be able to impose sanctions. Dr. Gowlland-Debbas writes about re-reading the Charter.[3] In my view, the problem I have just indicated calls for such a re-reading, as otherwise sanctions would become impossible without the situation at hand constituting at the same time a threat to peace and security.

Nico Schrijver, in an earlier version of his contribution, distinguished three functions for sanctions: '(a) a way of expressing condemnation of certain unlawful behaviour; (b) a form of punishment and retaliation for unlawful behaviour; and (c) a method of persuading or forcing a change of policy'. In my view, the first function cannot be classified as a separate category because sanctions will always operate,

---

[*] Dr. K.C. Wellens is Professor of Public International Law at the University of Nijmegen.
[1] See their contributions to this volume at p. 35 ff. and p. 51 ff. respectively.
[2] Case Concerning 'Questions of Interpretation and Application of the 1971 Montreal Convention Arising from the Aerial Incident at Lockerbie', (Libyan Arab Jamahiriya v. United States of America) *ICJ Reports* (1992), pp. 114-128.
[3] See her contribution at p. 163 ff. of this volume.

either as a form of punishment and retaliation or as a method of persuasion or forcing a change of policy. This seems to be more in line with the Rapporteur's point of view expressed *supra,* on page 146: 'With the exception of the Libyan and perhaps the Iraqi case, the sanctions were thus intended not so much to punish or repress the target State, but rather to coerce it to put an end to unlawful policies. In other words, they were meant to serve as collective measures to redress an international wrongful act and to restore legality.'

My final remark concerns *supra* page 156, where it is stated: 'Yet the cutting off of relations, whether commercial or diplomatic, may also eliminate opportunities for dialogue and public pressure.' That may very well be true at bilateral level, but there are of course the debates within the Security Council offering ample opportunity for public pressure on the target State, but we should keep in mind, as far as 'dialogue' is concerned, that 'due process of law' is often disregarded by the Security Council towards the accused State, as was clearly illustrated by the Iraqi and Libyan cases, in spite of the reference made this morning by Mr Heere, unintentionally I imagine, to the 'Security Council and any other international tribunal'.

SELECTED BIBLIOGRAPHY

Abi-Saab, G., 'The Specificities of Humanitarian Law', in C. Swinarski (ed.), *Studies and Essays on International Humanitarian Law and Red Cross Principles,* Geneva/The Hague 1984, pp. 265-280.

Ago, R., 'Seventh Report on State Responsibility', *Yearbook of the International Law Commission* 1978, Vol. II, Part One, pp. 31 ff.

Ago, R., 'Eighth Report on State Responsibility', Chapter V, 'Circumstances Precluding Wrongfulness', *Yearbook of the International Law Commission 1979*, Vol. II, Part One, pp. 27 ff.

Ago, R., 'Addendum to the Eighth Report on State Responsibility', *Yearbook of the International Law Commission* 1980, Vol. II, Part One, pp. 13 ff.

Akehurst, M., 'Reprisals by Third States', 44 *British Year Book of International Law* 1970, pp. 1 ff.

Back Impallomeni, E., *Il principio rebus sic stantibus nella Convenzione di Vienna sul diritto dei trattati*, Milan 1974.

Balladore Pallieri, G., *Diritto bellico*, 2nd ed., Padua 1954.

Barsotti, R., 'Armed Reprisals', in A. Cassese (ed.), *The Current Legal Regulation of the Use of Force*, Dordrecht/Boston/Lancaster 1986, pp. 78 ff.

Bayliss, J.F.T., 'The Law and Practice of Maritime Embargoes and Blockades in the Context of UN Security Council Enforcement Measures', in *Contemporary International Law Issues: Opportunity at the time of momentous change. Proceedings 1993 Joint Conference of the American Society of International Law and Netherlands International Law Association*, Dordrecht 1994, pp. 339-342.

Bergeijk, P.A.G. van, *Economic Diplomacy, Trade and Commercial Policy: Positive and Negative Sanctions in a New World Order*, Cheltenham 1994.

Bertram, A., 'The Economic Weapon as a Form of Peaceful Pressure', in *Transactions of the Grotius Society*, vol. 17 (1932), pp. 139-174.

Bianchi, A., 'Esportazione e transito di armamenti: profili di diritto internazionale', 75 *Rivista di diritto internazionale* 1992, pp. 65 ff.

Bierzanek, R., 'Reprisals as a Means of Enforcing the Laws of Warfare', in A. Cassese (ed.), *The Current Legal Regulation of the Use of Force*, Dordrecht/Boston/Lancaster 1986, pp. 232 ff.

Bindschedler, R.L., 'Neutrality, Concept and General Rules', 4 *Encyclopedia of Public International Law*, Amsterdam/New York/Oxford 1982, p. 9 ff.

Bindschedler, R.L., 'Permanent Neutrality of States', 4 *Encyclopedia of Public International Law*, Amsterdam/New York/Oxford 1982, p. 133 ff.

Blix, H., *Sovereignty, Aggression and Neutrality*, Stockholm 1970, p. 41 ff.

Bluntschli, J.C., *Das Beuterecht im Kriege und das Seebeuterecht insbesondere; Eine völkerrechtliche Untersuchung*, Nördlingen 1878/Amsterdam 1970.

Bohr, S., 'Sanctions by the United Nations Security Council and the European Community', in 4 *European Journal of International Law* 1993, pp. 256-268.

Borchard, E., 'War, Neutrality and Non-Belligerency', 35 *American Journal of International Law* 1941, pp. 618 ff.

Bothe, M., *Das völkerrechtliche Verbot des Einsatzes chemischer und bakteriologischer Waffen*, Köln/Bonn, 1973.

Bothe, M., 'Die Erklärung der General-versammlung der Vereinten Nationen über die Definition der Aggression', 18 *German Yearbook of International Law* 1975, pp. 127 ff.

Bothe, M., 'Chemical Warfare', in 3 *Encyclopedia of Public International Law*, Amsterdam/New York/Oxford, 1982, pp. 83 ff.

Bothe, M., Partsch, K.J., Solf, W.A., *New Rules for Victims of Armed Conflicts*, The Hague/Boston/London 1982.

Bothe, M., Cassese, A., Kalshoven, F., Kiss, A., Salmon, J., Simmonds, K.R., *Protection of the Environment in Times of Armed Conflict* (European Communities, Commission, Doc. SJ/110/85) 1985, p. 47.

Bothe, M., 'Neutrality in Naval Warfare. What is Left of Traditional International Law?', in A.J.M. Delissen, G.J. Tanja (eds.), *Humanitarian Law of Armed Conflict. Challenges Ahead. Essays in Honour of Frits Kalshoven*, Dordrecht/Boston/London 1991, p. 387 ff.

Bothe, M., 'Neutrality at Sea', in I.F. Dekker, H.H.G. Post (eds.), *The Gulf War of 1980-1988*, Dordrecht/Boston/London, 1992, pp. 205 ff.

Bowett, D.W., *Self-Defence in International Law*, Manchester 1958.

Bowett, D.W., 'Reprisals Involving Recourse to Armed Force', 66 *American Journal of International Law* 1972, pp. 1 ff.

Boyle, F.A., 'International Crisis and Neutrality: U.S. Foreign Policy Toward the Iran-Iraq War', in A.T. Leonhard (ed.), *Neutrality. Changing Concepts and Practices*, Lanham/New York/London 1988, p. 59 ff.

Bring, O., 'Comments', in I.F. Dekker, H.H.G. Post (eds.), *The Gulf War of 1980-1988*, Dordrecht/Boston/London 1992, p. 243 ff.

Broms, B., 'The Definition of Aggression', 154 *Hague Recueil* 1977, I, pp. 305 ff.

Brown, Th.D., 'World War Prize Law Applied in a Limited War Situation: Egyptian Restrictions on Neutral Shipping with Israel', 50 *Minnesota Law Review* 1965-1966, p. 849 ff.

Brownlie, I., *International Law and the Use of Force by States*, Oxford 1963.

Brownlie, I., *System of the Law of Nations. State Responsibility*, Part I, Oxford 1983.

Cadoux, C., 'La supériorité du droit des Nations Unies sur le droit des Etats membres', 63 *Revue général de droit international public* 1959, pp. 649-680.

Cahier, P., 'Le changement fondamental de circonstances et la Convention de Vienne de 1969 sur le droit des traités', in *International Law at the Time of Its Codification. Essays in Honour of Roberto Ago*, Vol. I, Milan 1987, pp. 163 ff.

Calogeropoulos-Stratis, S., *Le Pacte général de renonciation à la guerre*, Paris 1931.

Canadian Forces, *Law of Armed Conflict Manual* (Second Draft), Ottawa 1988.

Carver, J.P., in *Proceedings of the 85th Annual Meeting of the American Society of International Law*, Washington DC 1991, p. 183.

Cassese, A. (ed.), *The Current Legal Regulation of the Use of Force*, Dordrecht/ Boston/Lancaster 1986.

Cassese, A., 'Le droit international et la question de l'assistence aux mouvements de libération nationale', 19 *Revue belge de droit international* 1986, p. 307 ff.

Castrén, E., *The Present Law of War and Neutrality*, Helsinki 1954.

Cavaglieri, A., 'Belligeranza, neutralità e posizioni giuridiche intermedie', 13 *Rivista di diritto internazionale* 1919, pp. 58 ff. and 328 ff.

Chaumont, C., 'Nations Unies et neutralité', 89 *Hague Recueil* 1956, I, p. 1 ff.

C.J. Colombos, *The International Law of the Sea*, 5th ed., London 1962.

Combacau, J., 'The Exception of Self-Defence in U.N. Practice', in A. Cassese (ed.), *The Current Legal Regulation of the Use of Force*, Dordrecht/Boston/Lancaster, 1986, pp. 9 ff.

The Commander's Handbook on the Law of Naval Operations (NWP 9 Rev. A), Washington DC 1989.

Condorelli, L., Boisson De Chazournes, L., 'Quelques remarques à propos de l'obligation des Etats de 'respecter et faire respecter' le droit international humanitaire 'en toutes circonstances'', in C. Swinarski (ed.), *Studies and Essays on International Humanitarian Law and Red Cross Principles,* Geneva/The Hague 1984, pp. 17-35.

Condorelli, L., 'Le droit humanitaire dans la crise et la 'Guerre' du Golfe', in B. Stern (ed.), *Les Aspects juridiques de la crise et de la guerre du golfe*, Paris 1991, pp. 195-197.

Conetti, G., 'Società delle Nazioni', 17 *Enciclopedia del diritto*, Milan 1990, p. 1167 ff.

De Nova, R., *La neutralità nel sistema della Società delle Nazioni*, Pavia, 1935.

De Nova, R., 'Neutralità e Nazioni Unite', 1 *La Comunità internazionale* 1946, pp. 495 ff.

De Guttry, A., *Le rappresaglie non comportanti la forza militare nel diritto internazionale*, Milan 1985.

Dehejia, R.H., Wood, B., 'Economic Sanctions and Econometric Policy Evaluation: A Cautionary Note', in 26 *Journal of World Trade* 1992, pp. 73-84.

Delbez, l., 'La notion juridique de guerre', 57 *Revue générale de droit international Public* 1953, pp. 177-209.

Delbrück, J., 'Collective Security', 3 *Encyclopedia of Public International Law*, Amsterdam/New York/Oxford, 1982, pp. 104 ff.

Delivanis, J., *La légitime défense en droit international public moderne*, Paris 1971, pp. 148 ff.

Dinstein, Y., 'The Laws of War at Sea', *Israelian Yearbook of Human Rights* 1980, p. 56 ff.

Dinstein, Y., 'The Laws of Neutrality', 14 *Israelian Yearbook of Human Rights* 1984, p. 80 ff.

Dinstein, Y., *War, Aggression and Self-Defence*, Cambridge 1988, pp. 12 and 145 ff.

Dinstein, Y., 'Remarks', 82 *Proceedings of the American Society of International Law* 1988, pp. 606 ff.

Doswald Beck, L., 'The International Law of Naval Armed Conflicts: The Need for reform', 7 *Italian Yearbook of International Law* 1986-1987, pp. 251 ff.

Doswald Beck, L., 'Remarks', 82 *Proceedings of the American Society of International Law* 1988, pp. 599 ff.

Doxey, M., *International Sanctions in Contemporary Perspective*, London 1987, Chapter 3.

Doxey, M., 'Sanctions in an Unstable International Environment: Lessons from the Gulf Conflict', in 2 *Diplomacy & Statecraft* 1991, pp. 207-225.

Eisemann, P.M., 'Article 41', in J.P. Cot, A. Pellet (eds.), *La Charte des Nations Unies. Commentaire article par article*, 2e éd., Paris 1991, pp. 691-704.

Elagab, O.Y., *The Legality of Non-Forcible Countermeasures in International Law*, Oxford 1988.

Eustathiadès, C.T., 'La définition de l'agression adoptée aux Nations Unies et la légitime défense', 28 *Revue héllenique de droit international* 1975, pp. 5 ff.

Fabela, I., *Neutralité*, Paris 1949, pp. 156-157.

Fastenrath, U., *Lücken im Völkerrecht*, Berlin 1991.

Fenrick, W.J., 'The Exclusion Zone Device in the Law of Naval Warfare', 24 *Canadian Yearbook of International Law* 1986, pp. 91 ff.

Fenrick, W.J., 'Legal Aspects of Targeting in the Law of Naval Warfare', 29 *Canadian Yearbook of International Law* 1991, pp. 238 ff.

Fenrick, W.J., 'The Merchant Vessel as a Legitimate Target in the Law of Naval Warfare', in A.J.M. Delissen, G.J. Tanja (eds.), *Humanitarian Law of Armed Conflict. Challenges Ahead. Essays in Honour of Frits Kalshoven*, Dordrecht/Boston/London, 1991, pp. 425 ff.

Fenwick, C.G., 'Is Neutrality Still a Term of Present Law?', in 63 *American Journal of International Law* 1969, pp. 100-102.

Ferencz, B.B., 'Aggression', 3 *Encyclopedia of Public International Law*, Amsterdam/New York/Oxford 1982, pp. 1 ff.

Forland, T.E., 'The History of Economic Warfare: International Law, Effectiveness, Strategies', 30 *Journal of Peace Research* 1993, p. 151 ff.

Fox, H., Wrickremasinghe, C., 'UK Implementation of UN Economic Sanctions', in 42 *International and Comparative Law Quarterly* 1993, pp. 945-970.

François, J.P.A., 'L'egalité d'application des règles du droit de la guerre aux parties à un conflit armé', 50 *Annuaire del'Institut de droit international* 1963, I, p. 5 ff.

Franck, Th.M., 'The Powers of 'Appreciation': Who is the Ultimate Guardian of UN Legality?', 86 *American Journal of International Law* 1992, pp. 519-523.

Friedman, W., *The Changing Structure of International Law*, London 1964.

Gaja, G., 'Il Consiglio di Sicurezza di fronte all'occupazione del Kuwait: il significato di una autorizzazione', 73 *Rivista di diritto internazionale* 1990, pp. 696-697.

Gioia, A., 'Il ricorso alla forza armata da parte argentina e la reazione britannica', in N. Ronzitti (ed.), *La questione delle Falkland-Malvinas nel diritto internazionale*, Milan 1984, pp. 123 ff.

Gioia, A., Ronzitti, N., 'The Law of Neutrality: Third States' Commercial Rights and Duties', in I.F. Dekker, H.H.G. Post (eds.), *The Gulf War of 1980-1988*, Dordrecht/Boston/London 1992, p. 221 ff.

Gioia, A., 'Commentary', in A. De Guttry, N. Ronzitti (eds.), *The Iran-Iraq War (1980-1988) and the Dispatch of Western Fleets to the Gulf. A Collection of Documents and Related Commentaries on Naval Warfare*, Cambridge 1993, pp. 57 ff.

Gioia, A., 'The CWC and Its Application in Time of Armed Conflict', in M. Bothe, N. Ronzitti, A. Rosas (eds.), *Chemical Weapons Disarmament: Strategies and Legal Problems*, Stockholm 1993.

Giuliano, M., *I diritti e gli obblighi degli Stati*, Padua 1956.

Gowlland-Debbas, V., *Collective Responses to Illegal Acts in International Law. United Nations Action in the Question of Southern Rhodesia*, Dordrecht 1990.

Gowlland-Debbas, V. 'Security Council Enforcement Action and Issues of State Responsibility, 43 *International and Comparative Law Quarterly* (1994), pp. 55-98.

Greenwood, C., 'The Concept of War in Modern International Law', 36 *International and Comparative Law Quarterly* 1987, p. 283 ff.

Greenwood, C.J., 'Remarks', 82 *Proceedings of the American Society of International Law* 1988, pp. 158 ff.

Greenwood, C., 'The Twilight of the Law of Belligerent Reprisals', 20 *Netherlands Yearbook of International Law* 1989, pp. 35 ff.

Greenwood, C., 'Self-Defence and the Conduct of International Armed Conflict', in Y. Dinstein (ed.), *International Law at a Time of Perplexity*, Dordrecht/Boston/London 1989, pp. 273 ff.

Greenwood, C., 'Comments', in I.F. Dekker, H.H.G. Post (eds.), *The Gulf War of 1980-1988*, Dordrecht/Boston/London 1992, pp. 212 ff.

Greig, D.W., 'Self-Defence and the Security Council: What Does Article 51 Require?', 40 *International and Comparative Law Quarterly* 1991, pp. 306 ff.

Grelon, B., Gudin, C.-E., 'Contrats et crise du Golfe', 118 *Journal du droit international* 1991, pp. 633-677

Grob, F., *The Relativity of War and Peace*, New Haven 1949.

Gross, L., 'States as Organs of International Law and the Problem of Autointer pretation', in A. Lipsky (ed.), *Law and Politics in the World Community, Essays on Hans Kelsen's Pure Theory and Related Problems in International Law*, Berkely 1953, pp. 59-89.

Gross, L., 'Passage through the Suez Canal of Israel-Bound Cargo and Israel Ships', *American Journal of International Law* 1957, p. 530 ff.

Grotius, H., *De jure belli ac pacis libri tres* [1646], rep. in J.B. Scott (ed.), *The Classics of International Law*, Vol. I, Oxford/London 1925, Book I, Chapter III, iv; Book II, Chapter XIII, xiii, 5; Book III, Chapter III, i, Chapter IV, Chapter VI, ii, 1, Chapter X.

Grunawalt, R., 'The Rights of Neutrals and Belligerents', 19 *Ocean Development and International Law* 1988, pp. 303 ff.

Guggenheim, P., *Traité de droit international public*, Vol. II, Geneva 1954.

Guillaume, G., 'La crise du Golfe et son développement jusqu'au 15 janvier 1991', in B. Stern (ed.), *Les Aspects juridiques de la crise et de la guerre du golfe*, Paris 1991, pp. 123-130.

Haraszti, G., 'Treaties and Fundamental Change of Circumstances', 146 *Hague Recueil* 1975, III, pp. 1 ff.

Heintschell von Heinegg, W., 'Visit, Search, Diversion and Capture in Naval Warfare. Part 1: The Traditional Law', 29 *Canadian Yearbook of International Law* 1991, pp. 283 ff.

Heintschel von Heinegg, W., 'Kriegsentschädigung, Reparation oder Schadenersatz? – Die möglichen Forderungen an den Irak nach Beendigung des Golf-Kriegs', 90 *Zeitschrift für Vergleichende Rechtswissenschaften* 1991, pp. 113-129.

Henkin, L., 'Force, Intervention and Neutrality in Contemporary International Law', in R.A. Falk, S.H. Mendlovitz (eds.), *The Strategy of World Order*, Vol. II, *International Law*, New York 1966, p. 335 ff.

Higgins, R., *Development of International Law through the Political Organs of the United Nations*.

Huber, M., 'Die Fortbildung des Völkerrechts durch die II. Friedenskonferenz im Haag', *Das öffentliches Recht der Gegenwart. Jahrbuch 1908*, p. 586.

Hufbauer, G.C., Schott, J.J., Elliott, K.A., *Economic Sanctions Reconsidered: History and Current Policy*, 2nd. ed., Washington DC 1990.

Jenkins, M., 'Air Attacks on Neutral Shipping in the Persian Gulf: the Legality of the Iraqi Exclusion Zone and Iranian Reprisals', 8 *Boston College International and Comparative Law Review* 1985, pp. 517 ff.

Jessup, P.C., Deak, V., *Neutrality. Its History, Economics and Law*, Vol. I, *The Origins*, New York 1935.

Jessup, P.C., *Neutrality. Its History, Economics and Law*, Vol. IV, *Today and Tomorrow* [1936], New York 1976 (rep.), at p. 58 ff.

Kaempfer, W.H., Lowenberg, A.D., Mocan, H.N., Topyan, K., 'International sanctions and anti-apartheid policies in South Africa: An empirical investigation', in *The Use of Economic Sanctions in Trade and Environmental Policy*, OCfBE, Research Centre for Economic Policy, Erasmus University Rotterdam, Research Memorandum, No. 9307, 1993, pp. 1-36.

Kaikobad, K.H., '*Ius ad bellum*: Legal Implications of the Iran-Iraq War', in I.F. Dekker, H.H.G. Post (eds.), *The Gulf War of 1980-1988*, Dordrecht/Boston/London 1992, pp. 51 ff.

Kalshoven, F., *Belligerent Reprisals*, Leyden 1971.

Kalshoven, F., 'Commentary on the 1909 London Declaration', in: Ronzitti, N. (ed.), *The Law of Naval Warfare*, Dordrecht/Boston/London 1988, pp. 257-275

Kalshoven, F., 'Belligerent Reprisals Revisited', 21 *Netherlands Yearbook of International Law* 1990, pp. 43 ff.

Kaufmann, J., *United Nations Decision-making*, Dordrecht 1980.

Kaufmann, J., Leurdijk, D., Schrijver, N., *The World in Turmoil: Testing the UN's Capacity*, Academic Council on the United Nations, Reports 1991-4.

Kelsen, H., *The Law of the United Nations*, New York 1950.

Komarnicki, T., 'The Place of Neutrality in the Modern System of International Law', 80 *Hague Recueil* 1952, I, p. 395 ff.

Kooijmans, P.H., 'Zwijgt het recht als de Veiligheidsraad spreekt?', 27 *Nederlands Juristenblad*, 16 July 1992, pp. 847-851.

Kussbach, E., 'L'évolution de la notion de neutralité dans les conflits armés actuels', 17 *Revue de droit pénal militaire et de droit de la guerre* 1978, p. 19 ff.

Kussbach, E., 'Neutral Trading', 4 *Encyclopedia of Public International Law*, Amsterdam/New York/Oxford 1982, p. 7 ff.

Kuyper, P.J., *The Implementation of International Sanctions. The Netherlands and Rhodesia*, Alphen aan den Rijn 1978.

Kuyper, P.J., 'Trade Sanctions, Security and Human Rights', in M. Marescau (ed.), *The European Community's Commercial Policy after 1992: The Legal Dimension*, Dordrecht 1983, pp. 387-422.

Lagoni, R., 'Angary, Right of', 3 *Encyclopedia of Public International Law*, Amsterdam/New York/Oxford 1982, pp. 18 ff.

Lagoni, R., 'Gewaltverbot, Seekriegsrecht und Schiffahrtsfreiheit im Golfkrieg', in W. Fürst, R. Herzog, D.C. Umbach (eds.), *Festschrift für Wolfgang Zeidler*, Vol. II, Berlin/New York 1987, pp. 1833-1867.

Lagoni, R., 'Remarks', 82 *Proceedings of the American Society of International Law* 1988, pp. 161 ff.

Lalive, J.F., 'International Organization and Neutrality', 24 *British Yearbook of International Law* 1947, p. 72 ff.

Lamberti Zanardi, P., *La legittima difesa nel diritto internazionale*, Milan 1972.

Lamberti Zanardi, P., 'Indirect Military Aggression', in A. Cassese (ed.), *The Current Legal Regulation of the Use of Force*, Dordrecht/Boston/Lancaster 1986, pp. 111 ff.

Lattanzi, F., *Garanzie dei diritti dell'Uomo nel diritto internazionale generale*, Milan 1989.

Lavoyer, J.-P., 'Le CICR et le conflit du Golfe – quelques aspects juridiques', in B. Stern (ed.), *Les Aspects juridiques de la crise et de la guerre du golfe*, Paris 1991, p. 201.

Lauterpacht, E., 'The 'Legal Irrelevance' of a State of War', 62 *Proceedings of the American Society of International Law* 1968, p. 58 ff.

Lauterpacht, E. *et al.* (eds.), *The Kuwait Crisis: Sanctions and Their Economic Consequences*, Part I and II, Cambridge 1991.

Lauterpacht, H., 'Rules of Warfare in an Unlawful War', in *Law and Politics in the World Community. Essays on Hans Kelsen's Pure Theory and Related Problems in International Law*, Berkeley/Los Angeles 1953, pp. 89 ff.

Lauterpacht, H., 'The Limits of the Operation of the Law of War', *British Yearbook of International Law* Vol. XXX (1953), pp. 206-243.

Leben, C., 'Les contre-mesures inter-étatiques et les reactions a l'illicite dans la société internationale', 28 *Annuaire français de droit international* 1982, pp. 9 ff.

Leonhard, A.T. (ed.), *Neutrality. Changing Concepts and Practices*, Lanham/New York/London 1988.

Lowe, A.V., 'Commentary', in A. De Guttry, N. Ronzitti (eds.), *The Iran-Iraq War (1980-1988) and the Dispatch of Western Fleets to the Gulf. A Collection of Documents and Related Commentaries on Naval Warfare*, Cambridge 1993, pp. 241 ff.

Lowenfeld, A.F., *Trade Controls for Political Ends,* New York 1983, 2nd ed.

Mallisson, W.T., *Studies in the Law of Naval Warfare: Submarines in General and Limited Wars* (Naval War College, International Law Studies 1966), pp. 129 ff.

Martin, Lisa L., *Coercive Cooperation. Explaining Multilateral Economic Sanctions*, Princeton 1992.

Mc Dougal, M.S., Feliciano, F.P., *Law and Minimum World Public Order*, New Haven/London 1961.

Menefee, S.P., 'Commentary', in A. De Guttry, N. Ronzitti (eds.), *The Iran-Iraq War (1980-1988) and the Dispatch of Western Fleets to the Gulf. A Collection of Documents and Related Commentaries on Naval Warfare*, Cambridge 1993.

Meng, W., 'Contraband', 3 *Encyclopedia of Public International Law*, Amsterdam/New York/Oxford 1982, pp. 122 ff.

Meng, W., 'War', 4 *Encyclopedia of Public International Law*, Amsterdam/New York/Oxford 1982, p. 282 ff.

Meron, T., 'Remarks', 82 *Proceedings of the American Society of International Law* 1988, pp. 164 ff.

Meron, T., *Human Rights and Humanitarian Norms as Customary Law*, Oxford 1989.

Meron, T., 'Prisoners of War, Civilians and Diplomats in the Gulf Crisis', 85 *American Journal of International Law* (1991), pp. 104-109.

Meyrowitz, H., *Le principe de l'égalité des belligérants devant le droit de la guerre*, Paris 1970.

Miele, A., *L'estraneità ai conflitti armati secondo il diritto internazionale*, 2 Volumes, Padua, 1970.

Migliazza, A., 'L'évolution de la réglementation de la guerre a la lumière de la sauvegarde des droits de l'homme', 137 *Hague Recueil* 1972, III, p. 143 ff.

Momtaz, D., 'Commentary', in A. De Guttry, N. Ronzitti (eds.), *The Iran-Iraq War (1980-1988) and the Dispatch of Western Fleets to the Gulf. A Collection of Documents and Related Commentaries on Naval Warfare*, Cambridge 1993, p. 19 ff.

Neuhold, H., 'The Neutral States of Europe: Similarities and Differences', in A.T. Leonhard (ed.), *Neutrality. Changing Concepts and Practices*, Lanham/New York/London 1988, p. 97 ff.

Nordquist, M.H., Wachenfeld, M.G., 'Legal Aspects of Reflagging Kuwaiti Tankers and the Laying of Mines in the Persian Gulf', *German Yearbook of International Law* 1988, Vol. 31, pp. 138-164.

Norton, P.M., 'Between the Ideology and the Reality: The Shadow of the Law of Neutrality', 17 *Harvard International Law Journal* 1976, p. 249 ff.

Nwogugu, E.I., 'Commentary', in N. Ronzitti (ed.), *The Law of Naval Warfare*, Dordrecht/Boston/London 1988, p. 353 ff.

O'Connell, D.P., 'International Law and Contemporary Naval Operations', 44 *British Yearbook of International Law* 1970, pp. 19-85.

O'Connell, D.P, *The Influence of Law on Sea Power*, Manchester 1975.

O'Connell, D.P., *The International Law of the Sea*, Vol. II, edited by I.A. Shearer, Oxford 1984.

Oppenheim, L., *International Law. A Treatise*, Vol. II, *Disputes, War and Neutrality*, 7th ed. by H. Lauterpacht, London/New York/Toronto 1952.

Orvik, N., *The Decline of Neutrality 1914-1941*, Oslo 1953.

Ottmüller, R., *Die Anwendung von Seekriegsrecht in militärischen Konflikten seit 1945*, Hamburg 1978.

Ottolenghi, G., *Il rapporto di neutralità*, Turin 1907.

Oxford, T., 'Exclusion Zones at Sea: Some Observations on the Conduct of the Falklands War 1982', 2 *Sea Changes* 1985, p. 91 ff.

Padelletti, M.L., *Pluralità di Stati nel fatto illecito internazionale*, Milan 1990.

Partsch, K.J., 'Armed Conflict', in R. Bernhardt (ed.), 3 *Encyclopedia of Public International Law* 1982, p. 27.

Politis, N., *La neutralité et la paix*, Paris 1935.

Presutti, F., 'L'uso della forza per garantire l'applicazione di misure non implicanti l'uso della forza: il caso della risoluzione n. 665 del Consiglio di Sicurezza', 73 *Rivista di diritto internazionale* 1990, p. 380 ff.

Quigley, J., 'Complicity in International Law. A New Direction in the Law of State Responsibility', 57 *British Year Book of International Law* 1986, p. 77 ff.

Rambaud, P., 'La définition de l'agression par l'O.N.U.', 80 *Revue générale de droit international Public* 1976, p. 835 ff.

Rauch, E., *The Protocol Additional to the Geneva Conventions for the Protection of Victims of Armed Conflicts and the United Nations Convention on the Law of the Sea: Repercussions on the Law of Naval Warfare*, Berlin 1984.

Roach, J.A., 'Missiles on Target: The Law of Targeting and the Tanker War', 82 *Proceedings of the American Society of International Law* 1988, pp. 154 ff.

Robert, E., 'Le statut des Etats neutres dans le Golfe', in *Entre les lignes. La guerre du Golfe et le droit international*, Bruxelles 1991, pp. 91 ff.

Roelofsen, C.G., 'Grotius and State Practice of His Day', 10 *Grotiana* 1989, p. 3 ff.

Röling, B.V.A., 'International law and the maintenance of peace', in 4 *Netherlands Yearbook of International Law* 1973, pp. 1-103.

Röling, B.V.A., *Volkenrecht en Vrede*, 3rd rev.ed., Deventer 1985.

Röling, B.V.A., 'The 1974 Definition of Aggression', in A. Cassese (ed.), *The Current Legal Regulation of the Use of Force*, Dordrecht/Boston/Lancaster 1986, pp. 413 ff.

Ronzitti, N., *Le guerre di liberazione nazionale e il diritto internazionale*, Pisa 1974.

Ronzitti, N., 'Use of force, Jus Cogens and State Consent', in A. Cassese (ed.), *The Current Legal Regulation of the Use of Force*, Dordrecht/Boston/Lancaster 1986, pp. 147 ff.

Ronzitti, N., 'La guerre du Golfe, le deminage et la circulation des navires', 33 *Annuaire français de droit international* 1987, pp. 647 ff.

Ronzitti, N. (ed.), *The Law of Naval Warfare*, Dordrecht/Boston/London 1988.

Ronzitti, N., 'The Crisis in the Traditional Law Regulating International Armed Conflicts at Sea and the Need for Its Revision', in N. Ronzitti (ed.), *The Law of Naval Warfare*, Dordrecht/Boston/London 1988, p. 1 ff.

Ronzitti, N., 'Forza (Uso della)', 7 *Digesto delle discipline publicistiche*, Turin 1991, pp. 1 ff.

Rousseau, C., *Le droit des conflits armés*, Paris 1983.

Russo, F.V., 'Neutrality at Sea in Transition: State Practice in the Gulf War as Emerging Customary Law', 19 *Ocean Development and International Law* 1988, pp. 381 ff.

Russo, F.V., 'Targeting Theory in the Law of Armed Conflict at Sea: The Merchant Vessel as Military Objective in the Tanker War', in I.F. Dekker, H.H.G. Post (eds.), *The Gulf War of 1980-1988*, Dordrecht/Boston/London 1992, pp. 153 ff.

Schachter, O., *International Law in Theory and Practice*, Dordrecht 1991, Chapter XI.

Schachter, O. 'United Nations Law in the Gulf Conflict', 85 *American Journal of International Law* 1991, pp. 452 ff.

Schindler, D., 'Aspects contemporains de la neutralité', 121 *Hague Recueil* 1967, II, p. 221 ff.

Schindler, D., 'L'emploi de la force par un belligerant sur le territoire d'un Etat non belligerant', in *Estudios de derecho internacional. Homenaje al Profesor Miaja de la Muela*, Madrid 1979, pp. 847 ff.

Schindler, A., 'State of War, Belligerency, Armed Conflict', in A. Cassese (ed.), *The New Humanitarian Law of Armed Conflict*, Naples 1979, p. 3 ff.

Schindler, D., 'Commentary [on 1907 Hague Convention XIII]', in N. Ronzitti (ed.), *The Law of Naval Warfare*, Dordrecht/Boston/London 1988, p. 211 ff.

Schindler, D., 'Transformations in the Law of Neutrality Since 1945', in A.J.M. Delissen, G.J. Tanja (eds.), *Humanitarian Law of Armed Conflict. Challenges Ahead. Essays in Honour of Frits Kalshoven*, Dordrecht/Boston/London 1991, p. 367 ff.

Schlittler, G.B., 'Sanctions Procedures at the United Nations', in *Proceedings of the American Society of International Law*, Washington DC 1991, pp. 175-183.

Schrijver, N., 'The United Nations and the Use of Sanctions During the Gulf Crisis', in 22 *Georgia Journal of International and Comparative Law* 1992, No. 1, pp. 40-53.

Schwarzemberger, G., 'Clausula Rebus Sic Stantibus', 7 *Encyclopedia of Public International Law*, Amsterdam/New York/Oxford 1984, pp. 22 ff.

Schwebel, S.M., 'Aggression, Intervention and Self-Defence in Modern International Law', 136 *Hague Recueil* 1972, II, pp. 411 ff.

Sciso, E., 'L'aggressione indiretta nella definizione dell'Assemblea Generale delle Nazioni Unite', 66 *Rivista di diritto internazionale* 1983, pp. 253 ff.

Sciso, E., 'Legittima difesa ed aggressione indiretta secondo la Corte internazionale di giustizia', 70 *Rivista di diritto internazionale* 1987, pp. 627 ff.

Scott, G., *The Rise and Fall of the League of Nations*, 1974.

Scott, J.B. (ed.), *The Hague Conventions and Declarations of 1899 and 1907*, New York 1915.

Scott, J.B. (ed.), *Resolutions of the Institute of International Law dealing with the Law of Nations*, New York 1916.

Seidl-Hohenveldern, I., *International Economic Law*, Dordrecht/Boston/London 1989.

Sereni, A.P., *Diritto internazionale*, Vol. IV, *Conflitti internazionali*, Milan 1965, p. 2077 ff.

Sharma, P., *The Indo-Pakistan Maritime Conflict 1965. A Legal Appraisal* 1970.

Shihata, I.F.I., 'Destination Embargo of Arab Oil: Its Legality Under International Law', 68 *American Journal of International Law* 1974, pp. 591 ff.

Sico, L., *Gli effetti del mutamento delle circostanze sui trattati internazionali*, Padua 1983.

Sperduti, G., *Influenza della necessità nei rapporti fra i belligeranti e i neutrali*, Rome 1939-1940.

Sperduti, G., *L'individuo nel diritto internazionale*, Milan 1950.

Stodter, R., 'Convoy', 3 *Encyclopedia of Public International Law*, Amsterdam/New York/Oxford 1982, pp. 128 ff.

Stone, J., *Legal Controls of International Conflict*, Sydney 1954, at p. 381 ff.

Tavernier, P., 'Le caractère obligatoire de la résolution 598 (1987) du Conseil de Sécurité relative à la guerre du Golfe', 1 *European Journal of International Law* 1990, pp. 278 ff.

Thürer, D., 'Comment: UN Enforcement Measurers and Neutrality. The Case of Switzerland', 30 *Archiv des Völkerrechts* 1992, p. 63 ff.

Torrelli, M., 'La neutralité en question', 96 *Revue générale de droit international public* 1992, p. 5 ff.

Tucker, R.W., *The Law of War and Neutrality at Sea* (Naval War College, International Law Studies 1955), Washington 1957, at p. 165 ff.

Venezia, J.-C., 'La notion de représailles en droit international public', 64 *Revue générale de droit international public* 1960, pp. 465 ff.

Venturini, G., '*Ius in bello* nel conflitto anglo-argentino', in N. Ronzitti (ed.), *La questione delle Falkland-Malvinas nel diritto internazionale*, Milan 1984, pp. 210 ff.

Venturini, G., *Necessità e proporzionalità nell'uso della forza militare in diritto internazionale*, Milan 1988.

Venturini, G., 'Commentary', in A. De Guttry, N. Ronzitti (eds.), *The Iran-Iraq War (1980-1988) and the Dispatch of Western Fleets to the Gulf. A Collection of Documents and Related Commentaries on Naval Warfare*, Cambridge 1993, pp. 523 ff.

Verdross, A., 'Neutrality Within the Framework of the United Nations Organization', in *Symbolae Verzijl*, The Hague 1958, p. 410 ff.

Verdross, A., *The Permanent Neutrality of Austria*, Vienna 1978.

Verzijl, J.W.H., *Le droit des prises de la Grande Guerre*, Leyden 1924.

Verzijl, J.W.H., *International Law in Historical Perspective*, Vol. X, *The Law of Neutrality*, Alphen aan den Rijn 1979.

Verzijl, J.H.W., Heere, W.P., Offerhaus, J.P.S., *International Law in Historical Perspective*, Vol. XI, Part IX-C: The Law of Maritime Prize, Dordrecht/Boston/London 1992.

Waldock, C.H.M., 'The Regulation of the Use of Force by Individual States', 81 *Hague Recueil* 1952, II, p. 451 ff.

Walters, F.P., *A History of the League of Nations*, 1952, vol. II.

Weber, L., 'Blockade', 3 *Encyclopedia of Public International Law*, Amsterdam/New York/Oxford 1982, pp. 46 ff.

Wehberg, H., 'L'interdiction de recours à la force; le principe et les problèmes qui se posent', 78 *Hague Recueil* 1951, I, p. 7 ff.

Weiss, T.G., Minear, L. (eds.), *Humanitarism Across Borders. Sustaining Civilians in Times of War*, Boulder and London 1993.

Wellens, K.C., 'Apartheid, an international crime', in L. Heyde *et al.*, *Begrensde Vrijheid* (Liber Scheltens), Zwolle 1989, pp. 288-311.

Wengler, W., 'L'interdiction de recourir à la force. Problèmes et tendences', 7 *Revue belge de droit international* 1971, p. 401 ff.

Whitton, J.B., 'La neutralité et la Societé des Nations', 17 *Hague Recueil* 1927, II, p. 453 ff.

Williams, W.L., 'Neutrality in Modern Armed Conflicts: A Survey of Developing Law', 90 *Military Law Review* 1980, p. 9 ff.

Wright, Q., 'The Present Status of Neutrality', 34 *American Journal of International Law* 1940, p. 391 ff.

Wright, Q., 'The New Law of War and Neutrality', *Varia Juris Gentium. Questions of International Law*, Leyden 1959, p. 412 ff.

Yearbook of the International Law Commission 1979, vol. II (Part Two).

Zacklin, R., *The United Nations and Rhodesia. A Study in International Law*, New York 1974.

Zacklin, R., 'Les Nations-Unies et la crise du Golfe', in B. Stern (ed.), *Proceedings of Colloque sur les aspects juridiques de la Crise et de la 'Guerre' du Golfe*, Paris 1991, p. 68.

ZDv 15/2, *Humanitäres Völkerrecht in bewaffneten Konflikten* – Handbuch, Bonn 1992.

Zoller, E., *Peacetime Unilateral Remedies: An Analysis of Counter-Measures*, Dobbs Ferry 1984.

Zourek, J., *L'interdiction de l'emploi de la force en droit international*, Leyden 1974.

Zourek, J., 'Enfin une définition de l'agression', 20 *Annuaire français de droit international* 1974, pp. 9 ff.

Zourek, J., 'La notion de légitime défense en droit international', 56 *Annuaire de l'Institut de droit international* 1975, pp. 1 ff.

LIST OF ARBITRATIONS AND JUDGMENTS

LIST OF UN SECURITY COUNCIL RESOLUTIONS

SUBJECT INDEX

Angola
    sanctions, use of, 142-143
Armed conflict
    arms and war materials, trade in, 82-84, 109
    belligerent rights, exercise of, 86
    changes in State behaviour, effect of, 47
    economic warfare, as precondition for, 8
    enemy character, determination of, 9
    equal application of laws, 22-23
    Geneva Conventions, application of, 58
    international economic law, relationship with, 2
    international law, conduct in violation of, 18
    large-scale, 24
    law as *lex specialis*, 17
    lawful conduct of, 18
    laws of, 55
        compliance with, 59
        law of war as, 59
    legal status, views of parties as to, 61
    outbreak, effect of, 56
    principles of necessity and proportionality, laws not superseded by, 18
    regulation of conduct during, 18
    relations between belligerents, rules governing, 56
    self-defence, use of *jus ad bello* in, 19
    victims, protection of, 23
    visit, search and diversion, rights of, 9-11, 16, 20
    war, amounting to, 64
    war distinguished, 8
Auto-interpretation
    principle of, 43-44
    Security Council, power of, 45-46

Belligerents
    neutral vessels, attacking, 85
    non-belligerents, relations with, 77, 79